The Psychology of Music

The Psychology of Music

John Booth Davies

Stanford University Press
Stanford, California

Stanford University Press
Stanford, California
©1978 by John Booth Davies
Originating publisher: Hutchinson of London, 1978
First published in the United States by
Stanford University Press in 1978
Printed in the United States of America
Cloth ISBN 0-8047-0980-7   Paper ISBN 0-8047-1057-0
Last figure below indicates year of this printing:
88   87   86   85   84   83   82   81   80   79

Contents

6   *Contents*

Figures

8 *Figures*

Acknowledgements

To Mr B. Bett and Dr P. Aitken for advice on various parts of the text. To Mrs Irene Gilligan for typing the manuscript quickly. To numerous friends in the musical profession.

'If only I could play something. It must be marvellous to be able to stand up there, and help to make a sound like that. I'd give my right arm to be able to do that.'

Electronics engineer

'I would rate my job about the same as any other job: at least, any other skilled job. I'm just a musical engineer.'

Member of a symphony orchestra

'Glad you liked it. Thanks very much. Where's the bar?'

Modern jazz saxophonist

'Music is a language of feeling. We none of us know, or speak it, in its full perfection as yet. An earnest endeavour to attain some richer appreciation of its charms, or to acquire some higher power in the expression of its meaning, will undoubtedly bring with it a reward of inestimable worth. Exalt art, and art will elevate you.'

Josiah Booth

'The second horn tore his part up and walked off. It really is a load of old rubbish.'

Member of a symphony orchestra, speaking about a well-known composer

Introduction

This book covers various topics concerning the psychology of music. The relationship between the topics is sometimes obscure. However, they are, in the main, subjects which have not been covered by existing texts on the psychology of music, or else things which have not been dealt with for some time. The approach taken differs from some previous treatments in being primarily a psychologist's view of music, rather than a musician's view of psychology; though it is the hope that such a treatment is not unsympathetic to the musician's view. Indeed, the aim is to give a realistic musical account, in which the real-life musician features from time to time.

The book makes the initial value-assumption that a parsimonious, scientifically based view is ultimately more satisfying and enriching than a view based on the approach of the art critic. Nobody can tell the art critic he is wrong; they can only disagree.

It is the hope that certain topics will appeal to almost all tastes. Thus, whilst the material on testing musical aptitude will be mainly of interest to those concerned with testing, other areas such as experimental aesthetics (why people like the tunes they do), the use of rhythm in Western music, the importance of events of the past, and so on, should be of interest to anyone who takes pleasure in music of any kind. From time to time, examples are given by diagrams, a few involving musical notation. This should not deter any reader, since the point being made is readily comprehended from the text, and the musical examples are merely bonuses for those who are able to use them.

J.B.D.

1 Psychology and music

This book is principally concerned with some of the facts, fantasies and speculations that have emerged as a consequence of the scientific study of music. The application of the scientific method to topics within the general area of aesthetics is by no means the only useful approach, and, as we shall see later, it does not meet with universal approval. On the other hand, much of the work on aesthetics is of a highly subjective nature, and frequently confuses empirical fact with pure opinion. Many of the so-called musical laws, for example, are not laws in the physical sense (e.g. the law of gravity) but are conventions (e.g. laws of harmony) which musicians have simply agreed upon. Furthermore, whilst the scientific study of music might with some justification be seen as a rather dull, unexciting and concrete-minded thing to undertake, in the sense that it has none of the beauty or poetic appeal of the actual subject matter, it can serve a very useful purpose in exposing certain beliefs as pure mysticism; hopefully, in this process, making such things as 'good taste', 'sensitivity', 'musical understanding', and so on, into comprehensible entities common in varying degrees to almost all people, rather than magical properties of some sort of musical priesthood.

Close contact between the author and musicians from all walks of life has revealed that the world of the professional musician is indeed more down-to-earth than many of us would perhaps believe. Consider the following extract from a diary of Franz Schubert: 'Thus beautiful impressions remain in the soul, which are soothing to our existence, and which neither time nor events can efface. In the darkness of our life they throw a light, bright and beautiful future, which fills us with fervent hope. O Mozart! Immortal Mozart! How many, yea, innumerable impressions of a brighter and better world have you imprinted on our souls.' There can be no doubt that this passage is a true attempt on the part of Schubert to express his feelings about the works of a very great composer, and there is no intention here to belittle them. There is a danger, however, that such powerful sentiments become a model for the way one ought to feel about Mozart, perhaps even accompanied by the belief that this is in some absolute sense the right way to feel. Contrast the above extract with the following incident which occurred when the author encountered two members of a nationally famous symphony orchestra in a Glasgow pub, shortly before a concert. The question 'What's on the programme tonight?' elicited the baleful reply, 'Bloody Mozart'.

These two reactions to Mozart are equally valid, and, more important, potentially equally explicable. If we know sufficient about the people who expressed these opinions, about their states of mind, and about their styles of life, both reactions become in some way more logical. Thus the first extract can be seen as the outpourings of a shy, retiring, and extremely sensitive individual, who in his overt behaviour is reputed to have been undemonstrative, and who perhaps expressed his inner feelings covertly rather than overtly. (It is said that when he visited Beethoven shortly before the latter's death in 1827, he simply stared at him for some time in silence before bursting into tears and quickly leaving the room.) The latter statement, on the other hand, represents the reaction of an overworked orchestral musician who has played a particular composition many times in the past, and who frankly doesn't want to play it again. It is, furthermore, not merely the opinion of someone who is musically unskilled, uninformed, or insensitive (the same musician goes into ecstasies about Sibelius). Neither of the two statements is 'right', but both are equally valid indicants of the reactions of two different people, in different sets of circumstances. The conclusion should be clear. Regardless of what critics or experts say about the way a piece of music 'is', it is in fact all things to all men.

In the past, many books about music have appeared, but in some cases there is a lack of clarity about what is fact (i.e. that which is shown to have objective support in empirical studies, and which is also verifiable by such means) and that which looks like fact, or is described as though it were fact, but which is based on opinion or evaluation. There is clearly plenty of room for both modes of treatment, but the blurring of the distinction between the two has some unfortunate consequences. This issue is admirably, and uncompromisingly, dealt with in Berlyne (1971). This writer sees the objective study of aesthetics as having been persistently impeded by the failure to distinguish between normative and factual questions. Furthermore, Berlyne points out that the writings of psychologists and others, on artistic topics, frequently suffer from the intrusion of artistic values and preconceptions. Too often, he claims, writings in the area of aesthetics serve not merely the function of objective analysis, but also serve the desire of the writer to demonstrate that he is a man of culture, taste and sensitivity, who can tell the difference between good and bad art. If, for example, one wishes to illustrate a point with an example, and equally good examples are available from Berlioz's 'Symphonie fantastique' or 'Roll out the barrel', the tendency has been to choose the former, even though relatively speaking hardly anyone has heard of it.

Music, and to a large extent the other arts, have also acquired a supernatural or mystical quality which tends to make any analysis of these activities seem sacrilegious, especially if it is seen that the standpoint for such analysis is fundamentally the same as that adopted in studying the operations involved in putting sardines into tins. This mystical quality may conceivably be an example of extended cultural lag, and have its roots in the association between music and religious ceremonies during early times. Certainly, there is much evidence of close association between music and religious practice from many epochs and many parts of the world. One may therefore feel a certain uneasiness about dismissing a particular piece of sacred music as boring or tuneless without first knowing how the Almighty feels about it. The fear of many musicians would appear to be that a scientific analysis of music will in some way render it less wonderful than it was before, and that its magical quality will be in some way diminished. This is not the view taken here.

In historical terms, the position of the creative artist has frequently been a rather elevated one. Mankind is seen as reaching its highest pinnacle of achievement, and hence being most godlike, when involved in the act of artistic creation. Although perhaps today only a few people would make such an extravagant analogy, the feeling that there is something special about music and musicians persists. And of course there is – but this 'specialness' lies not in terms of metaphysical entities or magical qualities, but in terms of processes and forms of behaviour which are actually or potentially amenable to precise and objective description, and which are, in theory at least, explicable ultimately at a physiological level. Such an approach by no means denies the importance of social influences upon musical performance, or upon musical preference either. Clearly, one's musical tastes are to a considerable extent influenced by the musical tastes of one's family and friends, one's workmates, one's peer group and so on. None the less, social cognitions, like musical cognitions, are not metaphysical or magical in nature, and are again underpinned by physiological processes which may one day be capable of explanation at such a level.

It is perhaps by now apparent that the approach taken in this book is largely empirical, in so far as it concerns itself for the most part with various kinds of observation and evidence; and also physical, in so far as it assumes that musical behaviour of all sorts is explicable without resort to abstract or metaphysical entities. It is not claimed that there is any absolute virtue in such an approach, but simply that it has pragmatic value, and also that it makes a change from some other more mystical interpretations. The claim to pragmatism stems from the belief that a more satisfactory, deeper, and ultimately more sensitive understanding of musicality and musical experience will emerge from a standpoint of parsimony and humility than from one which starts with an initial series of value-laden assumptions about the subject matter. The dangers of the latter approach have been exposed admirably by Arthur Koestler in his book *The Act of Creation*. Speaking of the aesthetic snob, he writes, 'When he reads Kierkegaard he is not moved by what he reads, he is moved by himself reading Kierkegaard.' In an analogous way, there are perhaps individuals who are not directly moved by music, but who are very moved by the taste and sophistication they show in going to a symphony concert. The same is also true for jazz music, where a distinction is sometimes made between 'real punters' and 'scene-diggers'.

At the same time, it must be conceded that there are limitations and dangers inherent in the approach adopted. In later chapters, several instances will be cited in which the very application of a rigorous experimental method has caused the phenomenon under investigation to disappear like mist before the rising sun.

Examples of this include investigations into the nature of consonance and dissonance which remove context and use only isolated chords, thereby casting light only on a particular laboratory situation, and saying little about music. Or the erroneous application of information theory, in which a sequence of tones picked at random from a particular major scale is assumed to be a musically random sequence. Such shortcomings, however, are often of value in themselves since they demonstrate what music is *not*. The harmoniousness of a consonant chord and the unpleasantness of a dissonance, for example, are not invariant relationships, but vary depending on the musical context and the musical culture in question. This has only become apparent through the performance of context-free studies, leading to the realization that the experimental situation did not reflect the musical experience.

One consequence of the scientific study of music has been the undermining of beliefs about the basis of Western musical theory, and the growing realization that other music forms which violate these principles are not necessarily inferior. The supposed superiority of music in the Western classical tradition over other forms is apparent in the writings of many authors, who make the distinction between Western music and primitive music, as though the latter were at some lower and inferior level of development; thus any development must automatically be towards the true light of Western music. This tendency is not unique to the field of music, however. Because of the rigidity, and frequently the absurdity, of our criteria (which are arbitrary), it is almost habitual to think of New York as a civilized part of the world, whereas the 'savage' society of the African pygmy would be described as uncivilized. There are very good reasons for arguing precisely the opposite. It has been assumed in the past that musical theory, as we know it, has a firm physical basis, and that consequently laws of harmony, counterpoint, fugue and so on are 'real' in the sense that they are underlaid by physical laws. Such a notion, if true, would provide support for musical theory, since an example of bad harmony or incorrect counterpoint would be not just a departure from an arbitrary rule, but would run counter to nature. Unfortunately, the assumption of a straightforward physical basis is not justified. There are very few musical universals, and the story of the development and evolution of music is better expressed in terms of the progressive and systematic violation of rules than in terms of adherence to them. 'It seems that the voluminous edifice of musical theory rests on sand', wrote Moles (1968).

A good example of the discrepancy between theory and practice is given by Pederson (1975). This author performed fascinating research into twelve-tone composition, the theory of which involves the supposition that 'the notes of a series can be used in any octave position. As long as the succession of notes is unchanged, each note can be played in any register' (Brindle 1966). The above theory is based on the notion of 'octave equivalence', and claims that particular notes of the scale are equivalent regardless of the octave in which they fall. In a series of experiments involving random transposition of octaves, Pederson concluded that, although it was possible to learn the notes of a twelve-tone series, 'random octave transposition of the members of a series of twelve different pitch classes destroys the perceptibility of the series'. The author states, with great perceptiveness, 'The controversies that have arisen over serialism have probably resulted from critic and composer alike often failing to distinguish between compositional working techniques and perceptible musical structure. The composer cannot assume that because a technique is logically consistent it will necessarily result in perceptible sound structures.' In other words, the working method adopted by the composer in such a case is a purely arbitrary law, and the fact that his composition obeys the self-imposed rules is no guarantee at all that the composition will have any perceptual unity. This example is, of course, fairly extreme.

To say that musical theory is based on a set of largely invented rules rather than on a set of natural laws is not to diminish it, however. The rules define the area within which the artistic endeavour takes place. They make possible such things as aesthetic deviation, confirmation or disconfirmation of expectancy, and the deliberate violation of rules for aesthetic effect, all of which are critical events as far as musical cognition is concerned. The game of cricket, for example, is in the same way precisely defined by its rules, and without the rules the game cannot take place. In the absence of rules there is a state of utter liberty in which pure chance reigns, and a chain of purely chance events is without meaning. In summary, there can be no art without some kind of constraint.

In large part, the psychological study of music involves examination of the relationships between the rules of music and the laws of perception and cognition, in so far as these latter are understood. The area of study thus defined is surprisingly large, and includes areas of research which have practical, as well as theoretical, implications. Thus, in addition to the traditional areas of research into the perception of tones, the nature of musical ability and its assessment, and emotionality and music, there is an expanding literature on the uses of music in industry, music as therapy with handicapped groups, and the application of certain principles to the teaching of musical skills.

The role of music in the service of industry ranges all the way from the use of piped music in supermarkets (a practice which does not meet with universal approval), through to more precise studies of the effects of different types of music upon work rates. The use of music in industry to induce people working at mundane jobs to work harder, or to make the time pass more easily, is not an entirely happy alliance, and involves some ethical problems. None the less, the finding of a relationship between music and task performance is in itself of interest. Music in industry seems to have enjoyed a heyday in the years 1940 to about 1944, particularly in the USA. At that time, a number of forays were made into this area, many of which are difficult to interpret in the light of the confounding variable of a world war. For example, Hough (1943) claimed not merely an increase in production, but also a 35 per cent reduction in accidents after the introduction of industrial music. Halpin (1943-4) showed, or rather claimed, major improvements in morale due to music. However, a study in the same year by Kerr showed that people liked patriotic songs as much as dance music, a state of affairs almost certainly related to the world situation, and very different from today's apparent preference for pop music. Increasing production, safety, and morale appear to be things more easily achieved during war than in peace-time.

There are reasons for supposing that some of the claims made by less rigorous investigators, or people with a commercial interest, are often overly optimistic. More careful studies reveal less striking, or non-existent, improvements. A detailed study by Kerr (1945) investigated effects of music upon performance of repetitive tasks in an electrical factory. Using a counterbalanced design, involving periods of music and no-music, Kerr found slight improvements in production and slight reduction in scrappage. In groups of employees containing more than twenty-five individuals, production was increased by only 1·86 per cent and scrappage reduced by 3·53 per cent. Moreover, these differences were not statistically significant (they fall within the range of chance), though, in a subsequent note, Kerr claims that his statistical analysis was 'overly conservative'. Research by McGehee and Gardner (1949) investigated the effects of music on what they describe as a 'complex industrial job' to contrast with earlier studies where the task was often repetitive and uncomplicated. The job involved the setting up of looms for rug-making. In this instance, the authors concluded that the music had no effect, favourable or otherwise, upon production. If individuals were favourably affected, then such favourable effects must have been masked by unfavourable effects on other workers.

In 1947 Cardinell and Burris-Meyer were moved to comment on the 'music in industry' boom, and pinpointed four misconceptions. These were:

1 The basic concept: music in industry is defined as a good thing. That is all there is to it.

2 The benefits: it works like a slot machine. You put in the music and out comes your production increase.

3 The sop to labour: feed the people the auditory equivalent of candy and they will be grateful to you.

4 Programmes: give them what they ask for; after all, the purpose is to keep them happy.

An excellent paper by Uhrbrock (1961) gives a broad coverage of what has been achieved in this area. It is apparent that some claims are simply unsubstantiated. Some studies claim success on the basis of irrelevant criteria. For example, production increases have been demonstrated by such methods as playing music to employees, then asking them whether they like it (it appears that a majority say 'Yes'), and finally asking them whether they *think* they produce more when the music is playing. In another study, a work team in an aircraft factory happily agreed to an eighteen-hour overtime shift, during which a good production rate was maintained. The result was attributed to music, which it was claimed, sustained the workers. However, the researcher also reports that they received coffee and sandwiches during the shift. Studies like these have little scientific value, but appear in large part to be responsible for the 'music in industry' myth. Uhrbrock also has some amusing things to say about the claims of Muzak (1958), a firm which supplies music to many commercial undertakings. An up-to-date opinion cannot be given, however, as it has proved difficult to obtain information from the firm.

It is clear that a free-for-all approach is unlikely to have the required effects. For example, the author quite recently received an enquiry on behalf of a large catering organization, who had encountered a problem after they had given a group of working girls a choice of music. The girls had apparently requested Radio 1, and subsequently output had gone down since the girls preferred to listen more and work less. The employers reacted with some dismay as DJs instructed their audience to 'stop whatever you're doing, put your feet up, and relax for five minutes', and so forth. The dilemma remained unresolved. Finally, in some industrial settings, high levels of background noise interact with the background music which itself has to be, consequently, very loud. Even so it is often only heard indistinctly or intermittently. Though noise has been much studied, this type of interaction has not.

Recent, precise, studies have been performed in that bastion of industrialization, Japan, where the role of music in industry is taken quite seriously (Yoshida 1965).

The use of music as therapy, especially with handicapped children, is an application which would probably meet with more universal approval. Since the founding of the National Association for Music Therapy in the USA in 1959, this subject has made large steps forward, both with respect to the assessment of its own effectiveness, and in scientific rigour. None the less, there is still a tendency for much of the work, and the evaluation of effectiveness, to take place at an intuitive level (though this does not necessarily mean that the work is thereby rendered of no value. It might be of great benefit, and certainly appears to be so in many cases). A recent book by Nordoff and Robbins (1973) illustrates with great sensitivity some of the results of music therapy with handicapped children, and contains some very powerful photographs. However, the work is totally descriptive, so that it is impossible to specify why the therapy appears to work in some cases but not in others, or whether the effects are specifically musical or could be achieved by any type of therapy involving prolonged close contact with a sensitive adult. Finally, the statements that the therapy produces increased awareness, increased responsibility, or greater social ability, for example, are based on subjective impressions. On these kind of issues, Madsen and Madsen (1970) write, 'To state that patients singing side by side are "socialising" is somewhat misleading; . . . and to assume that this "socialising" is monolithically good appears extremely questionable', and later, speaking of the rationale for employing this type of therapy, they write perhaps a little facetiously, 'To place a patient in the hospital chorus for specific reasons pertaining to his particular malady appears wise. If the reason the patient was institutionalised was in part that he could not sing songs side by side with other people, then the speculative positive benefits from this experience seem advisable.' Despite these comments, there can be no doubt that music therapy has been of great benefit in many cases, even if the benefit sometimes appears diffuse rather than specific. This is a fascinating and expanding area. There are recent reports of its use in the USSR (Brusilovsky 1972). Brusilovsky recommends a 'differentiated' approach, which he finds to be an 'effective means of overcoming autism in schizophrenic patients and of eliminating their inertness and their negative attitude toward work'. The 'differentiated' approach involves devising a programme for a patient which becomes gradually more complicated and demands progressively more active participation. Tasks used involve, for example, passive listening, active listening, choir singing, individual singing, ensemble work, and playing the piano. Again, however, the results are in the form of subjective report.

On the whole, the teaching of musical skills, especially in this country, tends to follow traditional lines; psychology does not appear to have penetrated very far into these realms, perhaps because it has achieved relatively little. Interesting issues have been raised, but with the exception of test construction (a topic covered in some detail in later chapters) none of them seem to have gathered much momentum. For example, various forms of feedback have been shown to be effective in improving pitch discrimination. These methods involve presenting the subject with information about the accuracy of his judgements in various types of pitch matching or discrimination tasks, leading to subsequent improvements in performance. Perhaps the most sophisticated example of this kind is the voice tonoscope, a device which presents a singer with a pictorial representation of the notes he is singing, on a television-type screen (Seashore 1906). Any inconsistencies are reproduced visually on the screen. In the field of assessment, Lamp and Keys (1935) examined the feasibility of predicting aptitude for playing *specific* musical instruments, a fascinating idea, but again one which has received little subsequent study or application. Perhaps the most famous (or infamous) example of the application of particular teaching/learning methods to the teaching of musical skills comes from the work of Shinichi Suzuki in Japan. Under his intensive methods, very small children acquire instrumental techniques vastly in excess of what one would expect for their age group, though some critics have suggested that the final results sound a little mechanical. Suzuki has produced literally thousands of tiny, competent violinists during recent years, a fact which one might view with some alarm in view of the somewhat astringent nature of early violin-playing endeavours. The methods used are highly concentrated and intensive, and run to the extent of small children having tape-recorders strapped to their backs (or, as a musician friend described it, of small children being strapped to the front of tape-recorders) so that they can hear the tunes they are to learn, constantly, at almost any time of night or day. Although Suzuki's results are in many ways outstanding, the approach is perhaps a little too regimented for some tastes. None the less, Suzuki's basic tenet, that a person's environment governs his artistic skill and sense, makes a change from some of the more traditional, and exclusive, views of musicality as a purely hereditary trait. There have been many and varied studies of musicality as a hereditary trait, ranging from Shuter's scientific investigation to more ambiguous evidence from family-trees of famous families like the Bach family. This topic will be mentioned in a later chapter, but, suffice to say, the problem remains one of separating environmental from genetic factors. If one is musical, and one's father and mother are musical, this could be because one has inherited the musicality from one's parents, or because one was made to practise five hours a day since the age of zero; or both sets of factors could contribute. Whatever the truth of the matter, the Suzuki war-cry, that everywhere talent is common, but favourable environment is not, is a most optimistic one.

On the topic of music in education, it is worth while noting that some music educationists have aims and ideals which go far beyond the mere teaching of musical skills. Music lessons are seen not just as music lessons, but as education for living generally. For example, in an essay on 'The place of music in education', Nickson (1967) writes, 'Music affects every pupil and contributes more than any other single experience to the well-being of the growing child', and also, 'Without the presence of music a school lacks a soul. Here is the early training ground of character and personality.' There are other examples of such idealism. Suzuki is reported as saying, 'Music has an invisible but mighty living power to save mankind', and urges that music policy should be a primary national concern. Zoltán Kodály, who has worked with and written extensively for children, says, 'We must look forward to the time when all people in all lands are brought together through singing, and when there is a universal harmony.' The belief seems to be that musical education has effects upon character and personality that generalize to other situations, and affect almost all other aspects of life in a favourable way. Such traits as self-discipline and social awareness are also taught, it is claimed, by a proper musical education. Unfortunately, there is very little to support such claims, and for the most part they remain matters of idealistic belief. Whilst there is no doubt that many music educators hold such beliefs very deeply and sincerely, it is also unfortunately the case that they are the kinds of platitudes which, in the mouths of others, win loud applause at music conferences. It is important to take a less passionate view of music, if objectivity is to be preserved. For example, some children actually *dislike* music, and music lessons may consequently be a source of very great anxiety for them. We may in fact be tormenting some children by forcing music lessons on them. Also, the bringing of nations together in song seems to occur at least as much in times of war as in times of peace; and nearer home, mass singing is a frequent accompaniment to some of the worst conflicts between rival football supporters. In other words, song can not only unite people together, it can apparently help in uniting them *against* someone else. Finally, the notion that musical harmony leads, as Kodály suggests, inevitably to social harmony, is simply not true. It is not difficult to find petty jealousies, or even more positive dislikes, between members of the same symphony orchestra. In summary, one can say that in so far as such beliefs lend fire and determination to music educators, they are wholly admirable. However, to make such claims into the overt and explicit aims of music education is to make the subject appear ridiculous to those not intimately involved. Why such claims should be made for music, rather than botany, geography, painting or ceramics is not clear. In short, regardless of what we believe, we must distinguish between belief and fact, and not publicly lay claim to the unsubstantiated or the fantastic.

The three areas outlined in the above paragraphs, namely music in industry, music therapy, and music education, are from many points of view important, especially as they are three areas in which knowledge about the psychology of music can actually be applied. This book, however, is concerned almost wholly with music from the standpoint of the listener, rather than with practical applications in these three applied areas, and no further mention will be made of them. This limiting of the coverage to the main theoretical, experiential and sensory aspects of music is made without intending to imply that other areas are unimportant. It is simply that another book would be necessary to cover the uses to which music might be put. The immediate concern here is with music and musicality *per se*, and with the evidence and the theories which have been put forward to support various notions about musicality, and to explain some of the phenomena which occur when people listen to music. With this purpose in mind, the next chapter concerns itself with a highly simplified introduction to the physics of musical sound, as an introduction to some of the more equivocal topics.

What is music?

Music is something of a mystery. Most people spend considerable amounts of time listening to music of one sort or another, and some people dedicate the major part of their lives to musical pursuits. Yet, unlike other activities such as reading, talking, or watching television, where the transmission of a more or less unambiguous message is readily apparent, music does not appear to pass on any message we can readily identify. Music does not really satisfy the requirements that would completely justify its being called a 'language', since we tend to use the word 'meaning' rather differently in the context of music than in the context of language. In addition, music seems to have something in common with simple forms of sensory experience like warmth, taste, or the smell of jacket-baked potatoes. For example, one can, in a sense, appreciate the taste of a good steak, although the question 'What does it *mean*?' is hard to answer. By the same token one can ask 'What does Beethoven's "Fifth symphony" *mean*?' and again be at a loss for a satisfactory reply. Any answer we might attempt would be couched in terms of our own reactions and feelings, and these are not identical with another person's responses to the same piece of music. By contrast, the message 'The cat sat on the mat' is fairly precise in its meaning, and relatively unambiguous. However, it is not the kind of message that most of us would become excited about.

Despite these elusive qualities, people in all parts of the world indulge in musical pursuits with great enthusiasm, and their lives are often profoundly affected as a result. Individuals can be stirred to great and glorious sentiments by the sound of a martial strain, moved to compassion by the sound of a lullaby, or driven to sorrow and despair by a symphony, or merriment and laughter when a jolly tune is struck up. Emotional responses apart, people's actual behaviour can be affected by music. Productivity in factories can be influenced by the music we play to the workers, the well-being of mental patients can be affected by the playing of suitable music, and warriors seem to forget their fear and rush into battle on hearing the sound of the bagpipes or the war drums. At a more fanciful level, it has even been claimed that cows give more milk, and that hot-house plants grow more rapidly, when we accommodate to their musical tastes.

The widespread influence which music undoubtedly has, has led some authors to describe it as a system for communication of emotions. Certainly, our responses to music are emotional. And yet can we describe as 'communication' something which produces dissimilar effects in different people, produces no effects at all in some, and produces in others a reaction which may be different from the state of the person who sent the message (i.e. the composer)? To explain how music can have such a diversity of effects, whilst being so universal in nature, and yet at the same time be so difficult to come to grips with at a scientific level, is a problem to which at present there is no entirely satisfactory answer. However, there is not a complete dearth of information and the present volume attempts to present some of the known facts about music and the ways in which we perceive it. As a starting point we may try to discover what physical attributes distinguish musical sounds from non-musical sounds (or noises), and draw attention to those attributes of musical sound that are important from the point of view of the listener.

In the course of everyday activities people experience little difficulty in discriminating between sounds which are noise and sounds which are music. The difference between the sound made by a jet aircraft, for example, and that made by a music programme on the radio is very obvious when we listen to them. However, people do more than merely detect the difference. They label one 'noise' and the other 'music'. This distinction, which seems so obvious to most people, is perhaps less obvious when the sounds are compared in terms of their physical properties. It should be clear from the outset, therefore, that the labelling of certain sounds as 'music' and others as 'noise' involves more than simple differences in physical properties. For example, in terms of certain physical measures, the music of certain extant 'pop' groups may have more in common with the jet aircraft than with other pieces of music that one could choose. Similarly, in some physical respects, the music of Stockhausen might have more in common with certain electronic noises than with other more conventional forms of classical music. This means that any consideration of the characteristics of music must take in the responses of the listener, and the intention of the composer or performer, in addition to the simple physics of the matter. In his book *Noise and Society* Rodda (1967) also implies the impossibility of adequately distinguishing between noise and music in purely physical terms, and implies that *intention* must be taken into account. He offers perhaps the best, simplest, definition of noise as 'any annoying or unwanted sound'. This, of course, leaves the door open for individual interpretation. After all, people complaining about pop festivals usually draw attention to the fact that they are too noisy, rather than too 'musicky'. Whether it is noise or music you are listening to thus depends on who you are and what you are doing; your music might be someone else's noise, and vice versa. However, the more complex matters of responses and intentions will be dealt with in later chapters; the present task involves the physical attributes, though this is in no way intended to suggest that other non-physical aspects are of less importance.

The phenomena we refer to as music and noise are both types of sound. Sound, as such, does not really exist in the world around us. What does exist is vibration. Sound is merely the subjective end-product of vibrations impinging upon the mechanism of the ear. In other words, there is no sound until we hear it. In the same way, colour only exists because the eye uses colour to help the perceiver organize and interpret a diverse pattern of electromagnetic radiations reflected from objects. Objects do not 'have' colours; human beings simply possess a receptor system that provides them with the sensation of colour. Thus, a violin does not emit music. It merely vibrates in such a way that the ear provides us first of all with a sensation of sound; armed with this sensory information, we might then decide whether the sound was musical or unmusical, pleasant or unpleasant, and so on. In a sense, therefore, 'music exists in the ear of the listener', and nowhere else.

Although sound can be transmitted to a greater or lesser extent by any elastic medium, people normally encounter sounds which are carried by vibrations in air. If there is no medium, there can be no mechanical transmission of vibrations. It follows, therefore, that there can be no sound in a vacuum. Given an elastic medium the normal course of events might be as follows. As a result of the application of some extraneous force, some object (or 'body') commences to vibrate. These vibrations of the object or 'body' serve as a sound source by transmitting vibrations to the air. The ear can pick up the vibrations in the air, and this in turn leads to their eventual interpretation as sound. The vast array of different types of sound which we are capable of hearing arises as a consequence of the fact that there are different kinds of vibrations, and the basilar membrane of the ear makes possible their differentiation. At this stage, the fundamental issue is to examine the ways in which one type of vibration in air can be different from another, giving rise to the sensation of different types of sound.

Transmissions of vibrations through air are sometimes referred to as 'sound waves'. Although the notion of 'waves' is perhaps not the best analogy, it will serve, with caution, for the present. If we throw a stone into a smooth pond, deformations of the surface layers are easily observed. A series of concentric circles is produced which radiate outwards, away from the point of entry of the stone. We may also observe that, with increasing distance from the entry point, the height of the waves becomes progressively smaller, until, at the edge of the pond, there may in fact be no disturbance whatsoever. Finally, if we observe the motions of a leaf situated on the surface a few feet from the point of entry, we can observe that, although the leaf is disturbed by the waves on the surface, it does not in fact move outwards as the apparent motion of the waves suggests it should. Instead it simply moves up and down. This analogy illustrates two points in a fairly obvious way. Firstly, a disturbance in an elastic medium is transmitted to other parts of that medium. Secondly, although the disturbance is transmitted, the particles or molecules comprising the medium are only displaced on either side of their original rest positions and do not rush about like tiny projectiles (i.e. the radiating waves are not formed by molecules rushing from the point of disturbance towards the periphery of the pond. If they did this, they would carry the leaf with them.)

The propagation of sound in air differs in a crucial way from the propagation of waves on a pond. The waves on the pond are deformations which, as far as the observer is concerned, take place on a flat surface. The air, however, is all around us. Thus, a suspended firecracker produces, on detonation, not waves in a flat plane, but a disturbance which is spherical. This spherical disturbance radiates outwards, losing power as it does so, for the same reason that the ripples on the pond gradually die away towards the periphery (i.e. mechanical resistance caused by particles rubbing together).

Although sound waves can travel great distances through the atmosphere, the actual displacement of individual air molecules is very small. In normal speech, heard from a distance of about three yards, for example, the particles move only one or two millionths of an inch in each direction. How is it that such small movements can transmit sound over large distances? In the most simple terms, the movement of one particle disturbs adjacent particles, which in turn disturb others. The disturbance is thus transmitted from one particle to the next, and so on. To illustrate this, place a row of pennies in a line on a desk top. Tapping the one end results in a displacement of the penny at the opposite end. Thus, although the individual pennies have hardly moved at all, the displacement has travelled over a distance of several inches from one end of the row to the other. As noted earlier, however, sound waves do not travel in a flat plane, but take the form of spherical radiation.

It is the fact that air molecules can vibrate in a variety of different ways that gives rise to the different kinds of sounds we hear. It is conventional to represent different kinds of particle motion in the form of graphs, which give information about frequency, amplitude, phase and complexity, and it is the explanation of these terms, and their graphical representation, which now concern us.

From the outset, it is essential to remember that wave-form graphs are merely a convenient mode of description. They do not provide a picture of the ways in which particles move, nor do they show what a sound wave would look like if we could see it. To make sense of these graphs, we therefore need to be familiar with certain conventions: to illustrate these we shall take the simplest form of steady state wave-form graph. Steady state simply means that the sound is going on steadily and continuously; thus bangs, clicks, rumbles, or any sound which is variable, or non-continuous, is not steady state, whereas tones of certain kinds are.

The steady state example given in fig. 1 is known as a 'sine wave'.

In fig. 1 the line AB is used as a symbol to denote the passage of time. Thus, if A represents a particular point in time, different positions between A and B

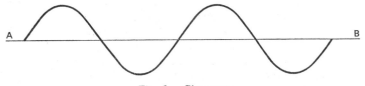

Fig. 1.   Sine wave

represent different points in time subsequent to A. The wavy line represents symbolically the movement of particles (air molecules), and indicates therefore, when considered in conjunction with the line AB, that particles occupy different positions at different points in time. The only remaining problem now is to understand how the to-and-fro movement of the particles is represented by a wavy line, and this is easily done. In the example given, the simplest type of vibration is shown, in which the particle path can be described as the projection of a circle. The wave-form graph simply shows the motion of a point moving around a circle, in a 'spaced out' form. Examination of fig. 2 might make this clearer. Assume that point 'p' moves around the circle at a constant rate, commencing at position 'p' in fig. 2. As 'p' rotates to position 1 on the circumference of the circle, it becomes equivalent to position 1 in fig. 2a. In the same way,

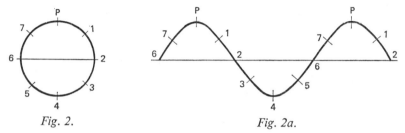

Fig. 2.   *Fig. 2a.*

Sine wave as the projection of a circle

the different positions of 'p' as it moves around the circle are shown by the matching numbers in fig. 2a. Note that position 4 is opposite the starting point, and is the point at which the wave-form graph begins to change direction; also note that the particle passes through positions 2 and 6 in opposite directions.

It should now be apparent that differences in the size of the circle, or alterations to its shape, will result in differences in the graphical representation. In fact only the purest tones (a pure tone, or sine wave, is a tone in which all the energy goes into the production of a single frequency) conform to the example above. Most tones are less pure (the energy is distributed among a number of different components, referred to as 'harmonics' or 'partials'), and their graphical equivalents more complex as a result, but the way in which we obtain the graph from the motions of the particles is fundamentally the same.

Our subjective experience tells us that tones can be of differing pitches, i.e. some tones sound higher or lower than others. This sensation of pitch is a function of the frequency of the sound we are hearing. Frequency simply indicates the speed of vibrations, and is normally expressed in terms of cycles per second, or Hertz (Hz). A cycle occurs when the particle moves from its rest position to maximum displacement left, back through the rest position to maximum displacement right, and back to rest. (The representation of this oscillatory movement in terms of a circular projection is just a matter of convenience.)

A cycle is represented by the distance XY in fig. 3a. An increase in the frequency of the vibrations results in the sensation of an increase in the pitch. Fig. 3b illustrates a sound of higher frequency than that shown in fig. 3a. The reduction in the length XY is readily seen.

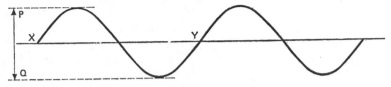

Fig. 3a.   Cycle, amplitude, wavelength

Considered together, figs. 3a and 3b illustrate how an increase in the frequency (number of cycles) per unit time interval results in a decrease in the wavelength XY.

However, figs. 3a and 3b differ in one more respect, namely the distances

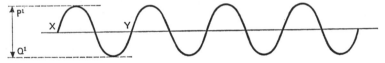

Fig. 3b.   Cycle, amplitude, wavelength

PQ and P^1Q^1. This distance describes the amplitude of the sound wave, and differences in amplitude lead to differences in intensity, and the sensation of differences in loudness. With loud sounds, the magnitude of the particle vibrations is greater than with softer ones; or, to put this another way, the particles in a loud sound move further than with quiet sounds. Increasing the loudness is equivalent to increasing the size of the circle in fig. 2. Looking again at the figs. 3a and 3b, it should now be clear that fig. 3a represents particle motion employing a larger circle than does fig. 3b, i.e. its amplitude (PQ) is greater. It therefore represents a sound which is louder (i.e. of greater amplitude) and, as we have seen previously, of lower pitch and therefore of lower frequency than fig. 3b.

Finally, consider the two wave-forms illustrated in fig. 4.

It will be noticed that the upper wave-form (a) has its maximum displacement downwards at the instant that wave-form (b) is maximally displaced upwards (see point P). Conversely, at point Q the upper wave-form (a) is maximally displaced upwards, whilst (b) is maximally displaced downwards. The notion of 'phase' is used to describe the relationship between two wave-forms. In the example given, the two wave-forms are in an opposite phase relationship. It will be apparent that the phase relationship can range all the way from 'in phase', where the two coincide, right through to opposite or reversed phase, with all the stages in between.

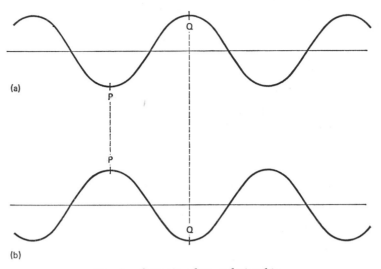

Fig. 4. Opposite phase relationship

The brief description of phase, amplitude and frequency serves as an elementary introduction to the physics of sound. More detailed descriptions are readily available elsewhere. Phase, amplitude and frequency are three of the most central characteristics for describing, and distinguishing between, sounds in physical terms. The wave-forms described so far, however, have been simple pure tones (sine waves), in which all the power goes into the production of a particular, unique frequency. Most sounds we hear in everyday life and, in particular, the sounds we encounter when listening to music, are not of this simple type, and the paths followed by the air molecules are more complicated than the simple oscillatory paths described so far. Instead, most sounds are a compound of a number of simple sounds occurring simultaneously, in a phase-related manner. In other words, the power which goes into producing the sound is divided between a number of tones of different frequencies, i.e. the sounds are complex as opposed to the simple ones we have considered up to this point. Musical instruments, for example, produce their characteristic sounds because they produce complex tones which have a more or less unique, and typical, structure. The actual 'pitch' (the subjective sensation of frequency) of the tones they produce is perceived normally as being a function of the 'fundamental'. The fundamental is usually the component of the complex tone into which most of the energy is directed, and in most cases this fundamental is also the lowest of the tones produced. The other tones present in addition to the fundamental are referred to as harmonics, or partials. Precisely speaking, the terms 'partial' and 'harmonic' are not synonymous, though for most intents and purposes they are. In fact, however, any component of a sound is a partial, *including the fundamental*. A harmonic, however, is a partial occurring at any frequency which is an integral multiple of the fundamental, but *not including* the fundamental. A complex tone can thus be described as a number of partials, or as a fundamental and harmonics. Consequently, the first harmonic is, to be very precise, the second partial.

There are some special cases in which the ear does not perceive the fundamental as the lowest tone produced. The phenomenon known as the 'missing fundamental' demonstrates that the pitch of a tone is related to the frequency difference between partials, which does not have to be the same as the frequency of the lowest component, although it usually is. For example, in experiments by Schouten, Ritsma and Lopes-Cardozo (1962), subjects presented with an artificially synthesized tone containing partials of 1,200, 1,400 and 1,600 Hz heard a tone with a pitch equivalent to 200 Hz, the constant frequency difference between the partials. In other words, subjects heard a sound where the fundamental ought to have been. This has also been demonstrated by Houtsma and Goldstein (1971) in experiments involving recognition of musical intervals. In many sounds, particularly musical ones, tones are produced in addition to the fundamental, at frequencies which are always multiples of the fundamental. Thus, if the fundamental has a frequency of 100 Hz, additional tones may occur at 200, 300, 400 . . . n × 100 Hz. Tones produced in addition to the fundamental are harmonics; since the number, placement and relative intensities of the harmonics produced are different for different musical instruments, each instrument has a characteristic sound. The following examples in figs. 5 and 6 should help to make this clearer.

Fig. 5 shows the fundamental and three harmonics produced by a bassoon playing an E of 329 Hz (cycles per second). The table gives the proportions, in percentages, of the total energy going into the production of the fundamental and harmonics. Harmonics having less than 1 per cent of the energy are not listed, so the cumulative total is 99 per cent instead of 100 per cent. The

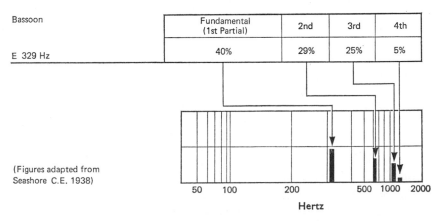

Bassoon	Fundamental (1st Partial)	2nd	3rd	4th
E 329 Hz	40%	29%	25%	5%

(Figures adapted from Seashore C.E. 1938)

50   100   200   500 1000 2000

Hertz

Fig. 5.   Partials present in bassoon tone

same applies to fig. 6. Although the precise location of harmonics and their relative intensities changes according to the amplitude and frequency of the note in question, there is usually sufficient consistency for the observer to recognize the tones as characteristically 'bassoon-like'. Fig. 5 also presents a graphical representation of the same tone. Note the large percentage of energy present in frequencies other than the fundamental. The sample bassoon tone may now be compared with a sample clarinet tone, shown in fig. 6. Note how, by comparison, the clarinet has more of its energy in the fundamental, making it more 'pure' and more like the examples given in figs. 1, 2, and 3. The clarinet tone in question has been chosen specially to illustrate this, and not all of its tones are so pure; conversely, others are more pure. Because of the nature of construction and mode of operation of musical instruments, the tone quality varies depending on which note is being played. Overall, however, the clarinet may be noted for the relative dominance of its fundamental which gives it its characteristic sound.

On modern electronic organs, or the more recent tone synthesizers, it is possible to add or subtract harmonics, and adjust their relative strengths, and so try out for oneself the kind of things referred to in the preceding paragraphs.

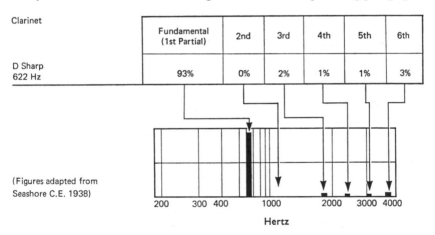

Clarinet	Fundamental (1st Partial)	2nd	3rd	4th	5th	6th
D Sharp 622 Hz	93%	0%	2%	1%	1%	3%

(Figures adapted from Seashore C.E. 1938)

200   300 400   1000   2000   3000 4000

Hertz

Fig. 6. Partials present in clarinet tone

When sounds are complex, as in the case of the bassoon or the clarinet, the simple wave-form graph (figs. 1, 2, and 3) is no longer an accurate description, because we know that more than one simple tone is present. Fortunately, it is possible to represent a fundamental and its harmonics in a single wave-form graph by a particular type of addition process. Some of the resulting wave-forms look extremely complicated, but basically they come about simply as a result of certain portions of the constituent tones adding together, and other parts cancelling out. Given a particular complex wave-form, such as might appear on an oscilloscope screen, an electronic device which is capable of producing a pictorial wave-form graph to describe a sound fed into it, it is possible to reverse the process and apply a technique known as Fourier analysis in order to discover what the simple constituent tones of a more complex form might be. An example of complex wave-form, in this case a violin producing a tone of frequency 196 Hz, is given in fig. 7a below. Fig. 7b then gives the simple tones which go together to produce it. The addition of simple wave-forms results in the

Fig. 7a.   *Violin tone (196 Hz)*

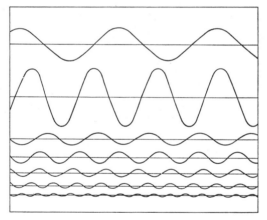

Fig. 7b. Partials dominant in the production of the wave-form in fig. 7a

complex wave-forms which give each musical instrument its characteristic tone quality or timbre.

Now that the main physical aspects of sound have been introduced, we may return to the topic introduced at the beginning of this chapter, namely the difference between sounds defined as noise and sounds defined as music. In terms of frequency, the range of sounds is potentially just as great in music as in noise. However, although the upper limit for the perception of sound lies for most individuals in the range 16,000 Hz to 20,000 Hz, musical sounds do not approach this limit. The top note on the piano, for example (four octaves above middle C), has a frequency of 4,186 Hz. (In musical terms, an octave is the distance between two notes having the same musical name, e.g. the distance between two consecutive As is an octave.) The ear could probably handle six octaves above middle C, if frequency response was the only consideration. Interestingly enough, however, research by Attneave and Olson (1971), in which subjects performed pitch transposition tasks, revealed that the judgements of musical and non-musical subjects became unreliable at frequencies over 5,000 Hz. It appears that there is a quite sudden loss of musical quality once this frequency is exceeded. The authors write, 'The empiricist may argue that tones above 5,000 Hz are unmusical because they do not occur as fundamentals in music, and the nativist may counter that they do not occur in music because they are unmusical.' The authors confess that their data shed no light on this puzzle. However, the finding is consistent with the fact that, in terms of frequency, music does not exploit the upper end of the audible pitch range. On the other hand, the low notes on the piano keyboard do in fact begin to encroach on the area where pitch perception becomes difficult, or breaks down. There is some difficulty about determining the frequency at which a periodic stimulus ceases to have a pitch, and becomes a series of discrete stimuli (Guttman and Pruzansky 1962; Guttman and Julesz 1963). Guttman and Julesz, for example, give 19 Hz as the lower limit for pitch perception, and the bottom note on a piano has a frequency (periodicity) of 27·5 Hz. Apart from the range of frequencies employed, music also differs from noise in so far as the frequencies employed in music are, in theory, discrete and precisely located (i.e. involving only the notes of the musical scale) whereas noise may contain frequencies at any point on a continuous scale. In fact, of course, musical tones may contain many aesthetic or accidental deviations from the tones present in the scale; none the less, the notes of the scale do have precise, formal locations. Finally, the frequencies present in musical sounds are selected to give particular effects such as consonance or dissonance, as a result of the way different instruments blend together. The frequency spectrum of noises, by comparison, does not normally suffer from such aesthetic constraints and is largely accidental.

In terms of amplitude, or subjective loudness, music and noise may be differentiated towards the upper limit. Until recently, it could be safely said that musical sounds did not approach closely to the upper threshold of loudness, or pain threshold. Measured in terms of decibels, a person standing in fairly close proximity to a jet aircraft about to take off would be subject to a sound-pressure level of about 150–60 dB. A rocket engine approaches 180 dB. Since sounds in excess of 130 dB are painful, exposure for even fairly short periods to excessive loudness levels such as these would be both unpleasant and likely to cause actual structural damage to the mechanism of the ear. (The decibel is a measure of the ratio of two powers. With respect to hearing, the decibel indicates the power of a particular sound as a ratio of the lowest level which the ear is capable of hearing. This lowest perceptible intensity level is conventionally taken to be equivalent to a rate of energy flow of 10^{-16} watts, or a pressure of 0·0002 dynes per square centimetre. The decibel scale has logarithmic properties, such that the addition of about 3 dB indicates an approximate doubling of power. A sound of 60 dB, therefore, has about one million times more power than a sound at the threshold of hearing (0 dB). For the sake of illustration, a 1,000-fold increase in voltage would have to be applied to a loudspeaker system i.e. the voltage or current ratio is the square root of the corresponding power ratio).

Instrumentalists sitting in the middle of a symphony orchestra do not experience sound levels as great as those of a jet aircraft or rocket. For example, an orchestra playing a *pianissimo* passage probably produces about 40 dB. This sound level is roughly the same as the ambient noise in an average office. The sound of the orchestra can, on occasion, be quieter than the background noise present in the theatre itself. Fortunately, human beings can direct their attention to different aspects of the sounds they encounter, and filter out the music (or, in general terms, the 'signal') from the background noise, even when the noise is louder. On the other hand, a symphony orchestra playing at its loudest would be unlikely to exceed 90 or 100 dB. Since an increase of 20 dB represents a hundredfold increase in actual power, the orchestra's *fortissimo* is about 90 or 100 thousand times less powerful than the noise of the jet engine. It should be noted, however, that modern amplification systems such as are commonly used by rock or pop groups may be collectively rated at many hundreds, or even thousands, of watts. With this equipment, three or four musicians can produce sound intensity levels many times greater than a 150-piece symphony orchestra. Health warnings and speculations about possible auditory damage as a result of prolonged exposure have appeared at times in the press and in the medical literature. At a recent Glasgow concert by the Mahavishnu Orchestra, some members of the audience made the interesting comment that they 'could not hear the music because it was so loud'. This is a fascinating comment, as it is apparently contradictory. A few members of the audience left the concert with feelings of dizziness and nausea. The sheer intensity of the sound had apparently made listening difficult for them, so much so that the task of attending to the excellent underlying music became impossible. The five musicians, interestingly, though closest to the sound source, appeared unaffected. One facetious spectator hypothesized that this was because they were already deaf.

There has been a very great deal of research into the effects of noise, and problems of noise control, and good summaries are available (e.g. Taylor 1970). Interesting papers, however, include research into sonic bangs of the Concorde variety by Broadbent and Robinson (1964). These authors investigated the annoyance of sonic bangs, relative to conventional piston-engine or jet aircraft. They found that the three sounds were *not* equally annoying when their perceived sound levels (PNdB) were simply matched. As intensity increased, the annoyance caused by sonic bangs increased more rapidly than did the annoyance of the other two aircraft noises. Thus, it appears that the subjective response to noise depends not merely on its perceived sound level, but also upon the type of noise. With respect to sound levels produced by rock groups, an excellent coverage of the possible effects upon hearing is given in Whittle and

Robinson (1974). Points raised are the differences between permanent impairment and temporary threshold shift (TTS), and the wide individual differences in susceptibility to temporary and permanent impairment. The point is made that impairment affects listening to music before it affects communication. It appears that musicians are at greater risk than audiences, because of more prolonged exposure, and also that some musicians are unwilling to accept auditory examination despite hearing difficulties. It is clear that more data are needed on this topic, but this paper makes fascinating reading, and contains an excellent bibliography. (A more general coverage of the noise problem appears in the Wilson Report 1963). Some groups have adopted an interesting strategy, one effect of which is to safeguard themselves against the high noise levels. A set of small slave amplifiers/speakers is located behind the musicians to enable them to monitor their own sound. A different output is directed to massive banks of speakers placed at the edge of the stage or platform (though, increasingly, it is the practice for the main speakers to be balanced by an extra member of the group situated at the rear of the auditorium with a mixer, linked to the main banks by remote control cables). The musicians do not therefore stand immediately in front of their own main speaker banks. Such a setting-up pattern is illustrated below in fig. 8, though at the present time this layout is not typical.

Fig. 8. Sample stage layout (aerial view)

In general terms the amplitude of music does not approach the threshold of pain, whereas noises do, and can even exceed this limit on occasion. However, the modern amplification used by certain rock bands makes this distinction less clear than formerly.

The position with regard to phase and complexity is rather more complicated. As we have seen in figs. 5 and 6, a single instrument playing a tone of a particular frequency produces not one, but several tones of different intensities and frequencies. These tones comprise a fundamental and harmonics. Normally, however, we encounter music in which not one but several instruments are playing at once. Discounting extremely modern or *avant-garde* music for the present, we can say that generally the notes produced by the different instruments are selected to produce particular pleasing effects by virtue of the fact that their fundamentals are related in much the same way as the harmonics are related in an individual instrument, i.e. the constituent notes of the chord are all multiples, or functions of multiples, of a fundamental frequency. In fact, all combinations of tones can be shown to be related in terms of functions of multiples of a fundamental. In general terms, however, the most 'consonant' chords comprise tones which are related to the lower rather than the higher harmonics of that fundamental. Thus, the elementary chord CEGC comprises a fundamental, plus functions of first, second and fourth harmonics of that fundamental. By contrast, the dissonant sound of B and C struck together comprises C and a function of its fifteenth harmonic. All harmonics up to the fifteenth beat with each other and create dissonance. Note, however, that consonance and dissonance are not completely explicable in these terms. Even the above is not strictly true, due to complications caused by the adoption of the equal-tempered rather than the natural scale.

If the fundamentals of different instruments are related, this immediately raises an important difficulty. If a single instrument produces several tones, how can the listener tell the difference between several instruments and a single instrument? For example, how can he tell that a particular piece is a duet between a violin and a trumpet rather than a solo by an instrument of strange timbre? It would appear that the precise way in which people distinguish between 'timbre' and 'harmony' in real life settings (i.e. in the concert hall) is still a subject of some debate. There is evidence, from laboratory experiments, to show that people can discriminate between sounds on the basis of phase differences. On the other hand, some workers have performed experiments showing that phase differences have no effect. In order to make sense of the evidence, consider first the operation of Ohm's law (not to be confused with the other Ohm's law, relating electrical current, voltage, and resistance). We have seen earlier how a complex tone is built up from a number of simple tones occurring in a phase-related manner. The law laid down by G. S. Ohm, whose major contributions to science took place in the first half of the nineteenth century, states that the ear analyses any composite mass of tones into its simpler components. By so doing, the observer can 'analyse out' the sound of a trumpet from that of a violin. However, the law goes further. If this auditory analysis is capable of breaking sounds down into their simple components, this can take place regardless of whether we are listening to a complex sound compounded from a number of different sources or to a tone of particular timbre from a single source. Hermann Helmholtz (1885), a supporter of the Ohm hypothesis, states, 'If the ear is able to analyse a composite musical tone produced by two tuning forks, it cannot but be in a position to carry out a similar analysis when the same motion of the air is produced by a single flute or organ pipe.' In other words, Ohm's law argues that the analysis of tones into their simple components takes place independently of whether such tones come from single or multiple sources. In order to support this notion, Helmholtz performed a large number of experiments in which he trained subjects to apply auditory analysis to complex tones from single sources. He showed beyond all contradiction that people can attend to the upper partials of complex tones from a single source. Helmholtz also showed that changing the phase relationships of the upper partials did not affect the perceptual quality of the sound. This is interesting because complex tones from single sources produce fundamental and harmonics which are phase-related whereas sounds from multiple sources are normally not phase-related. It has sometimes been assumed that the ear hears a single percept when sounds are phase-related and multiple percepts when sounds are not phase-related. Helmholtz's experiments, in which it is shown that people can attend to individual harmonics in single complex tones, demonstrate that such an assumption is at best an over-simplification.

Contrary to Ohm's law stands a different body of evidence, some scientific and some rooted in common sense. Dealing with the common-sense arguments first, our own subjective experience tells us that we do not hear a trumpet as a mass of simple tones, but rather as a single tone of particular quality or timbre. If this were not so, the instrument would appear to produce chords, a musical sound perceived as comprising several tones of different fundamental frequencies, and we know that this is not true. On the other hand, we can attend to an individual instrument in an orchestra and perceive its own characteristic complex tone although it is part of a chord comprising many complex tones. If Ohm's law were true, there could be no sense of timbre or tone quality, since all tones would appear to be just a conglomerate of pure (sine wave), simple sounds, and this would apply to an entire symphony orchestra. The Russian musicologist B. N. Teplov (1966), writing on this topic, expresses disagreement with the analytic approach to timbre in no uncertain terms. 'To say that such a notion is inexact or even erroneous would be too feeble. It must be said that it is in direct opposition to the facts.' (Translation from French by author, p. 72.) And later, 'The perception of timbre and the perception of harmony are two exclusive and opposed operations' (p. 75). In addition to this common-sense argument, there is scientific evidence to show that people can in fact detect changes in perceptual quality as a result of changes in phase of upper partials. This is in opposition to the findings of Helmholtz described earlier. Thus, Stevens and Davis (1938) write, in connection with some of their experiments, 'Not only does the phase of a harmonic that is present in the stimulus have an effect upon the threshold for distortion, *but it may also influence the subjective effects of a complex tone.* This statement is contrary to the usual assertion that, under Ohm's auditory law, the ear tends to analyse the components of a complex sound, regardless of their phase-relations.' Compare this with Helmholtz, 'Differences in musical quality of tone depend solely on the presence and strength of partial tones and in no respect on the differences in phase under which these partial tones enter into composition.'

More recent research by Rosenzweig (1961) seems conclusively to demonstrate, however, that phase differences are an important cue in auditory localization, especially for tones of about 1,000 Hz and below. Above this frequency, intensity differences seem to provide the main localization cue. If phase and intensity differences serve to locate sound sources, they could be used to locate different musical instruments which occupy different points in space. The listener might then know, for example, that a particular sound was produced by an oboe and a trumpet playing together, because he hears the sounds coming from two different places, rather than because of an ability to do particular types of spectral analysis. However, this still leaves us with a difficulty, since people can identify instruments, one assumes, when these are played over a mono hi-fi system, and where there are apparently no position cues. Two points are worth bearing in mind, however. Firstly, position cues (especially distance cues) are not totally absent from mono reproductions; secondly, knowledge of what orchestras sound like live probably affects perception of recorded music. We probably learn that very high pitch noises come from flutes or piccolos, loud strident noises from trumpets and lower ones from trombones, and so on. In other words, familiarity with the live situation enables us to make correct identifications under conditions where cues are degraded, as in a mono record (or to a lesser extent, a stereo record). Evidence for this point comes from Eagleson and Eagleson (1947) who asked musical and non-musical subjects to identify sounds made by different instruments played in isolation, when heard both directly and over a public-address system. Some instruments were more readily identified than others (e.g. bells, cymbals, trumpet were easy; saxophone, clarinet were difficult). Although, as one might expect, the musicians were better at the task than non-musicians, both groups made more errors than one would expect. Despite their previous experience, the musicians made many wrong identifications when instruments were heard through the loudspeakers. Identification was easier when instruments were heard direct. Thus, instruments heard in isolation over a public-address system are not always correctly identified, even by musical people. The authors concluded, 'Music, as such, is more than the discrete sounds that were used in the experiment. As is well known among musicians and other interested persons, music is best considered in terms of a total response. Hence, when separate sounds were taken out of the kind of pattern with which the musicians were acquainted, they were difficult to recognise. . . .' The importance of familiarity with the total context is thus implied. In addition, recognition was harder when loudspeakers were used.

In trying to resolve this debate, it is important to distinguish between what people *can* do and what they *do in fact*. For example, suppose we seat a blindfolded person in front of a large dinner plate, and place chips at one side, roast beef in the centre, greens at the other side, and so on. With practice, we might demonstrate that he *can* discover the location of the food on his plate by olfactory cues (sense of smell). Under normal circumstances, however, this is not the way he locates his food. In the same way, laboratory experiments which show that people *can* perform perceptual tasks do not necessarily show that they do them all the time. With this in mind, the disagreements pointed out above lose some of their importance for the task in hand, which is to say something about the way people *do* listen to music. From this standpoint, one can say, firstly, that people do not in fact break down the sounds produced by different instruments into a fundamental and its partials. They hear integrated sounds of a particular quality. Secondly, in distinguishing between instruments, it is possible that people use phase differences as cues, but various other cues exist. For instance, different instruments occupy different points in space, and people can locate sound sources in front of them (in the horizontal plane) with a high degree of accuracy (Sivian and White 1933), due to differences in the sound arriving at the two ears. They can often also see the instrument in question. In addition to localization cues, it is also possible that familiarity with the sound of different instruments affects their perception, and makes it more probable that a particular sound will be heard as a combination of two known instruments, rather than a new one of strange timbre; this latter may happen in the case of unusual combinations.

Returning again to the consideration of differences between musical sound and noise, we can say that there are definite phase relationships between the harmonics or partials contained in the tones of particular instruments. However, the phase relationship between different instruments playing at the same instant is a matter of chance alone. In this respect, there is no difference between music and noise. Thus, the noise of a bus with a squeaky brake involves a fundamental and a series of phase-related partials. However, there is only a chance phase relationship between the squeaks of two buses each with a squeaky brake. With respect to timbre, or the actual nature of the partials, however, the position is different. The aspect of timbre gives colour and richness to music, and the relative stability of partials makes instruments identifiable. As seen earlier, there is variability in the partials even on one instrument, but not so much that the instrument becomes completely unrecognizable. This fact, a number of variable fundamentals each having a fairly consistent set of partials, even at different fundamental frequencies, is not normally a characteristic of noise; with noise, frequencies and partials are more liable to non-organized fluctuation, and/or the stable elements tend not to change in any dimension at all (as in humming or droning noises).

So far, the main emphasis has been on certain physical characteristics of sounds, both musical and non-musical. Little more will be said with specific reference to this topic. To conclude this section, however, attention will now be directed at certain characteristics of the listener, as a result of which some of the complexities involved in musical perception might be revealed. The physical properties discussed so far have included frequency, amplitude and complexity. It is important to understand that these are all physical, objective dimensions, which give rise to the subjective sensations of pitch, loudness, and tone quality. Note, however, that these terms are not interchangeable. Thus pitch is not the same as frequency, loudness is not the same as amplitude. Though it may appear rather surprising, it is simply not true to say that the frequency of a tone specifies its pitch, nor that the amplitude of a tone specifies its loudness. *It is the very fact that the physical properties of sound fail to define the subjective response that makes music possible.* Without this fact, orchestras could never play in tune, trumpets could never play with pianos, and music as we know it could hardly exist at all. How can we explain this apparent paradox? The answer lies in the field of psychological study known as 'psychophysics'. Psychophysics is simply the study of the relationships between the physical properties of stimuli and the sensations they produce. A one-to-one relationship between stimulus and sensation does not exist. Scientists such as E. H. Weber, G. T. Fechner and more recently S. S. Stevens have searched for mathematical formulae to describe these complex relationships. Weber postulated that sensation was a constant fraction of stimulation; Fechner proposed a logarithmic relationship, and Stevens a 'power law' relating stimulus and sensation. The issue is still not completely resolved, though Stevens's law seems to be the most powerful. (There are many good accounts of these three psychophysical 'laws', e.g. Galanter 1962.) The precise nature of the relationships postulated by these workers is, however, less important here than the notion that the way we perceive things is subject to considerable variation even though the stimulus remains constant. Thus our sensation of colour varies with the colour of the background, or with varying light conditions; the apparent difference between the size of two objects varies with the absolute size of the objects, and our ability to detect small sounds or dim lights varies, depending on how alert or how inattentive we are, or depending on what we expect to happen. There is an almost limitless number of similar examples.

Psychophysical investigations of the way people perceive sounds show that in this area, too, there is considerable variation. In the first place, it has been shown that the pitch of a tone of given frequency is affected by the amplitude of the tone. Conversely, the loudness of a tone is influenced by its frequency. Put simply, if we increase or decrease the amplitude of a given tone without altering frequency, a change of pitch results. This effect of an interaction between loudness and pitch (amplitude and frequency) has been well documented by Stevens (1935). In order to investigate this effect, he devised a task which seems incredible to many musicians. He presented the subject alternately with one of two electronically generated tones of slightly different frequency; the subject could adjust the amplitude (and hence the subjective loudness) of one of the two tones. It was found that the subject could match the pitch of the two tones, compensating for the frequency difference by altering the loudness. In the graph below, adapted from Stevens, the relationship between pitch and intensity (amplitude) may be seen.

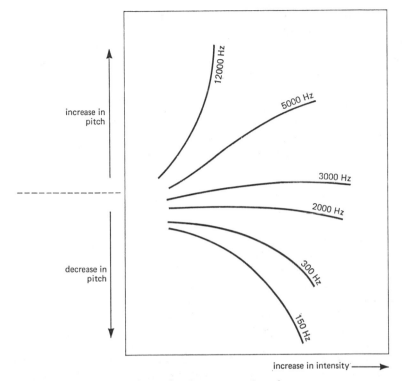

increase in
pitch

decrease in
pitch

12000 Hz

5000 Hz

3000 Hz

2000 Hz

300 Hz

150 Hz

increase in intensity ⟶

Fig. 9.   Relationship between pitch and intensity

The graph shows the effects upon pitch of increasing amplitude, for tones of different frequencies. Put very simply, tones of high pitch appear to go higher as they become louder, and low tones appear to become lower. There is a range in the middle of the audible frequency band where there is little effect upon pitch as a result of intensity change. It is worth while noting that other workers (Fletcher and Munson 1933) have performed similar experiments the other way round, i.e. they have constructed graphs which show what happens when intensity (amplitude) is held constant for a tone of 1,000 Hz, and subjects are asked to match another tone in terms of loudness, by changing the frequency. Again, tones of different pitches are set at different intensities in order to make them sound equally loud. This confirms the nature of the interaction between pitch and loudness. Using methods such as those above, changes of pitch in excess of a full musical tone have been shown to occur as a result of changes in intensity. It should be noted in passing, however, that the tones used in these experiments were isolated tones devoid of any context, and also that there may be individual differences in susceptibility to this effect. Even the same subject shows variable pitch judgements on different occasions, and the variability of the phenomenon suggests that a straightforward physiological explanation is unlikely. The subjective pitch phenomenon was quantified by Stevens, Volkmann and Newman (1937), who produced a scale of subjective pitch called the 'mel' scale. Stevens's methods with respect to pitch scaling are not without controversy, however (see recent work by Franzen, Nordmark and Sjoberg 1972). In a study of subjective musical pitch, Ward (1954) found significant differences in subjects' pitch judgements on different days. A good review of music from a perceptual point of view is given by Ward, in Tobias (1970). The differences between psychophysical scales like the mel scale, and what musicians mean by pitch, is again discussed. Ward also refers to research by Elfner (1964), who showed that subjects deprived of sleep required a 5 per cent increase in frequency separation before two tones would be judged to be an octave apart. Pitch thus also seems to vary depending on the state of the listener.

When we consider the complex tones produced by musical instruments, further complications occur. Firstly, as with any kind of tones, extremely high or extremely low notes tend to sound less loud than those of the middle register, even though intensity is kept constant. This basic effect is easily understood when one considers that the ear can respond to tones only within a certain band of frequencies. Thus, most people are unable to hear sounds with a frequency higher than about 18,000 or 19,000 Hz. (The upper limit for the young, good human ear is about 20,000 Hz.) Conversely, it has been found that tone perception ceases at frequencies below about 20 Hz, though the findings here tend to be more variable than for the upper limit. Between these limits, however, the ear is not uniformly sensitive. We do not suddenly begin to hear sounds at 19,000 Hz; if we listen to a tone of continuously descending pitch but of constant amplitude which starts at about 30,000 Hz we become dimly aware of its presence when it approaches the upper threshold, and more positively aware as it descends further. With further descent, the tone moves through a maximally sensitive area at about 3,000 to 1,500 Hz and then into less sensitive areas towards the lower limit. The subjective effect of this is to make the tone sound louder in the more sensitive areas, and quieter in the less sensitive areas. Now, this raises an important issue with respect to complex musical tones; namely, a tone with a certain constant harmonic structure cannot subjectively sound the same in terms of quality, at different fundamental frequencies. For example, imagine a tone has a fundamental frequency of 1,000 Hz and three strong harmonics at 2,000, 3,000 and 4,000 Hz. Such a tone will appear to the listener to have a strong overtone structure which will impart a timbre of a certain richness. However, the same tone (i.e. with the same harmonic structure) sounding a fundamental of 6,000 Hz will produce its three harmonics at 12,000, 18,000 and 24,000 Hz of which the latter will be inaudible. Since musical tones usually comprise rather more than four partials, the loss of audible harmonics with increases in the fundamental frequency is correspondingly greater. This change in timbre with change in frequency is a necessary concomitant of the operation of the mechanism of the ear. In the experience of the author, many music teachers stress the importance of 'keeping the tone constant' at all points in the register, and claim that a characteristic of a master instrumentalist playing a fine instrument is an ability to do just this. It will be readily appreciated that, unless an instrument produces absolutely pure tones (sine waves), which they do not, such a feat is impossible. Perhaps what is meant is that one should strive to make the best use of the natural resonance regions of the instrument (in physical terms, attempt to produce an ideal 'formant'), thus avoiding, for example, thin or squeaky high notes and rough or breathy low notes. (Note, however, that squeaky high notes and breathy low notes are used to good aesthetic effect in some music.) The loss of perceptible harmonic content with increases in frequency contributes to the subjective effects of a loss in loudness which we have already noted, and also the impression that high notes are in some way thinner and clearer than low notes, which appear to be fatter and duller. Some authors describe high tones as being 'denser' and 'less voluminous' than low tones (e.g. Stevens 1934). This change in the subjective perception of tones as one proceeds from lower to higher tones has led Teplov to propose that the perceived pitch of a tone is based on two components ('*Théorie des deux composantes de la hauteur*'), namely a component arising as a result of change in frequency, and a component deriving from the sensation of clearness or dullness of the tone. One could perhaps use this latter component speculatively to explain the very fact that we use terms like 'high' or 'low' to describe sounds, when these terms are normally only meaningful as descriptions of concrete objects. Why tones of increasing frequency should give the sensation 'up' rather than 'down' is a fascinating problem but beyond the scope of this present chapter.

Finally, it remains only to note that the pitch of a tone can be influenced by its harmonic content, and that the loudness can also be similarly affected. It can be seen therefore that, when considering pitch, loudness, and tone quality (the subjective aspects of frequency, amplitude and complexity), we have an extremely complicated relationship in which the perception of any one is affected by the nature of the other two. To conclude this chapter, we are, therefore, left with something of a dilemma. At the outset, we might have imagined that music consisted of the production of a series of sounds having definite pitches, and standing in certain relationships to each other. However, now we are left with a state of affairs whereby every time we change the loudness we change the timbre and vice versa; every time we change either of these we alter the pitch; every time we alter the pitch we change the loudness, which in itself might further alter the pitch, and so on. In addition, we have seen from our coverage of timbre and harmony that it is not clear how people distinguish between a chord produced by several instruments and a complex tone from a single instrument; given this uncertainty we ought not to have any clear notion as to how many people are involved in the production of this mêlée of sound. Such a state of affairs should by all accounts result in an auditory percept similar to a herd of angry bulls of indeterminate number in an ironmonger's shop. And yet we know from our own experience that this is not the case. Orchestras *do* appear to play in tune, notes *do not* veer and change with every variation in loudness, and we *can* identify the characteristic sound of the oboe at different points in its register. The problem, then, is to explain how people can organize this auditory material and extract form and meaning from an array of sounds which, according to scientific evidence, should be cacophonous to a high degree.

3 The musical present

When we consider the physical aspects of music, certain problems are encountered. As we have seen, the precise physical nature of the sound (e.g. its frequency, intensity or complexity) fails to specify the exact nature of what we hear. A change in any one of these physical dimensions affects the listeners' response to other dimensions, although these latter remain unchanged physically. It should be apparent, therefore, that a person's response to a piece of music will be more fruitfully explored in terms of what he or she subjectively hears, rather than in terms of the purely physical characteristics of the musical sound. The basic building blocks of music thus consist not of simple physical events, but of people's responses to those events. This fact goes a long way to explaining why it is so difficult to distinguish between music and noise in purely physical terms.

The reason for dealing, in this chapter, with basic 'building blocks' is to pick out the important ingredients which combine to create an overall structure. In the end, it is the perception of overall form and structure which is important; when we look at a great cathedral we do not see the individual blocks of stone, but rather an edifice having a sense of wholeness. None the less, by examining individual blocks or keystones, we can find out more about cathedrals if we so wish. In a similar sense, we can look at the subjective building blocks of music, though these are barely noticed when we listen to a symphony.

The crucial quality about music, which distinguishes it from most of the visual arts, is a temporal one. If we look at a painting we can build up an impression of its wholeness in a very short space of time. Although we perhaps cannot direct our attention to every aspect of it simultaneously, our field of vision is such that we can 'take it all in' in an instant. We can see its boundaries, and its extent, and make judgements about its various qualities. Further, we can scan and re-scan particular elements of the painting whenever we wish, since it is permanently before us. Finally, if we leave the room for a while, we can return at leisure to examine the picture further, and can indeed find it exactly as it was before, apart from changes due to the processes of decay in the picture and in ourselves, which would normally be imperceptible. None of this is possible with music, however. Nobody has ever seen (perceived) a symphony in its entirety, since as soon as a note is played it is gone, vanished, and all we have left is its memory. We can only make judgements about music by comparing recent memories with less recent memories, all concerning events which have taken place in the past. If we enter a concert in the middle, and stay for only a short time, we can have no notion of the boundaries or extensiveness of the work (unless we happen to remember from a previous occasion when we heard a similar but not identical piece of music). Finally, if we leave the hall for a time, there is no way of examining again the things which took place while we were away. They are lost for ever. If we infer from memory what took place in the interim, we could easily be wrong. The pianist might have forgotten his part, and improvised a section; or the 'cellist might have fallen off the stage with a great crash.

At any one instant (let us call this instant the 'present') all that is perceived is a single input of sound which in itself is meaningless. Such events of the present have little consequence for music when considered individually; yet music comprises nothing more than a series of such events of the present. These events come together to form something which is always an event of the past. We have not heard a symphony until the last note is played; but no sooner is the last note played than the symphony no longer exists, except perhaps in memory. Clearly, the score for the symphony still exists. However, it is assumed that the symphony was written because the composer intended to create sounds of a certain aesthetic quality, rather than a set of aesthetically pleasing hieroglyphics on a piece of paper. The score is thus a coded plan, or blueprint, which enables the symphony itself to be recreated in approximately the same form; in itself it is not the symphony. (The Channel Tunnel does not exist simply because the plans for it exist, though it may do so at some time in the future.) As soon as it is complete, it vanishes into the past, and can never reappear in exactly the same form. This is especially true of music like modern jazz, for example, where the emphasis on improvisation means that every performance is unique, and the actual live performance is irretrievable.

A distinction has thus been made between events of the past and events of the present, and the intention is to treat these two types of events separately, commencing with events of the present.

To start with, it may be helpful to consider a particular way in which events of the present can be described. It is well known that if a light is flashed on and off sufficiently rapidly, an observer sees not a flashing light but a source of continuous illumination. This effect is employed in the cinema projector where a series of quite separate and distinct images are projected at a rate at which the individual images cannot be observed, and where the separate frames of film appear to fuse into a continuous, animated scene. The exact speed at which such fusion takes place depends on a variety of factors, including the size and brightness of the image, the wavelength and intensity of the light, and several other parameters (Kling and Riggs 1972), but generally it appears that, notwithstanding other factors, fusion takes place at rates of between fifteen and sixty presentations per second. Now, the ability to distinguish between closely spaced flashes of light is a function of temporal acuity; on the basis of the above type of evidence, it has been argued (Moles 1968) that a definition of 'the present' can be offered in terms of people's ability to tell the difference between successive events. If two events take place so rapidly in succession that we cannot perceive them as separate, then they must be perceptually simultaneous. In terms of this definition, therefore, the present is conceived as comprising an endless series of units of time of finite length; two successive events which are so fleeting as to fall within one of these units will both occur in the present, i.e. they are not separable in time. (Further elaboration of the 'psychological moment' theory of perception is given in Stroud (1955) and in the context of auditory recognition processes, in Massaro (1972).)

The notion that time constants govern the perception of events has some interesting ramifications. Different species of animals have different time constants. For example, it takes a Siamese fighting fish about 1/30 second to become aware of sensory stimulation. A general overall figure of 1/18 second has been suggested for humans. By contrast, the time constant for a snail is about 1/4 second. Insects appear to have a value of only 3–4 milliseconds (about 1/250 second). Creatures with short time constants will thus 'live faster' than those with longer time constants, and their perception of events will be accordingly very different (James 1890). Snails, therefore, only seem slow to creatures operating on shorter time constants, and not to other snails.

In terms of the above definition, events of the present will therefore be events falling within one of these postulated units of time; since all events falling within such a unit appear simultaneous, each unit will appear completely homogeneous (i.e. no perceived change will occur within a unit) and it will thus approximate closely to a steady state (see page 28) of brief duration. This definition has certain other implications. For example, two clicks separated by only two or three milliseconds (a millisecond is one-thousandth of a second) can be perceived by most people as two separate events, and only at separations less than these approximate values does fusion take place (Green 1971). It is notable that the performance of this task demonstrates a higher degree of temporal acuity for hearing than for seeing. It is implied therefore that the 'length of the present' for the ear is of shorter duration than for the eye. No doubt there are still different lengths of present for other sensory modalities. Note, however, that when sounds of such very brief durations are presented, we are not able to say a great deal about the pitch of the tones involved. Indeed, a tone of 1,000 Hz presented for one millisecond cannot have any pitch since there is only time for one cycle or pulse, and a single element, logically, cannot occur at a frequency (Miller 1948). However, with higher tones for which a frequency can be meaningfully specified, we are still able to report correctly that there are two successive 'bleeps' at speeds where we can say very little about their pitch. Pitch discrimination tends to become poorer with high frequencies, especially those over about 4,000 cycles per second (4 KHz), but this does not affect the present argument. With short presentations, we are able to say even less about their pitch. Thus, even within the hearing modality there are different time constants depending upon which attribute of the sound we are concerned with. Since, with music, pitch is a crucial dimension, our definition demands that this remain constant for a number of consecutive lengths of present before we can unambiguously interpret the pitch information as distinct from information about the discreteness or simultaneity of the units. In other words, we can tell that tones are not simultaneous before we can describe their attributes. In addition there is certain experimental evidence which presents us with an even more perplexing problem. It has been shown (Warren and Warren 1970, Warren and Obusek 1972, Bregmann and Campbell 1971) that when auditory stimuli are presented at certain rates, the experimental subjects are able to identify the sounds, but cannot tell in what order they are presented. This suggests that more time is needed to extract 'order' information than to identify the sounds. Thus, in an investigation into perceived order in different sensory modalities, Hirsh and Sherrick (1961) suggest that temporal resolving power has two components, one involving the perception of successivity of events, which is a necessary but not a sufficient condition for the second, which involves perception of order.

Now, in order to obtain the fullest benefit from a piece of music, we need to obtain information from a number of different dimensions. We need to know about the pitch of notes, their loudness, the order in which they come, their duration, and so on. Although we have not examined every one of these dimensions individually, the examples given might suggest that there is considerable variation in the times taken for the listener to extract each type of information. As far as music is concerned, therefore, a definition of 'the present' based on the ability to discriminate successivity of two auditory events is rather inadequate, since within such a time unit there is a paucity of information other than successivity or simultaneity. A more meaningful definition will be obtained if we use as our base the time taken to interpret that type of information which takes the longest to process, and which at the same time is important for our understanding of music. The length of such a time period is not too well defined, probably because it has not been investigated scientifically with this question in mind. However, Moles has suggested an overall value of about 1/20 (or 0·05) second, on the basis that pitch and loudness become less clearly defined with any shorter duration. The implication is that within such a period more and more information is becoming available as time passes. If we accept Moles's value for the duration of the musical present, then it follows that any piece of music with individual tonal elements having durations less than the postulated period will appear to be degraded, in the sense that there will be insufficient time to find out all the relevant subjective facts about the notes involved. In other words, if the notes occur more rapidly than do the postulated units of time, the listener is going to know less about them. (In fact, the situation is rendered less clear-cut by the intrusion of auditory decay. Upon cessation of a sound stimulus, the auditory sensation takes a finite length of time to decay to zero. This process imposes constraints on the temporal resolving power of the ear, e.g. Plomp (1964).) It is tempting to speculate that the well-known rubric invoked by many teachers of musical instruments when stressing the importance of slow practice, which may be roughly transcribed as, 'If you can't play good, play fast', is a response to precisely this state of affairs. However, this seems unlikely, since the durations involved are still extremely short in musical terms (if Moles's estimate is correct), and the 'Minute waltz', played at this sort of speed, lasts about thirty seconds. However, there are occasions when notes of this speed, and a good deal faster, do occur, as for instance when a harp or a piano player runs a finger from one end of the instrument to the other, in a *glissando*. If done fast enough, the effect produced has a continuous quality, although oddly we may at the same time be aware that the noise is composed of successive events. As an experiment, one can try running a finger between two Cs on the piano whilst keeping the eyes closed. If a friend can be persuaded to hold down one note so that it will not sound, it is possible to find a speed at which one is aware that a note is missing, but unable to say which one. The explanation may be that, at this speed, we can deal with information about the separateness of the notes, but cannot extract the pitch information. The only way we can say which one is missing is to locate the pitches of the notes on either side and infer that there is too large a gap in between. If the notes follow each other too rapidly, this becomes impossible.

Summarizing, it has been argued that it is useful to conceive of the present, at least so far as music is concerned, as a unit of finite length, rather than as a theoretically dimensionless point in time analogous to a point in geometry. The reason for proposing this is that pieces of music are made up of series of tonal events, and it takes people finite lengths of time to analyse the components of these events. If the events take place faster than they can do this, then a greater or lesser degree of confusion results depending on how much information they are able, or unable, to extract. If a study of musical events of the present is to be more than a study of confusion, we must define these as units during which time in fact passes, which is perhaps paradoxical, but also rather necessary.

In terms of our revised definition, a musical event of the present will thus be a sound having a quality which is a function of the frequencies present; if these frequencies consist of a fundamental and upper partials, the sound will appear to have a definite pitch. It will also have a certain loudness. (For the time being, certain issues are being laid aside; for example, the transients of musical instruments which prove to be a great aid in identification, though of very short duration (Taylor 1965); also the fact that a tone takes a certain length of time to grow to its full perceived loudness (Von Bekesy 1960).) Now we have already seen in the previous chapter that these different attributes of sound interact so that the pitch we hear depends to some extent on the intensity of the tone; the loudness varies with the frequency; and, finally, the quality or timbre of the sound alters with changes in the other two dimensions. Yet, when we think of a piece of music as a whole (i.e. as an event that we remember), we are not immediately struck by such vagaries of pitch, loudness or quality. In fact, the scientific findings seem directly to contradict our own everyday experience.

The experiments which show that the pitch of a tone can be altered simply by altering its intensity are well documented, and have already been described in the first chapter. However, it has also been convincingly demonstrated that different types of tones show this effect to differing extents. Tones which are pure (sine-wave tones) are found to be far more prone to pitch change as a result of alterations in intensity than are complex tones. In other words, when we alter the intensity of a complex tone, such as that produced by a violin, the pitch appears to remain more stable than for a pure tone of the same frequency. It has been suggested (Fletcher 1934) that a complex tone of 200 Hz, comprising five partials, is about five times more stable than a pure tone of the same frequency. As an explanation for the apparent stability of the pitch of music, it has been pointed out that the instruments of the orchestra produce complex tones rather than pure tones. The notion is that the presence of upper partials in a tone assists the listener in arriving at a more stable perception of its pitch (Ritsma 1966a, 1967) and that this is so because a complex tone will contain partials which fall within the frequency region at which there is little interaction between pitch and intensity (Stevens and Davis 1938; see fig. 9). On the face of it, such an explanation seems to tidy up all the loose ends quite nicely. The instruments of the orchestra produce tones which are complex, and so, on the basis of the foregoing argument, we predict that the tones of musical instruments will have more stable pitches than do artificially generated sine-wave tones. Therefore, music sounds in tune at all intensity levels. There are, none the less, still one or two minor difficulties. Firstly, complex tones are not completely stable in pitch when the intensity varies; they are simply more stable than sine tones. The evidence from the laboratory suggests that pitch changes do take place with complex tones, and that these ought to interfere with the perception of music. Secondly, orchestral instruments produce tones of widely differing complexities, and the tonal complexity even varies within an individual instrument. For example, the tone of a flute playing in the upper register contains virtually no overtones, and might be considered virtually pure. According to Olson (1967) the overtones are practically non-existent. Therefore, flutes should not be able to play consistently in tune in this region. On the other hand, the oboe is very rich in harmonics, and should be very stable in pitch. Other instruments might have tones with degrees of complexity greater or less than the examples given.

It is not clear just how much the addition of a single overtone to a pure fundamental increases the stability of its pitch (Ritsma 1966b). For example, it could be that the addition of a single overtone is all that is necessary to increase the stability to a maximum; or it could be that stability increases with the addition of every subsequent overtone. Since the explanation for the greater stability of complex tones rests on the supposed effect of tones falling in the frequency region where there is little interaction between pitch and intensity, we might suppose that only the addition of tones in this region will have such a stabilizing influence. The addition of tones not falling in this region will have no such stabilizing effect. This suggests that the simple addition of more overtones will not *per se* produce greater stability of pitch. We must know where the overtones fall; and, from what we already know about the nature of overtone structures, we can guess that whether the important overtones fall in the stabilizing region will depend on the fundamental frequency of the note in question, and also upon the instrument producing it. There are other implications from the above, but these do not concern us here. The aim has been merely to show that the explanation offered for the greater stability of musical tones is not a completely comprehensive explanation of what happens in musical performance.

A clue as to the resolution of this problem comes from some research performed by Lewis and Cowan (1936) though at first glance the results are still baffling. These two scientists made measures of the interaction between intensity and pitch using skilled performers playing the 'cello and the violin. This contrasts with the electronically generated tones used by the other workers mentioned. As a consequence, one can infer that the type of experimental testing situation would be rather different, and that the degree of control over extraneous factors would be less. After all, musicians are not machines (some conductors might disagree!) and they cannot be switched on and off precisely, and at will. There is also a degree of uncertainty introduced by variations in bowing (Cardozo and van Noorden 1968), the presence of transients, extraneous mechanical noise and so on. Using live performers in this way, it was found that there was very little influence on the pitch as a result of intensity changes, and that any such effects found were rather unreliable and inconsistent. Lewis and Cowan concluded that either 'intensity has no consistent effect on the pitches of violin and 'cello tones, or that the effect is so slight as to be counteracted by other factors in performance'. This conclusion offers a definite clue, namely, that what takes place in a sound-proof laboratory is not necessarily what takes place in a live concert.

In order to explain the two conflicting bodies of evidence, namely one which implies that musical instruments should sound out of tune, and another based on our own experience which tells us that this is not necessarily the case, the following suggestions are offered. Evidence about the nature of actual musical instruments suggests that explanations of why they sound in tune or out of tune, which are based on studies using electronic sound sources in an audio laboratory, may at times be of only marginal relevance, and at worst complete red herrings. In a review of the literature on audition, prior to 1967, Lawrence (1968) hints at this problem when he writes, 'one might well wonder just how meaningful a subjective report of the sensations resulting from many of these presentations can be', and later, 'When some weird type of signal is presented to him, he [the subject] may have to invent an explanation of what it sounds like.' The argument is based on the notion that there can be subjective pitch deviations (out of tune) even though the tone in question is accurate (in tune) in terms of frequency. There is a fundamental misconception here. Orchestras and orchestral instruments simply do not reproduce frequencies accurately. With most orchestral instruments (there are a few exceptions) the performer has a degree of latitude over the notes he plays. He can bend the note until it sounds in tune. Now, in the audio-laboratory, the confusion arises because there are two criteria by which a note may be judged: namely, the way it *sounds*, and the way it *is*. The scientist becomes confused because he tries to reconcile the one with the other. On the other hand, the musician has only one criterion, and provided it sounds right nobody has the slightest interest in what it is. For example, if a violinist plays a note which sounds out of tune, sharp let us say, he does not check it with an electronic counter to find out if it is accurate in terms of frequency. He simply shifts his finger down a bit. Furthermore, the mode of construction of certain musical instruments is in some cases such that the underlying physical principles involved make it actually impossible for that instrument to play naturally in tune. Even individual instruments often have a note which is always out of tune, and for which allowance must be made. For example, the Boehm clarinet (McGinnis and Pepper 1945) has a natural tendency to be out of tune (i.e. inaccurate in terms of frequency) at certain parts of its range. In a similar fashion, the three-valve system employed in trumpets results in lengths of tubing which simply cannot naturally resonate at the required frequencies towards the bottom of the range (Noble 1964, Webster 1954). The notes C sharp and D in particular are always sharp to a noticeable degree. In all these cases the onus falls on the performer to make the instrument sound in tune, by shifting the pitch with his lips, or whatever means of compensation are at his disposal. In other words, he has to make the instrument produce a note that it is not really 'happy' with.

Even on fixed-pitch instruments, like the piano, where the performer has no control over the state of tuning of the instrument during a performance, there is no unanimity about the frequencies to which it is tuned. There is considerable variation between different pianos any one of which might individually be considered in tune (e.g. White 1937, 1939; Martin and Ward 1954). After all, when the piano tuner comes to tune the instrument, he tunes it until it sounds right to him, not until it is right. He uses his ear and his experience, not an electronic counter. It appears in fact that the stresses on a piano string (particularly what are referred to as 'loading effects' and 'end effects') produce a slight distortion of certain partials, particularly the second, from their natural frequency. In tuning octaves, beats are minimized when the upper note coincides with the second partial of the lower tone, and this arrangement appears to sound more in tune than perfect frequency accuracy. The degree of 'detuning' necessary is a function of the particular strings being used, and the bridges at either end of the vibrating length. Given this fact, any given piano can only truly be in tune with itself, or with another which has the identical physical characteristics. Two such completely identical instruments cannot exist.

In addition, notes may not be tuned in the same way. The terms 'equal temperament' and 'just intonation' describe types of musical scale in which the notes are tuned according to different systems. In the system of just intonation, the scale steps are determined by the smallest whole-number ratios possible, e.g. 1/2, 2/3, 3/4, which ratios specify the octave, fifth, fourth, and so on. In the scale of equal temperament, however, the octave is simply divided into twelve equal steps, a procedure which produces ratios slightly different from the simple ratios of the just scale, e.g. a fifth is specified by the ratio 2/2·996614, a fourth by the ratio 3/4·00452. The reason for the adoption of the equal-tempered scale is that such a system allows the pitch ratios to remain constant in all keys. Regardless of which note you start from, the ensuing scale intervals have exactly the same pitch ratios. This is not the case with just intonation, and a piano tuned to this system could only be justly tempered in one key. Other keys would have different frequency ratios for the scale intervals, and would sound most strange.

For example, in just temperament, the interval of a fourth is specified by the ratio 3/4. Thus, if the interval were from C to F, then the frequencies of the two tones would be 264 Hz and 352 Hz respectively. Suppose now that we consider a different key and a different interval, for example, a major seventh in the key of G flat. The major seventh in just intonation is specified by the ratio 8/15. Since a justly tuned G flat has a frequency of 185·4 Hz, the ratio tells us that an F in this key must have a frequency of 347·6 Hz. There is the problem. We have seen how, in the key of C, the note F should have a frequency of 352 according to just intonation. In the key of G flat, however, it ought to have a frequency of 347·6. Equal temperament, therefore, is a compromise which makes it possible to play in different keys without having a keyboard containing all the alternatives necessary under just intonation. In return, some slight precision in tuning is sacrificed, though the listener usually does not notice this. Some experts, however, claim that the just scale has a beauty which is lost under equal-tempered tuning. It is often claimed, for example, that 'The well-tempered clavier' (a group of forty-eight preludes and fugues by J. S. Bach) sounds much better played on a well-tempered (i.e. justly tempered) instrument. It is difficult to know exactly how great the difference is, in perceptual terms.

Interestingly enough, from time to time energetic persons have assembled keyboards containing all or many of the alternative tones necessitated by just tuning. In an Appendix, Helmholtz (1885) describes a number of strange keyboard instruments which take just intonation into account, including his own 'harmonical' (a type of harmonium manufactured by Messrs Moore and Moore of London, and then retailing for the princely sum of 165 shillings), Mr Brown's 'voice harmonium', General Perronet Thompson's 'enharmonic organ', and Mr Bosanquet's 'generalized fingerboard'. This latter is illustrated on page 429 of Helmholtz's book. There are fifty-three notes in each octave, an array sufficient to cause any pianist to leap from the nearest tall building. Helmholtz claims that the difference between just and equal temperament is instantly discernible, and that the latter is 'unpleasant to uncorrupted ears'.

(It is worth noting, in passing, that there have been a great many other hilarious musical inventions from time to time. The pages of the Journal of the Acoustical Society of America contain descriptions of patents filed for such gems as a trumpet mouthpiece with built-in chin rest, 'musical gloves' [*sic*] and a 'bass-viol cart'.)

Although, as every musician knows, Western music uses the scale of equal temperament, the physical principles underlying the construction of certain instruments are fixed and immutable. Decisions about whether to use a scale of equal temperament or a scale of just intonation do not affect the way such instruments operate. The tones produced by brass and wind instruments, for example, are governed by the laws of resonance and of harmonics, and not by the mathematical abstractions underlying the scale of equal temperament. The equal-tempered scale is itself based on the notion of compromise and ought to sound consistently out of tune.

Finally, on this point, it has been shown that violin players show deviations from the correct frequency when performing a piece (Seashore 1938; Shackford 1961, 1962a, 1962b). Consider then a violin section in an orchestra, with every individual applying his own accidental or deliberate deviations and at the same time employing a vibrato which may or may not be synchronized with the vibrato of others, and which will involve his own personal degree of frequency modulation (frequency modulation is what gives vibrato its 'wobble'). In producing a vibrato, the player causes the note to alter rapidly in pitch, from one which is slightly higher than that required to one slightly lower. The pitch thus moves rapidly up and down, moving about an average or 'mean' position which has the required pitch. The actual speed of these modulations or wobbles, and the distance moved on either side of the mean position, are highly personal characteristics of individual players. Vibrato should not be confused with the roughly similar tremolo, which involves amplitude (loudness) modulation. In tremolo, it is the loudness of the note which fluctuates, not its pitch. All the above are subject to the vagaries of individual bowing technique. In the light of such a large number of sources for individual variation, the notion that musical performance demands frequency accuracy must be revised, and brought into its proper perspective.

In the end, we can do little better than echo a statement by Winckel (1967), referring to written music, in which he states, 'The essential point is not to be prejudiced by the written page of music, and to rely on the *ear as the sole authority and court of appeal.*' The statement stems from the idea that musical notes do not specify sonic events of precise and invariant frequencies and durations, so that what we actually hear is the most important factor rather than the written specification. Winckel's statement then seems equally applicable in the realm of frequency and pitch accuracy. So far as music is concerned, being in tune means sounding in tune to the listener. It is clear that context has an important part to play for the listener in determining what sounds in tune. Meyer (1962b) has shown how the pitch ratio 51:87 can be made to sound like either of two truly melodic intervals, simply by manipulating the context. An earlier paper (Meyer 1962a), dealing with the seeming misperception of the ratio 55:32 has been criticized by Ward (1962). Boomsliter and Creel (1962), however, performed experiments with the musical director of the Albany Symphony Orchestra, and found that, during Mozart's 'Serenata notturna', the subject insisted that a note was right (i.e. in tune) when it was considerably in error judged by the physical criterion of cycles per second. They concluded, 'This, and many other special tunings, equally stable in the subject's replayings and equally insisted upon as "right", are not insisted upon as "the" tuning for Do or Re or Mi, but as the tuning for a particular note in the phrase at hand.'

In our coverage of the units which comprise music, we have so far neglected an important type of sound event, namely that in which more than one fundamental is present (i.e. sounds resulting from several instruments playing simultaneously). It seems almost certain that one of the factors which prevents performers from slipping into regions of excessive pitch deviation, and producing marked shifts in tonality, is the nature of the interactions between simultaneously sounding tones. When tones of the musical scale are sounded together in the form of chords, particularly if they comprise simple intervals, the success (for want of a better word at this point) of the blend or fusion depends not on whether the constituent tones sound individually in tune, but on their actual physical frequency. This means in fact that we can have situations in which two tones individually sound out of tune, yet come together and form a perfect harmonious fusion; reciprocally, we might come across two tones which individually sound to be in tune but which produce an unpleasant or dissonant effect when sounded together. (The problems of consonance and dissonance will be dealt with later in chapter 11.) In other words, if we perceive an individual instrument, its degree of 'in-tuneness' or 'out-of-tuneness' will be judged solely in terms of what we hear. However, if we perceive several instruments playing together to produce an overall chordal texture, the 'in-tuneness' of the intervals involved will depend much more on the frequency accuracy of the constituent tones. The reason for this, it is usually argued, is that beats are produced when intervals are not tuned accurately in terms of frequency, and this results in a feeling of roughness in the sound which makes it unpleasant to listen to. (An excellent and imaginative attempt to describe dissonance in terms of words was made by Winckel, who employed the phrase 'a sort of audible friction' to describe the effects of the phenomenon.) The nature of beats has been much discussed by many eminent authors, and it is not proposed here to give a thoroughgoing description. However, a very brief summary may serve to illustrate the meaning of the term.

If we refer back to chapter 2, and fig. 4, we see a description of what happens in a situation where two identical wave-forms occur in an opposite phase relationship. In such a set of circumstances, wave-form (a) will be competing directly with wave-form (b), in the sense that the motions of the two are opposite. In other words, when one molecule moves one way, the corresponding molecule in the second wave-form moves in an exactly opposite manner. To put this in another form, the rarefactions of wave-form (a) are counterbalanced by rarefactions in wave-form (b). Similarly, the compressional stages also work in an opposite manner. The effect of such perfectly opposed motions (which in fact hardly ever exist in reality) is to cancel each other out completely. Therefore, all other things being equal (which they hardly ever are) a person subjected to tones (a) and (b) would hear nothing at all, since the two types of vibration would cancel each other out perfectly. It is possible also to conceive of the opposite state of affairs, where two identical wave-forms occur in a perfect ('in phase') relationship. In this case, the motions of molecules are complementary; when one molecule moves in a certain fashion, its motion is identical with that of the corresponding molecule in the second wave-form. In such a set of circumstances, the two wave-forms, far from cancelling each other out, will in fact summate to produce a resultant wave-form of twice the amplitude of either of the constituents. This is illustrated in fig. 10 below, where the resultant sound will be louder than either of the two individual sounds.

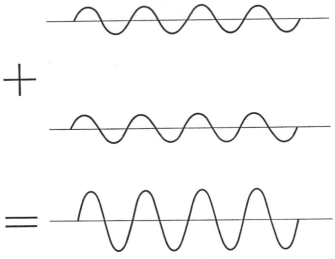

Fig. 10.   Addition of simple wave-forms

Now, as has been stated previously, wave-forms can occur in a range of phase relationships, all the way from 'in phase' to 'opposite phase'. Thus, there is also a range of phase relationships from complete cancelling out all the way through to perfect summation. With this in mind, the simplest way to conceive of the beat phenomenon is to imagine two tones which are of not quite the same frequency. In this case, the two tones will move from positions of perfect in-phase relationships to exactly opposite phase, at a rate which is determined by the difference in the frequency of the two tones. An example is given in fig. 11 facing. Wave-form (a) has a frequency slightly higher than wave-form (b). It will be noted that when these two occur together, a range of phase relationships all the way from in phase (PI) to opposite phase (PO) is produced. The positions PO

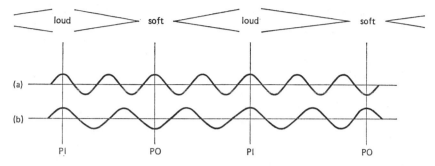

Fig. 11. Frequency difference, producing 'beats'

indicate where the two wave-forms compete, so there will be a reduction in amplitude, and hence in loudness at these points. (Theoretically, as stated previously, this cancelling process should be perfect.) Conversely, at point PI there will be summation, producing an increase in amplitude and hence in loudness. Therefore, when the two tones are sounded simultaneously there will be a fluctuation in loudness as the state of the resulting tone varies between PI and PO. The actual speed at which this loudness fluctuation takes place will be determined by the frequency relationship of the two tones concerned. If the frequencies of the tones are very different, beats are not usually heard very clearly. (This is an oversimplification, since the upper partials of tones can beat with each other. For the purposes of this explanation, the statement will serve for the present.) With two tones of nearly equal frequency, the prominence of beats will decrease as the frequency difference between them is reduced. Tones of the same frequency will therefore not beat. In addition, if the speed of the loudness fluctuations resulting from two different tones is so great that it takes place within one of our 'present' time units, the fluctuations will cease to exist for the perceiver, and only a resultant *quality* will remain. Now, one of the cues to 'out-of-tuneness' of intervals, and one of its most important consequences, is this phenomenon of beats. In a typical situation, two violinists might produce a unison which is out of tune, resulting in beats. The beats give the resulting sound a particular coarseness or roughness which, if it is not intended, will be judged unpleasant. When Helmholtz argues that beats of this type always produce sounds which are 'distressing and exhausting', he overlooks the effects of a changing musical culture which cause sounds to be judged dissonant at one point in time (and therefore to be avoided) and not dissonant (and therefore not to be avoided) at another. For example, major chords comprising doh, me, soh, plus a sixth, or a major seventh, or a ninth, are widely used in popular music. These are nowadays judged to give a rather sweet or 'slushy' type of sound; in fact, in jazz parlance they are sometimes referred to as 'night-club' or 'mickey-mouse' chords in a disparaging sense. People do not normally go to night-clubs to be 'distressed and exhausted', at least not as a result of simply hearing the music. According to Helmholtz, chords like those described should always have an intrinsic dissonant quality, but it is clear that there are other factors at work than those considered by Helmholtz. Nevertheless by a process of mutual accommodation the two violinists will attempt to eliminate the beats, attending to their own sound and the sound of their companion, and adjusting the frequency they are producing so as to eliminate the undesired changes in phase relationship which are producing the beats. When the beats have disappeared, the instruments will not only *sound* in tune with each other, but they will also be in tune in the sense of having the same frequency. (Of course, instruments cannot produce tones of perfect periodicity, that is tones which are perfectly constant, but within the limits imposed by the combination of the instrument and performer the above will be true.)

We have seen, then, that music is a highly ephemeral and fleeting art form. The portion of music which exists at any point in time occupies a tiny slice of a second, during which the listener extracts as much information as he can. If the actual music moves at a rate faster than these tiny time slices, the listener can extract only a correspondingly smaller amount of information. Now, it has been suggested that, although the page of written music presents a series of sound events which are in theory of precise duration and frequency, in fact there are constant essential deviations from this state of exactness. The scientist might argue that things ought to sound wrong, but bases his arguments on certain assumptions which are not entirely satisfactory. The way musical information is imparted depends not on the page of music, but on the performer who uses his ears as the final arbiter; the way the information is construed depends on a listener who uses the same criterion. Our previous comment, 'Music is in the ear of the listener', thus becomes even more meaningful. We might also add 'the performer', since we have seen the essential part he also plays in shaping the event of the present. At the risk of sounding tautological, we might now see the scientists' question 'Why doesn't music sound out of tune?' in a slightly different light. Music does not sound out of tune, because if it did it would *sound* out of tune. If it does sound out of tune, the performer (unlike the electronic tone producer, or audio-oscillator) does something about it to make it sound in tune. In considering musical events of the present, therefore, the ear reigns supreme.

However, when we judge a piece of music, we do not base our assessment on the last time slice we heard. We make a judgement about the whole thing, so that we must necessarily take into account events of the past. The consideration of past events is of paramount importance, since it involves organizing a series of discrete present events into something with overall form and shape. We do not merely remember a series of separate events. In fact, experiments into the ways in which people remember all manner of things suggest that, wherever possible, individual units are grouped together to form larger units. This process has been called 'chunking' and is described by Miller (1962). A most obvious example of chunking involves immediate memory. In experiments, it has been found that, if people are asked to remember individual letters of the alphabet, the average number remembered is about six or seven. If, however, the letters form words, a person can then remember five or six words which, together, might consist of twenty or thirty letters. Similarly, if the words form sentences, a person may then remember five or six sentences, perhaps containing four or five words each. Although these are very obvious examples, the chunking process can take place in a more sophisticated fashion, and in other areas. There is little doubt that chunking takes place when people listen to music. Thus, whilst most of us would find it difficult to remember eight or nine notes selected randomly, most of us can remember a number of tunes comprising many notes. The tunes become the units, because we can see their overall shape and form, rather than the individual tones comprising them.

In addition, we remember not only the overall shape and form of the musical event. Our memories often encompass more than the whole work, so that we also remember how we felt when we heard it. This consideration of how people perceive entire musical pieces which in fact never have any present existence is perhaps of more importance to musical understanding than the 'present' events, and will be the subject of the next chapter.

4 Events of the past

We have already noted, in the previous chapter, how the musical event of the present is a steady state tone or tonal complex occupying a temporal space of finite duration. One way of conceptualizing a piece of music is thus as a series of events of the present, each one succeeding the previous one in an orderly series, rather like beads on a string. From the point of view of the listener, however, the basic event of the present is not the basic perceptual unit, so the conceptualization is a bad one. A listener does not hear a series of discrete events. He hears whole phrases, recognizes entire tunes, becomes aware of particular patterns, and in general spends his time in perceptual tasks which involve the grouping together of the separate events. On the basis of research findings, Creel, Boomsliter and Powers (1970) conclude that the ongoing tonal event is, in fact, meaningless, and criticize the work of some investigators in this area for having undertaken experiments 'with the expectation that the patterns exist in the input signal and can be found there'. As we shall see later on, patterns exist in people and not in sequences of tones. Moreover, the all-important emotional response to music occurs as a consequence of events of the past, even though these may lead us to anticipate events of the future. By contrast, the event of the present is always an isolated tonal element, looking neither backwards nor forwards. It only has meaning once it becomes part of the past; in other words, paradoxically, perception of a tune (as distinct from sensation) involves memory. The basic problem is therefore to find out how events of the past come to take on such crucial importance in music, and to explain why they have the effects that they sometimes do.

As a forerunner, it is useful to consider what we mean by the term 'emotional response'. The nature of emotions is by no means a straightforward topic, and arguments have raged amongst psychologists almost since the time of that subject's inception. The basic starting point for the discussion is the common-sense view of emotions. This common-sense view relates the phenomena of perception, emotion (or affect), and behaviour in a particular way, such that there is a clear causal link between these three elements. Briefly, the notion is that, firstly, something is perceived and that this then produces an emotional feeling or mental affect, which in the end produces a particular kind of behavioural response. In other words, the man turns the corner of the street and sees the tiger; this causes him to feel fear, which in turn causes him to act by running away. To take a musical example, the woman hears Delius's 'Song of summer', feels sad, and begins to weep. In examples of this type, the emotional response comes midway between the acts of perception and behaviour, and the implication is that the behaviour is caused by the emotional state. Stated in this way, the common-sense theory seems so obvious that any attempt at alternative explanation appears almost impossible. A challenge to this view of the emotions came, however, in the shape of the so-called James–Lange theory of emotion outlined by William James (1884) in a previous paper, before the label James–Lange had been appended. He suggested that the ordering of the sequence described above was incorrect, and that the supposedly causal relationships between a percept and an emotional or affective state, and between such a state and a piece of behaviour, were in fact erroneous inferences. In essence, James altered the order so that the behaviour came between the perception and the affect or emotion. In other words we do not cry because we feel sad but rather we feel sad because we cry. In a similar way, James would argue that we feel fear because we run away, we feel angry because we punch someone, we feel shame because we hide, and so on. Stated in this way, we see a theory of the nature of emotions which stresses an inner rather than an outer cause. The emotions are not the result of seeing, hearing or otherwise perceiving an external stimulus, object or event, but are nothing more than the perceptions of our own bodily states brought about by external events. Skinner (1972), summarizing James's theory, suggests that it ascribes our emotional feelings to the perception of our own behaviour, though he clearly does not accept James's theory in this form.

What are the grounds upon which James turns topsy-turvy a notion which seems to have such high credibility in common-sense terms? In the first instance, James argues that if the bodily states associated with emotion did not follow immediately upon the act of perception, the latter would be an entirely cognitive act. There would be no emotional colour or feeling attached to the perception of a particular event. He argues that, if such were the case, the man would see the tiger and make a dispassionate decision to run away, but could not actually feel fear. Secondly, James points out that if we are asked to describe how we feel when in a particular emotional state, we are forced to describe physical, bodily feelings, or our perception of them. If we try to describe our emotional state, but take away all our consciousness of bodily symptoms, there is nothing left. Quoted in support of the theory are subjective reports from clinical cases, including cases of anaesthesia or loss of feeling from internal or external organs of the body, and cases of emotional insensibility or reduced emotionality. Although the evidence is rather ambiguous, there is some support for the notion that anaesthesia might be associated with lessening of emotional response, and that emotional insensibility might be associated with reduced sensation from the bodily organs. On the other hand, it is also a fact that there are a great many clinical cases in which this simply does not seem to be true. Clearly, if James's hypothesis were true, the one would always have to be associated with the other. Finally, in order to explain how the bodily changes follow directly from the perception, it was necessary for James to forge a link between the two. This he does by postulating that certain kinds of reactions are inbuilt, and have become inbuilt because of their evolutionary significance. In other words, there is an automatic bodily response to objects or situations of certain classes. He writes, 'Every living creature is in fact a sort of lock, whose wards and springs presuppose special forms of keys, which keys, however, are not born attached to the locks, but are sure to be found in the world near by as life goes on.'

In its original form, the James–Lange theory is no longer acceptable on scientific grounds, and there are reasons for supposing that the denial of a cognitive component in emotional behaviour might have been premature. So far as music is concerned, it is particularly difficult to conceive of a 'lock', to use James's analogy, which would have adaptive significance and yet vary from person to person so as to permit particular individual variations of the kinds we can observe in musical behaviour. For example, some people have a Beethoven lock, but not a Handel lock; others might have both; yet others appear to have no musical locks at all. Clearly, the kinds of locks talked about by James, such as the response of a bird to its eggs, the excitement of a dog on the scent, or the attachment of a hermit-crab to its whelk shell, which might reasonably be explained in terms of an innate locks system, are different in some way from pieces of behaviour which result in an emotional reaction to one piece of music but not to another. Evolution is wonderful stuff but, so far, no one has demonstrated the survival value of an emotional response to Bach as opposed to the Beatles.

There are other difficulties which arise from any theory of emotion which stresses the perception of inner physical states at the expense of cognitive processes. The purely physical manifestations of emotion are limited in number. Lange (1887), for example, attributed all emotional responses to the perception of changes in the vasomotor, or circulatory, system. James had a wider notion, which took in the feedback from the muscles, and skin, and especially the viscera. Other authors have stressed the importance of other physical components. The basic problem is to account for the vast range of emotional states which are experienced, in terms of a few physiological reactions whose number seems deficient for this purpose. One approach has involved the elaboration of the idea that the almost infinite number of felt emotions, each qualitatively different from the others, is derived from combinations of many different kinds, based on a relatively small number of basic emotions. It is the different combinations which give each emotional state its particular quality. Jorgensen (1950), for example, proposed six basic elements, namely Fear, Happiness, Sorrow, Want, Anger, and Shyness, which he believed constituted the basis of emotional life. Each of these components was believed to operate on a continuum, ranging from states of high excitement, when they would produce feelings of intense emotion, right through to states of light tone accompanied by feelings of repose. The six elements could combine at differing levels of activity and thus further extend the range of felt emotions. A similar type of model is proposed by

Wedin (1972) in a study of emotional expression in music. He proposes a three-dimensional model of subjective musical experience, comprising three factors, namely gloom *v* gaiety, solemnity *v* triviality, and tension/energy *v* relaxation. Applying this type of approach to the James–Lange idea might at first appear to offer some solution, since we now have only to find physiological concomitants for a few basic emotions rather than for the full range. Unfortunately, this does not solve our problem, since the basic axiom of the James–Lange theory, that the bodily changes take place automatically after the perception of an object or situation, is in conflict with other evidence.

For example, Hillman (1962) provides coverage of a range of views which see emotion as a distinct entity, rather than an attribute or function of other processes, and this is perhaps a crucial distinction. To paraphrase Ryle (1949), the two contrasted approaches appear to be centred respectively on a view of emotion as a consequence, and a view which sees emotion itself as a cause. In refutation of the former position, Cannon (1927) points out that particular visceral changes can occur in the *same* way when an individual is experiencing *different* emotions. In terms of the James–Lange theory, the same visceral state should result in the same emotion. Also, artificial induction of visceral changes which normally characterize particular strong emotions fails to produce them. Finally, he suggests that the viscera are too insensitive, and too slow of reaction, to serve the requirements of the James–Lange theory. Other objections are offered by Lehmann (1914). (In fact, however, not all of Cannon's criticisms are completely valid. Whilst he claimed that bodily changes in anger and fear were similar, it is now known that they are not. In particular, the two states are different pharmacologically.) From the musical standpoint, the experiences of musicians and music lovers also lend little comfort to any theory based purely on automatic physical responses. Different people can have different emotional responses to the same piece of music. In other cases, a tune which evokes an emotional response in one person fails to do so in another. It may well be that all hens feel the same way about eggs, or that all people feel the same way about meeting tigers in the street. There are other areas of emotional experience, however, where the reactions of individuals are more differentiated, and where the interpolation of some cognitive process between perception and emotion seems essential. For example, imagine the case where a man does not flee from the tiger because he knows it is harmless, it being his pet; or a situation at a cup final where the scoring of a goal plunges half the crowd into despair and the other half into euphoria; or a performance of a National Anthem which fills one man with patriotic fervour and another with distaste. These types of events are only explicable if the man recognizes the tiger before he does not flee, or is cognisant of the fact that Liverpool and not Newcastle have scored before he feels despair, or fits that National Anthem into his own left- or right-wing view of the world before his emotional experience. One might be prepared to accept a view of emotion as an automatic response to music if its manifestations were always predictable. If music always calmed the savage breast we might speculate that there was an innate lock that made this so. However, sometimes it renders savage the previously calm breast, sometimes it refreshes and invigorates, sometimes it depresses and so on. This lack of a homogeneous response makes the existence of a James–Lange type musical lock unlikely.

So far as emotional responses to music are concerned, virtually all the evidence points to the central importance of some form of cognition, or knowing, rather than simple sensation, or just hearing. Note, however, that such a conclusion does not prove that the James–Lange theory is wrong, but rather suggests that it is not always true. Much recent research of a physiological nature might be construed as support for the type of locks theory. For example, various reactions of the endocrine system to particular situations, and particularly the release of adrenalin (Gellhorn 1968) are often associated with emotional behaviour. For instance, experiments in which rodents are kept in overcrowded conditions demonstrate a deterioration in maternal behaviour (Calhoun 1962) and associated hormonal changes (Archer 1970). The maternal behaviour of pigeons has also been shown to be associated with the let-down of particular hormones, occasioned by participation in nest-building and courtship (Lehrman 1958 a and b). Even boxers have been found to have increased excretion of adrenalin as a result of pre-fight tension (Hoagland 1961). The investigation of such physiological mechanisms is of little help for the present inquiry, however, since we are here concerned with the qualitative differences which people (and possibly animals) experience in their emotional lives. These qualitative differences only exist as feelings, whereas the research mentioned above relates physiological states to behaviour. (McDougall (1928) has made particular distinctions between emotions and feelings. To use this distinction here would make for extremely tortuous explanation. The term 'feelings' is used here in a non-precise fashion, to refer to the subjective experiences of the subject; in other words, the way he feels.)

The problem of whether the feelings cause the physiological states or vice versa still remains. For example, animals which have been surgically operated on so as to destroy the connections between the brain and other organs such as the heart, lungs and viscera (as a consequence of which they can no longer feel their own internal states) still display emotional behaviour (Cannon, Lewis and Britton 1927). Though at first sight this seems like a death knell for the James–Lange theory, in fact it is not because it can be argued that the animals were only behaving *as if* they were responding emotionally. It is possible that situations merely triggered off particular types of emotional behaviour, with the animal not actually feeling any emotion. In other words, the animal might behave in an angry fashion without feeling anger, the behaviour being merely triggered in the absence of any associated feeling.

So far as emotion is concerned, therefore, the notion of feeling, or how an emotion feels, is the spanner in the works. On the grounds that feeling cannot be examined scientifically, but only indirectly through what people tell us, many theorists have abandoned it altogether. The claim is that feelings do not exist independently of particular bodily states. On the other hand, other workers have taken the view that feelings are central, and that, through feelings, emotions can be seen to have an independent existence (Hillman 1962). Though there is evidence on both sides, as we have seen, there is nothing so far to lead us to the definite conclusion that one approach is the correct one all the time. For music, however, most of our eggs must be put in the latter basket, but not quite all of them. Before setting out the reasons for this disposition of our eggs, it is useful to take a brief look at two more pieces of experimental evidence. The first comes from an experiment by Schacter and Singer (1962), which serves to emphasize the role of cognitive processes as causal influences in emotion. Briefly, the experiment consisted of injecting subjects with adrenalin, a hormone connected with emotional arousal which we have mentioned previously in connection with the boxers. The precise experimental controls need not concern us. The critical manipulation however consisted of exposing different subjects to two kinds of social conditions. In the first, the subject was seated with a stooge who acted in a silly, euphoric manner; in the second the stooge gave a display of anger and rage. Although the subjects in the two conditions had been given the identical injection, resulting in greater nervous-system activity than other subjects not so injected, the precise nature of their emotional reactions was found to be a function of the social conditions to which they were exposed. Thus, although the hormone had an arousing effect in all subjects, the exact quality of their emotional experience was dependent upon their perception of a particular social situation. The conclusion from the experiment was that cognitive factors were an important determinant of emotion type. To put this another way, it looks as though we can have different emotional experiences even when the physiological state is the same. We do not therefore have to search for a unique physiological state, or a unique combination of states, for every different emotion we experience. (Although the results of the Schacter and Singer experiment seem to be fairly convincing, they are not entirely unambiguous. For example, it is possible to argue that the actual social situation caused differing physiological states in the subjects, independently of the administered drug. For example, mice which watch other mice fighting show an increase in adrenalin.) Further evidence on this point comes from research with cats (Kopa, Szabo and Grastyan 1962) and involved the stimulation of parts of a cat's brain with small electrical currents. Depending upon whether the cat was standing on a floor through which it had in the past received an electric shock, or sitting on a shelf where it was safe, the identical stimulation of the brain produced either an attempt to escape, or a contented settling down, sometimes accompanied by purring. The cat's reactions were therefore closely related to the situation in which it found itself, rather than being a simple function of the brain stimulation.

Physiological states, then, may or may not be brought about automatically as a result of certain situations. Perhaps physiological changes are sometimes more automatic and sometimes less so. However, there can be little doubt that the precise nature of the emotional experience depends on where we are, what we are doing, and what we think of the situation. For all we know, and at risk of being highly anthropomorphic, it might be that the physiological arousal state of the tiger is basically the same as that of the man whom he is chasing. The quality of the emotional experience of each will, however, be different, because the tiger is aware that he is doing the chasing whereas the man is aware that he is being chased. In a sense, therefore, the quality of an emotion depends upon some sort of prior 'knowing', and the basis of the present argument is that emotional responses to music are also in the main dependent upon some sort of knowing. By extension, the offered explanation for the wide range of emotions an individual may experience to music, and the limitless differences between the reactions of individual people to musical material, is in terms of differences of knowing. The fact that different people know different things accounts for their differing reactions. Since knowing, in the sense in which we are using the word, refers to knowledge of things in the past, our argument comes full circle and we see that emotional response to music is only explicable in terms of events of the past. Recent research tends to reveal shades of physiological and pharmacological variation, suggesting that different emotional states may be more differentiated than was previously thought. This, however, is an inevitable consequence of more exact research techniques. Since knowing probably has physiological correlates, the distinction made between gross physiological or bodily states, and knowing, is probably a distinction between two types of physiological states. Even so, it is worth remembering that though perception of bodily processes probably does not have the central causal role assigned to it by James, there is little doubt that such perceptions are a component of emotional feeling.

One feature about the knowledge that a person brings to bear when listening to a particular piece of music is that it leads him to expect certain kinds of things to happen, and to expect that certain other things will not. Subsequently, his expectations may be confirmed or they may not. It is this process of confirmation or disconfirmation of expectancies which is at the centre of musical experience. Events of the past are the basic ingredients from which expectancies are formed, and this is why the past is of such importance. With no carry over from past events, a person could have no expectancies, and the world would be just a 'blooming, buzzing confusion'. This is true in other spheres of activity as well as in music.

Before proceeding to the more complex issue of specifically musical expectancies, there is, however, a more simple way in which music can cause emotional response or feeling in people. It is worth saying here that, in some ways, the term emotion is inappropriate in a musical context. Emotional states are usually of very brief duration, whereas music tends to produce states of greater duration. The term mood might be preferable. In any case, it appears that certain pieces of music can affect us emotionally through a process of conditioning. The idea here is that people learn certain associations, which in the end lead to an emotional feeling and/or response, in much the same way that Pavlov's dogs learned to salivate when they heard a tone from a tuning fork (1927). The classic example of this is perhaps the 'Darling, they're playing our tune' phenomenon. The lady from whose mouth this apocryphal saying is supposed to have emanated has acquired a specific emotional response to a specific tune simply because she heard it at a time when some other pleasurable business was taking place, at some time in the past. Now the tune itself makes her feel good simply because she associates it with the previous pleasant experiences. Even the most unmusical people usually have an associative response of this type to at least one or two tunes. (A man might therefore justifiably feel some alarm if his unmusical wife suddenly develops an apparently spontaneous liking for a new tune.) The point about this type of emotional response is that it is relatively simple to understand, and in its purest form depends in no way upon the musical content of the tune itself. In theory, Pavlov's tone would have served just as well; it just so happened that the thing the lady heard at her moment of crisis was a tune and not, say, a train. In practice, however, a great many people have a tune which is of special emotional significance to them, and relatively few experience this same state on hearing the sound of a train. From this point of view, the tune and the train are not completely equivalent therefore. As a partial explanation for this fact we may note that not even all tunes are equivalent in this respect. Tunes of the DTPOT (*D*arling, *T*hey're *P*laying *O*ur *T*une) type are usually drawn from the ranks of 'Songs for swinging lovers' or something similar, where the words and the mood of the music are somehow appropriate to the events with which they become associated. This, of course, begs another question, since moods are properties of people and not of music. None the less, people who use the overture 'William Tell' or 'The ride of the Valkyries' as a DTPOT tune are definitely in a minority. It is probable that people learn as a cultural norm that certain types of music are conventionally used in particular situations. Thus advertisements, films and so on typically use the same type of music to underscore scenes in which 'true love' is involved. As a result of this constant pairing of sentimental scenes with a particular type of music, the latter acquires sentimental connotations. When our lady herself falls in love she is thus more prone to associate events with a slushy tune than with a more vigorous one, or with the sound of the passing train. In addition, the words of the tune are often such of a nature as to make the associations even more explicit. After he had observed that he was being followed, Konrad Lorenz (1935) postulated that young goslings imprinted, or became attached to, the first large moving object they encountered after hatching. In an analogous way, we might frivolously postulate that at times of great emotion some ladies become attached to the first slushy tune they encounter, though, in the case of the lady, the attaching tendency is learned, rather than innate.

Through association with particular events, therefore, a tune can come to evoke emotional feelings. In addition, we have seen above how particular types of music can come to be associated with particular types of events, so that through a process known as 'generalization' a person may experience an emotion to a piece of music which he has not heard before. The processes of association and generalization would therefore help to explain why people experience an upsurge of pride when hearing a well-known nationalistic tune; or why we feel excitement and fear upon hearing a new, but particularly fearsome tune at a horror movie, which we immediately know to be the call-sign of the monster, because we have learned to associate the type of music with similar monsters as a result of our past experience, and which effectively announces his imminent appearance. More specifically, the processes of association and generalization explain why a girl-friend goes dewy-eyed whenever Andy Williams sings 'I left my heart in San Francisco' (or, if things have not run smoothly, why she nowadays throws a punch at your mouth). Almost any piece of music can, therefore, become associated with any emotional event regardless, to a great extent, of the nature of the event or the tune; people, however, learn that particular types of music are appropriate to particular types of event, a fact which puts certain constraints on this process.

The reader may be aware that to conceive of the emotional response to music in this way goes contrary to some cherished notions. 'But my patience and faith did not fail me, and today I felt that inexplicable glow of inspiration . . .; thanks to which I know beforehand that whatever I write today will have power to make an impression, and to touch the hearts of those who hear it.' So wrote Peter Ilich Tchaikovsky in 1878 (Newmarch 1906). The power to make an impression, and to touch the hearts of listeners, is attributed directly to the musical creation itself; whilst this might be true in a particular set of circumstances, it is not true as a generality. In the first place, the emotion felt has very little to do with the music itself but becomes attached to the music through a learning process. The feelings are not intrinsic in the music, but come, as it were, from outside. The second point is that there is nothing natural or inevitable about the emotional response. It, also, comes about as a result of learning. These conclusions run contrary to what many people believe. There is a widespread notion that feelings, emotions, or moods, lie inside the music, that is, they are thought of as properties of the music, and what the listener is doing is merely reflecting something that is in the music. Such a view is sometimes accompanied by the belief that there is something inevitable or natural about the experience of particular feelings as a result of listening to a particular tune. As a consequence, the inability of a particular individual person to be able to see (i.e. experience) those things which are thought to be in the music is often put down to factors such as deliberate perversity, refusal to attend, reluctance to admit, stupidity, or genetic defect on the part of a person who fails to get the message. The widespread nature of these beliefs is reflected in the way we tend to attribute emotions or moods to pieces of music. We talk about a happy tune, or a martial strain, or a sleepy lullaby. Such a view of music tends towards expressionism, since it is essentially a non-intellectual approach. However, we are not here denying that music affects people, but putting forward the not new proposition that to understand why it does so it is necessary to make reference to factors outside the music. This idea has been elegantly expounded by Meyer (1956), who contrasts 'formalism' with 'expressionism'. The former, he explains, sees the meaning of music as lying at a primarily intellectual level, and therefore demanding an understanding of the musical relationships contained in a given work. Expressionism on the other hand sees those same musical relationships as being capable of exciting moods or emotions in the listener. Meyer, however, elaborates on this distinction, and points out that an expressionist view does not necessarily imply that music produces human reactions without reference to the non-musical world. On the contrary, we can argue that music does have an effect of an emotional kind on people, but that the process by which it does so can best be understood by reference to non-musical concepts, events, and situations. In other words, music has its effect because of things we have learned or experienced. Finally, our own experience is sufficient to refute the notion that the mood or the emotion resides within the music. When we listen to music from a culture which does not use Western musical conventions, or with which we are very unfamiliar, it often sounds meaningless, and probably boring too. Oriental music or, to come nearer home, Scottish Pibroch, fall into these categories for many people. We cannot assume, however, that they are in some absolute sense really meaningless or boring, because they are neither of these things for the Chinese or the Scots. The reason is simply that we are unfamiliar with the musical system and the set of conventions employed.

So far, we have looked at instances in which moods and feelings can be evoked through the process of association or associative learning. There are a great many other ways in which feelings are evoked by music, most of which involve associative learning in some shape or form, but which are usually subsumed under the heading 'social and cultural factors'. We have already mentioned expectations as being of central importance, but before coming to grips with specifically musical expectations, we need to realize that people have expectations about situations as well as about music. For example, a person going to a jazz club to hear a Dixieland band will expect to spend a happy, ebullient kind of evening, and his expectations will affect the way he feels and the way he behaves. At appropriate moments, he might clap his hands, stamp his feet, and even shout jocular remarks at the performers, who will in turn probably shout back because they have the same set of expectations. He is likely to perceive the actual music, moreover, within this frame of reference. By contrast, a modern jazz concert might lead him to expect a more cool, possibly more introverted, type of setting. Instead of stamping his feet and shouting 'Play that thing', he is more likely to fiddle with his beads and quietly mumble 'Yeah man' as he lights another Gauloise. Finally, when he attends a symphony concert, he expects to feel soberly appreciative, and sets himself to experience some higher feelings. His expectations about the nature of all these situations will inevitably colour his perception and subsequent mood state, as well as his more overt behaviour. There is a vast amount of psychological evidence to demonstrate the fact that people do not merely perceive what is 'out there', but rather that they perceive what they expect to perceive. Bannister and Fransella (1971), for example, state that a basic fallacy of stimulus-response psychology is the notion that a man responds to a stimulus. In fact, they say, a man responds to what he interprets the stimulus to be. Since we have already taken the view that cognitive processes are of central importance in this area, and since our cognitions depend on our perceptions, it is not unreasonable to suggest that people do not simply feel things, but that they feel what they expect to feel.

In the field of drugs, for example, Barron *et al.* (1971) refer to studies in which people expecting to receive an hallucinogenic drug, but in fact given an inactive substance, have responded in ways contingent with an actual dose of drug. Bananadine, a completely inactive substance, was claimed to produce altered mood states in one particular study because subjects thought it was a drug which would have just such an effect. Even drunkenness and drunken behaviour is not a uniform phenomenon, but follows the cultural norms which prescribe how a drunk feels and behaves (Pittman and Snyder 1962). Returning to music, we can observe that, frequently, the programmes distributed at a symphony concert, or the notes on the back of a record sleeve, serve precisely this function of outlining the mood that is appropriate for a particular piece. Even more obvious is the role of tune titles in denoting the kind of mood, and its associated images, which we are meant to utilize. 'Claire de lune' (Debussy) sounds like moonbeams (in fact, of course, moonbeams do not sound at all, a paradox to be dealt with later) at least partly because of its title. Would anyone have argued if, at the time, Debussy had called it 'Snow'? Had he done so, one might speculate that the mental imagery which many people experience when listening to the music would be rather different. Interestingly enough, however, most of us would accept that not all titles would be equally appropriate as substitutes. For example, the title 'Rodeo' would for some reason seem highly inapt. Within a Western culture, a simple change of title is unlikely to cause a major re-construing of the tune as jolly or gay, rather than serene and contemplative. As an argument against the present thesis, therefore, one could point out that in this instance the change of title brings about changes in specific images rather than in general mood state. By way of rebuttal, however, it seems unlikely that a simple title change would be powerful enough to outweigh years of previous associative learning to the effect that tunes like 'Claire de lune' are serene and not jolly. Suppose the title were changed to 'Despair'; this might be more successful in bringing about an actual mood change from one of repose to one of anguish. Titles can therefore have the effect suggested, though they do not necessarily do so.

So far, we have looked at expectancies, and their role as inducers of mood states or emotion, only in terms of things external to the music itself. We have seen how a host of such external factors can be important in providing people with information about what mood states are appropriate. Record sleeves, programme notes, knowledge of the composer's life and times, the type of concert, even the dress of the audience and musicians, all have an influence.

No one, except a new-born baby, approaches a piece of music in the dark, as it were, and even this is debatable since babies *in utero* have been shown to respond to loud noises outside (Spelt 1948). In passing, it is worth while mentioning that musicians and performers are also affected by what they know about a piece of music, and that the quality of a performance can be affected by this knowledge. Research in Sweden by Nylof (1973) had previously shown how jazz fans made judgements about jazz records which were affected by the reported prestige of the performers, even though all subjects heard the same music. Thus, the information that the performers were well known and respected in jazz circles, or that they were coloured, caused people to make certain more favourable evaluations of the music. An adaptation of this procedure was used by Weick *et al.* (1973) to investigate the reactions of two jazz orchestras to compositions by reputable or little-known composers. The orchestras were presented with three compositions, one of which was described in such a way as to lead the musicians to believe that it was a 'serious' jazz composition, the second being described in terms that led the musicians to view it as a commercial and therefore non-serious composition. A third, neutral, piece acted as a control. The pieces were given to the two orchestras in opposite order, so that the serious piece for orchestra A was the non-serious piece for orchestra B, and vice versa. The experimenters found that the beliefs of the musicians about the seriousness of the composition had two main effects. On the first playing of the composition, the belief that it was non-serious led to a greater number of errors in performance suggesting that the musicians were less careful than with the piece they believed to be serious. Secondly, when one day later the musicians were tested to find out how much they remembered of the tunes they had played during the experiment, it was found that they had better recall for the serious composition than for the non-serious one. The experimenters interpret their results as indicating that the beliefs of musicians about the composer have the effect of producing a tendency to conservatism, rather than innovation, in music. This may or may not be the case, but it does lead us to speculate that a scrappy performance of a new piece by a little-known composer might to some degree be a reflection of the orchestra's attitudes to, and beliefs about, the composer in question.

However, we now turn from a consideration of external factors to those which are internal, that is those which involve the actual content of the music itself. As a preliminary, we might observe that people have expectations about the music itself, as well as about the circumstances that surround it, and it appears that these expectations might be instrumental in determining why Jack likes one thing and Jill likes another. Before tackling the notion of 'preference', however, we can look at some more mundane consequences of the degree of organization of musical material.

The fundamental premise is that people engaged in actively listening to music, as distinct from merely hearing it as background sound, are simultaneously doing two things: namely, looking backward into the past and forward into the future. The 'looking backward' involves processing of the musical sounds they have just heard, and the 'looking forward' involves making guesses as to what is likely to happen next. This looking into the future is not mere guesswork, but is more in the nature of a prediction based on the data currently available. In the way that an economist makes forecasts of future trade figures or market trends on the basis of information available to him at present about events that have taken place in the past, so the active music listener makes short-term predictions about what the musical future is likely to be. As noted previously, the important point about predictions is that they do or do not come true. Our economist, for example, will probably feel very pleased if he makes a string of correct predictions, but less happy if he puts together a galaxy of wrong ones. In a less obvious way, the notion is that confirmation or disconfirmation of our predictions affects the way we feel about a piece of music.

Consider the words, 'Baa, baa, black sheep'. Try to imagine that you have never seen them before, and that you therefore have a completely open mind as to what is likely to come next. The task is impossible. As a consequence, whatever comes next occurs not in a vacuum, but is inevitably evaluated in terms of what has gone before. Here are some examples:

'Have you any wool?' This is the most obvious continuation and, for some readers at least, probably the most boring, since what they expected was something rather more interesting than the mere redundant repetition of something they already knew. In other words, because we know what the obvious continuation is, in this book we perhaps expected some deviation from the obvious. The obvious is thus probably uninteresting. Note, however, that this is only obvious for people who know the poem.

'Its fleece was white as snow.' Within the confines of a psychology book, this might well be the type of thing that some readers expected. Their expectancy, that there would be a deviation from the normal continuation, is thus confirmed, although the exact form of the deviation was probably not predicted. In addition, the incongruity about wool colour is weakly humorous, and the phrase will, to most people, be recognized as something taken from another rhyme and here appearing in a different context. This will only be apparent to people knowing both rhymes.

'The mouse ran up the clock.' This again is an avoidance of the obvious continuation, and again involves the shifting of something already familiar into a new context. However, there seems to be very little carry over between the two intact lines, so we probably dismiss this continuation as merely silly because we can make no logical sense out of it.

'Noj wemb hivloth res?' We expected some deviation from the obvious, but we did expect any deviation to be in itself meaningful to us, rather than simply an absurd and meaningless collection of letters. However, what is meaningless for one individual is not necessarily so for another. The above phrase, for example, is in fact Martian for 'Have you any wool?', and thus, according to my scaly purple friend, does not even constitute deviation.

The principle of expectancy in music operates in an analogous way to the nursery-rhyme examples given above. To start with, the ability to make predictions depends on how organized the material used in making the prediction appears to be. There are thus two variables here. One is the degree of organization of the material, and the other is the knowledge of an individual person about the ways in which materials can be organized. For example, a schematic drawing of a complex electrical circuit is certainly not a random mass of lines and ciphers, although it may appear to be so to a non-electrician. On the other hand, a person with the appropriate knowledge of electronics can extract meaning from the diagram, and perhaps even predict what the functions and properties of the circuit will be. Similarly, many of us will be able to develop predictions about the kinds of things that are likely to happen when listening to Mozart, and perhaps fewer of us can make similar predictions for Schoenberg or Stockhausen.

An experiment by Miller and Selfridge (1953) concerned itself with lists of words, and the extent to which people could remember them. The lists of words used were compiled in a special way, so that the occurrence of any one word could, to varying degrees, be controlled by words that had gone before. For example, given the phrase 'Little Jack Horner sat in the . . .', the probability that the continuation will be 'corner' is very high, the probability that it will be 'jelly' is less, and the probability that it will be 'infamous' is very slight indeed. This process by way of which a given word or group of words exerts a probabilistic influence on a subsequent word is sometimes referred to as 'contextual restraint'. All that this means is that a given group of words which have already occurred exert some influence over those that are to follow, rendering certain words more likely to occur and others less likely. In the Miller and Selfridge experiments, the subjects were presented with word lists of different lengths, and also with different degrees of contextual restraint. The main finding was that people could remember the shorter lists better than the longer ones, as might be expected; also that they remembered the more organized lists better than the less organized lists. To understand this better, the most important point, as far as this discussion is concerned, is the method of producing the word lists. This was done by presenting a person with a word, or a group of words, and asking him to add one word which he thought might reasonably follow the last one given to him. The person might be given any number of words from one to seven, and asked to provide the next. For example, suppose the intention is to create a word list with a low degree of organization, we give our subject a single word, and ask him to write down one which he thinks might follow on. Suppose the first word we gave him was 'The'. Our subject writes down 'cat', to give 'The cat'. Now, suppose we cover up the first word 'The', and present our subject's word (cat) to a new subject, with the same instructions. Our new subject sees 'cat' and offers the word 'fell'. We now pass 'fell' on to a new subject who offers 'swoop'. A fourth person follows 'swoop' with 'down'. 'Down' is followed by 'amongst' and so on. The result so far is the rather garbled message 'The cat fell swoop down amongst', and a word list derived in such a fashion will be difficult to remember, since every word is only governed by the single word which precedes it. On the other hand, if we are constructing lists based on seven preceding words, the resultant list will be more organized and more easily remembered. For example, we present our first subject with the words 'One fine day the little boy was'. He offers the word 'going'. We now cover up the first word 'One' and pass it on to another subject in the form 'fine day the little boy was going', who offers 'to'. The message, 'day the little boy was going to' is then given to our next subject who adds 'the'. The next subject adds 'fair'. This leaves us with 'little boy was going to the fair' to be presented to the next subject, and so on. Clearly, the message based on seven preceding words is more organized than that based on one. By way of illustration, some word lists compiled by this method are given below:

Example 1
List produced on the basis of one preceding word only (first-order approximation).
'horse reins women screaming especially much was said cake love that school to a they in is the home think with are his before the want square of the wants' (Clearly in this example, some of the words amount to a virtual 'free association' with the preceding word.)

Example 2
List produced on the basis of three preceding words (third-order approximation).
'happened to see Europe again is that trip to the end is coming here tomorrow after the packages arrived yesterday brought good cheer at Christmas it is raining outside as'

Example 3
List produced on the basis of seven preceding words (seventh-order approximation).
'then go ahead and do it if possible while I make an appointment I want to skip very much around the tree and back home again to eat dinner after'

Comparison of the three examples should show there is an increasing organization in the lists as a result of increasing degrees of contextual restraint. In other words, the higher-order lists have more meaning. The experiment of Miller and Selfridge is hardly new, and their findings are fairly well-known in psychological circles. However, instead of presenting subjects with words, one can present them with notes, and construct note lists in a similar fashion. These note lists can be regarded as statistical approximations to Western music.

In some experiments performed by the author (1969), a group of musicians from different musical disciplines was assembled. The group included performing musicians from classical, dance band, and modern jazz backgrounds. The mixing of musical backgrounds was intended to prevent the dominance of any one Western musical idiom in the experiment, though the result was a confusion of musical styles rather than the removal of all stylistic bias. (The fact that the material derived proved successful in the experiment shows that the procedure works in spite of its heterogeneous nature.) Statistical approximations to music were produced by presenting a subject with either a single note or a number of notes, depending upon whether first, second, third, fourth etc. orders of approximation were required. These starting notes were selected from the melodic lines of a child's book of piano pieces with which all the musicians were unfamiliar. The notes were written on an 'endless belt' of manuscript placed in a special holder. By turning a handle, the manuscript could be made to move on one note at a time, leaving the required number of notes showing through a viewing slot. The subject was instructed to look at the note or notes given and to write in one more note that he thought might reasonably follow those shown. After he had accomplished this, the handle was turned so as to move the manuscript on one note, and the apparatus passed on to the next subject with the same instructions. The notion was that the musical material produced would reflect its order of approximation through varying degrees of organization. For example, sequences constructed when subjects had only a single note as a guide would be disorganized (i.e. un-tuneful) whereas those constructed on the basis of seven preceding notes would be more organized (i.e. more tuneful). The differing degrees of organization were subsequently reflected in the extent to which fragments of the tunes could be remembered by a new group of randomly selected subjects. For interest, some examples of the types of material produced by this procedure are given below, in fig. 12.

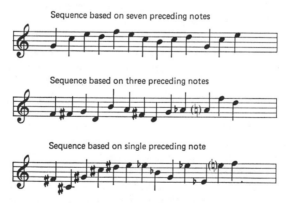

Fig. 12. Statistical approximations to music

Basically, the above method was simply used as a way of producing quasi-music for use in a number of different experiments and tests; what is of interest here is the finding that when subjects were played extracts of the quasi-music and at some later point in time asked whether they recognized the passages, they tended to recognize the more organized passages, i.e. those constructed on the basis of a larger number of preceding notes, more readily than those which were less organized. In an experiment by the author with 537 primary schoolchildren, aged seven–eleven years, in which the children were asked to listen to a number of extracts of 'quasi-music', the following percentages of correct recognition were obtained for tunes of seventh (most organized), fifth, third and first (least organized) orders of approximation.

Order of approximation	Difficulty (% correctly recognized)
7th	67·8
5th	60·36
3rd	53·8
1st	43·6

The main point to bear in mind is the effect of the organization of the music upon people's ability to recognize it at some subsequent point in time.

The organization of material also has an effect upon the people who play music. As one might expect, the less organized material is more difficult to play accurately. In an experiment with pianists, Quastler (1956) constructed a series of sight-reading tests of differing degrees of organization which had to be performed at varying speeds. It will come as no surprise to musicians that the number of errors increased as the pianists were required to perform faster. More interesting, however, were the findings with respect to organization. The material Quastler used consisted of sequences of tones each of which was selected from an 'alphabet' of a particular size. The smallest alphabet comprised only three notes, i.e. the entire sequence was made up using three tones only. By contrast the largest alphabet involved sixty-five notes. More errors were made as the alphabet size increased. One possible interpretation of these results would be in terms of expectancies. Where the pianist knows that every successive note is going to be one of a possible three only, he is going to be able to anticipate more correctly than when each successive note might be any one from a possible sixty-five. Experiments by Sloboda (1974 a and b) have shown that, in sight-reading, the musician reads ahead, that is, he is reading several notes ahead of the one he is actually playing. The more able sight-reader reads further ahead than the less able. Sloboda ventures the hypothesis that expectancy can influence the amount of sensory information necessary for identification, in the following manner: 'For example, if in the context of the previous notes of a musical phrase, only two notes have any great degree of probability of occurring in the next position, then the identifying processes will only need enough sensory information to distinguish between the two of them (say for instance that one note is high on the stave and the other one is low on the stave).' This conclusion is entirely compatible with the finding of Quastler, and with the results of the statistical music or quasi-music experiment described above. The more disorganized the material, the less we are able to guess what is likely to come next, and the more information we need in order to identify it. Thus, decreasing organization in Quastler's sight-reading tests might be expected to have its effect by preventing the pianists from anticipating what is coming next and thereby preventing them from reading ahead to the necessary degree. Similarly, in the recognition of, for example, first-order approximations, the subjects are again less able to anticipate what is coming next and thus require time to learn a new event, rather than simply confirm something that they might have to some extent already anticipated.

In the above paragraphs, it has been demonstrated that people's ability to anticipate coming musical events affects the way they listen to, and perform, music. This is the first step in showing that people respond emotionally (in terms of mood states) to aspects of the music itself as well as in terms of external factors described earlier. The second and more difficult step involves showing that the confirmation or disconfirmation of expectancies results in emotional responses. Without such a relationship, people's expectancies are mere curiosities. Unfortunately, it is just this relationship which is the most difficult to demonstrate empirically, since, as we have seen, the outward manifestations of an emotion (for example, heart rate, galvanic skin response, respiration, etc.) are insufficiently specific to allow us to differentiate between confirmation and disconfirmation. Similarly, although we might crudely demonstrate by inference that people do have expectancies in pieces of statistical music, it is much harder to isolate a particular very fleeting point in time, discover what the person expects, and observe the nature of his emotional response. Evidence on this point is thus less satisfactory, and the arguments in favour of the notion, that expectancy about specifically musical events leads to emotional response, though often subjective, are the main topic for the next chapter.

In summary, we have seen that people do not listen to music in a vacuum, but rather that they know certain things about it beforehand. This knowledge leads them to expect certain things to happen, and others not to happen. Events of the past are therefore central in enabling people to have expectancies. These expectancies concern not merely the music itself, but extend to a variety of other circumstances which surround the music, including the mood states which they believe to be appropriate in a particular musical context. As a corollary to this argument, it follows, as we shall see, that in musical situations where people do not have expectancies (such as when listening to music with which they are completely unfamiliar, and which therefore has no past as far as they are concerned) the music will be meaningless for them.

5 What makes a tune?

In previous chapters we have taken a look at the individual elements of which music is composed. The chief message concerning these individual elements is that they are interesting primarily on account of their perceptual characteristics which affect the way in which we experience them. These characteristics of tonal perception determine the type of sensory experience that a person is subject to when he listens to music. We have also seen that elements taken in isolation have nothing of the richness or depth, nothing of the emotional significance, or, if you prefer, none of the meaning of these same elements occurring in the context of a piece of music. The whole appears to be greater than the sum of the parts; furthermore, it is people who make it so. A string of more or less unremarkable and insignificant sounds only becomes a tune, or piece of music, as a result of the organizing capacities of the human brain. 'The central assertion is that seeing, hearing and remembering are all acts of *construction*, which may make more or less use of the stimulus information depending on circumstances', wrote Neisser (1967). It is these capacities which are central to any type of musical activity, especially that most widespread activity, listening to music. Furthermore, the human ear is, within very broad limits, of very little significance. Thus, people born with extremely sensitive hearing or an extraordinary capacity for discriminating sounds, are not automatically more musical than others with normal hearing. The reverse is also true. People with various species of auditory deficit can be extremely musical, providing that their hearing is not prohibitively bad. Herbert Wing, for example, administered his tests to a sample of boys who were considered sufficiently deaf to merit medical attention, and concluded that their disability had very little effect upon their performance on the tests (1948).

Unfortunately, in the popular imagination, the seemingly obvious relationship between musical ability and the human ear is probably perpetuated by some unfortunate figures of speech. People who find that they cannot perform some simple operation such as singing a tune, or saying whether a note is too high or too low, often say that they 'have not got the ear'. Music teachers describe their protégés as 'having a good ear' and their less successful pupils as 'having no ear'. Another term widely used as an explanation, although it is no such thing, is the phrase 'tone deaf', to describe someone's musical failings. Taken literally, the term 'tone deaf' would almost mean the same as deaf. A person who really could not discriminate between sounds of different pitches would be unable even to understand human speech, and would be likely to confuse Paul Robeson with Maria Callas, at least in terms of the sound of their voices. The term 'tune deafness', with its more specific connotations, has been wisely substituted for 'tone deafness' by Kalmus (1949), and refers to a more precise type of deficit. In fact, the attribution of poor musical performance to some straightforward malfunction of the peripheral auditory apparatus is probably wrong in the majority of cases. Several studies have shown that the sense of pitch, for example, can be considerably improved by suitable practice (a review of such findings is given in Shuter (1968), ch. 16), and there is little to suggest that other musical abilities might not be similarly amenable. This is not to imply that everyone is capable of becoming a musical genius, but simply that certain people might be capable of a higher degree of musicality than they in fact achieve. This implies that apparently poor musical ability may often be to some extent, at least, the result simply of inappropriate or non-existent training. Cleall (1968) has even pointed out that the singing of songs in schools, in a pitch range not suited to the young voices involved, may have detrimental effects, and by implication be sufficient to undermine the musical confidence of many of the children involved. Speaking of some hymn books, he quotes, 'the pitch seems to be chosen to display the excellence of the choirboys' upper register rather than to make the task of the man in the pew a pleasure'. In other words, a good way to convince someone that he is tone deaf is to put him in a situation where he has to sing, under conditions which make the task all but impossible. In the course of some experiments (1977) the author frequently observed people who were, with difficulty, trying to sing, hum or otherwise reproduce a tune which they 'knew', but who kept making errors. In many cases, the singer stopped in embarrassment, and said something like, 'No, that's wrong' or 'That's not right'. This creates a nice logical problem, since the person's correct statement that the singing is wrong implies that inside him is a little man, or homunculus, who *does* know the tune and who is telling the outer man that his performance is below par. In fact, what this probably means is that people can recognize something more easily than they can reproduce it. In this instance, however, the process is more interesting since it appears that the singer is applying a recognition process to the sounds he himself is making. There is a great deal of evidence to suggest that, in remembering (recognizing or recalling) tunes, people make use of an internal standard, or set of internal standards, possibly of a tonal nature, against which they match the perceived material. Something is recognized when the material they hear matches their internal representation. Creel, Boomsliter and Powers (1970) talk of this internal representation as an internal 'tonal matrix', whilst Ward (1970) describes it as 'an internal scale of relative pitch, a moveable conceptual grid or template, so to speak, that specifies the pitch relationships among the notes of our Western scale'. As implied by Ward, the precise nature of the set of internal standards would be learned, and hence different for different musical cultures. This topic will be dealt with in more detail in the chapter on memory for tonal sequences.

In the light of evidence, it is the opinion here that there is very little reason for looking at the ear as the seat of musicality. Davies and Jennings (1977) failed to find any significant difference between an unselected sample and a sample of musicians from a full-time national symphony orchestra, regarding their ability to correctly perceive the contour of tonal sequences. This indicates that explanations of poor musicality which invoke a general 'lack of a musical ear' might be wrong if taken literally. The differences between the groups appeared to involve storage and decoding, rather than perceptual abilities. Work by Sloboda (1974), involving memory for a visually presented array of notes, showed not surprisingly that 'the superiority of musicians over non-musicians is due to differences in coding or memory'.

The ear hears, but it does not organize, and the very essence of music is organization. We agree with Mursell (1937), therefore, that music is almost totally a mental ability. It is as absurd to consider the ear as central to musicality as it would be to consider that the secret of reading lies in having good eyesight. (Contrary evidence is reviewed by Shuter, but it is not convincing.) In answer to the question 'What makes a tune?', we must therefore reply that people make tunes when they listen to music by exercising certain mental abilities which they possess. Listening to a tune is therefore not a passive process of mere reception, but one of active construction. The ear simply picks up, or receives, the sound signal and thereafter the human mind constructs the tune from this raw material.

It follows from the above that, since people have different organizing capabilities, and also differ in the ways in which they organize things, a particular sequence of tones might constitute a different type of tune for one person than it does for another. Furthermore, for some people it may not constitute a tune at all. It will be evident that our definition of a tune in terms of a person's organizing abilities is rather different in type from some previous definitions which have concentrated upon the sound stimulus. In effect, we are saying that a tune is not a tune simply by virtue of its physical properties, but only when it is perceived as such by a person. This is a more sensible definition, since people are by no means in agreement about the tunefulness of different pieces of music. For example, an often-heard criticism of modern jazz is that it is untuneful. (*Avant-garde* jazz is rather different in its aims and purposes, and falls outside the scope of this discussion.) The modern jazzman, however, thinks differently. In other words, when we say that we can hear the tune in a piece of music, we are actually saying that we are able to organize it and make sense of it.

Before we continue to explore the ways in which people make sense out of the musical sound stimulus, we need to say a little more about the way in which we are using the word 'tune'. Within the context of this chapter, a tune is taken to mean any tonal sequence which can be organized into meaningful units of a number of tones, and which consequently does not sound like a mere random collection of isolated tonal events. Because of this definition, we cannot here use the word 'tuneful' or 'not-tuneful' to distinguish between particular musical styles, except in a special sense, i.e. to mean only that a smaller, or larger, number of people are able to make a tune out of it. On this point, we can do little better than quote from Mursell who writes, 'A melody is not something built up out of notes', and later, quoting from Bingham (1910), 'The unity, then, which marks the difference between a mere succession of discrete tonal stimuli and a melody, arises not from the tones themselves; it is contributed by act of the listener.' For example, to say that Mozart's 'Minuet in F' is more tuneful than Stravinsky's 'Rite of spring' is to use the word loosely. Provided I can make sense of both the Mozart and the Stravinsky, for me they are both tunes as opposed to nonsense. It is preferable, therefore, to distinguish between the two, not in terms of their tunefulness, but in terms of complexity, about which more will be said later.

The remainder of this chapter is now given to an elaboration of this idea, and especially to an explanation of terms like 'organize', 'make sense of' and 'complexity', for upon the elucidation of these terms our definition hangs. What do we mean when we say that a person 'organizes' or 'makes sense of' a string of notes? The answer lies in a person's ability to see complete units and structures within the tonal sequence, despite the fact that it is made up of individual elements. A necklace, for example, might be made up of a great many separate beads or stones, but when we look at it we see not the separate pieces but a necklace having a certain shape and form. In fact, what is really a collection of many separate pieces is perceptually unified. This propensity of people to see or hear not individual elements or sounds, but overall patterns and configurations, is one of the basic tenets of a psychological approach known as Gestalt psychology. What is implied, therefore, by the terms 'organize' or 'make sense of' is nothing more than a person's ability to see patterns (Gestalten) in strings of separate tonal events. In broad terms, the laws of Gestalt psychology are 'principles of grouping' (Forgus 1966), and there is much evidence to illustrate this.

Fig. 13 below shows three groups of circles, each group comprising eight. When viewing these, most people will not merely perceive three groups of eight circles, but will organize the groups as far as possible. Group (a) will thus appear as a square and group (b) as a diamond. Group (c), however, is less likely to be seen in terms of some overall configuration. None the less, it is still not seen as eight individual circles, but tends to break down into organized sub-units.

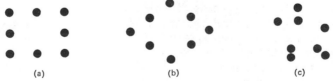

(a) (b) (c)

Fig. 13.   Patterns illustrating Gestalt organization

This tendency, to organize separate units into some sort of whole, is one of the central tenets of Gestalt psychology. Kurt Koffka (1935), one of the pioneers of the Gestalt approach to perception, further postulated the 'law of Pragnanz', or 'law of the best figure'. According to this, there is a natural tendency for observers to prefer the simplest and most stable figure available to them; unfortunately he does not offer an explanation for the terms 'simple' or 'stable'. Applying the law of Pragnanz to the Gestalt theory, Koffka reasoned that 'The psychological organization will always be as good as the prevailing conditions allow'. The act of perception therefore seeks to impose the best and most stable organization possible upon the percepts available; again, we are not absolutely clear about what 'best' means. (We may note in passing that symmetrical figures, which might be considered more stable than non-symmetrical figures, are by no means universally preferred to the latter.) The laws of Gestalt organization include specific effects due to similarity, proximity, inclusiveness, closure, good continuation, and others, all of which are relevant to this discussion, but which would occupy too much space to elaborate. We can make do with a grasp of the general principle outlined so far. In addition, it is important to realize that, as originally postulated, the laws of Gestalt perception were envisaged as natural laws, which automatically caused perception to take place along particular lines. It is clear, however, that the Gestalt assumption of innate and spontaneous organizational tendencies needs to be modified to take into account the learning and experience of the observer in forming his perceptual groupings.

So far as music is concerned, the argument from here on becomes more simple. The message is twofold. Firstly, when people hear a sequence of tones, they group these into perceptual units which will be as 'good as the prevailing conditions allow'. Assuming that they can do this with some success, the sequence of tones will become meaningful, and will be a 'tune' in the sense in which we have previously defined tunes. The argument for Gestalt organization in auditory perception is strongly put in Vernon (1934–5).

Secondly, one of the factors that will influence the 'prevailing conditions' will be the person's previous experience in organizing musical sequences into whole units. Speaking of the visual arts, Murch (1973) writes, 'The observer's familiarity with organizational tendencies may influence the tendency brought to bear on a particular situation. For example, the organization of a painting is probably different for the art critic than for the casual art observer.' In other words, the person who has a fund of experiences of ways of organizing particular types of material upon which to draw, is at a distinct advantage when confronted by new material which he has to organize. This applies not only to the visual arts, but also to music. Interesting evidence for both the above points is provided by two experiments on cerebral 'dominance', using musical material. In such experiments, the aim is very broadly to discover if the two sides of the human brain have different properties, and this can be done by finding out how well subjects perform various tasks in which aurally presented material is channelled to one ear or to the other. Since the two ears are contra-laterally connected to opposite sides or hemispheres of the brain (neurologically speaking, an oversimplification), any functional differences between the hemispheres should produce differential performance. Using this method, Kimura (1964) showed a superiority for recognizing tonal sequences when these were presented to the left ear of subjects, indicating right-hemisphere dominance. This contrasts with other findings using verbal material, where the right ear has been found to be superior (in right-handed people). More recently, however, Bever and Chiarello (1974) have hypothesized that the difference between the hemispheres does not correspond to the difference between verbal and non-verbal (or musical) material, but to a difference between 'analytic' and 'holistic' processing. Now it seems reasonable to suppose that musically sophisticated subjects can organize tonal sequences into integrated wholes rather better than musically naïve subjects, to whom a sequence is more likely to appear as a series of less organized tonal events. The left hemisphere (and hence, the right ear) is said to be the one responsible for holistic processing, and thus might be expected to have a superiority in the task of organizing a tonal sequence in terms of the internal relations of the constituent parts. Thus, a sample of musically sophisticated subjects should show right-ear superiority, whilst a sample of musically naïve subjects should show the left-ear superiority found by Kimura. This is in fact what Bever found, and he goes on to claim that being musical thus has real neurological concomitants. The point here, however, is that Bever's experiment provides further evidence for the notion that listening to music in a musical fashion involves the formation of perceptual groupings or 'wholes'.

Thus far, we have made the point that a person in some sense strives to make sense of tonal sequences by organizing the individual notes into groups or wholes, each constituting a psychological phrase. In addition, we have noted that a person's ability to organize the notes in this way is probably not innate or fixed, but subject to experience and learning. However, we have not given any detailed theory as to how these processes actually operate. There exists a body of psychological theory, known as 'information theory', which might cast some light on the nature of these processes. The basic assumptions of information theory stem from work by Shannon and Weaver (1949) who were originally interested in problems of communication. Here, however, we are more interested in their notion of 'uncertainty'. The term 'uncertainty' as used in information theory has nothing to do with a person's inability to make his mind up, or with his personal feelings of insecurity, but simply refers to the probabilities of different events taking place. In this sense, an event which is very likely to take place, for example, the probability that the word 'Queen' will follow the words 'God save our gracious . . .', will have a correspondingly low degree of uncertainty, i.e. it will be fairly certain. On the other hand, the probability that the word 'newt' will follow the same phrase is very low. Uncertainty is thus related to the likelihood of different events occurring. Furthermore, the larger the number of events which might take place, the higher is the degree of uncertainty. Thus, uncertainty will be greater where a particular event or chain of events has a great number of possible outcomes, than when it has relatively few possible outcomes. The final property of uncertainty states that, if an event has a fixed number of possible outcomes, uncertainty will be maximized when all these outcomes are equally likely to occur. For example, there is very little uncertainty about an event which, although it theoretically has a very large number of possible outcomes, has one particular outcome which is virtually certain to occur. Given the phrase, 'God save the . . .' there are thousands of words which might follow, but very little uncertainty since it is almost certain to be 'Queen'.

Imagine the situation in which one particular outcome is 100 per cent certain to occur. Such a situation would be one in which there was no uncertainty. On the other hand, there might be situations in which we can see any number of outcomes, each of which seems as likely to occur as any other, and in which uncertainty would be complete, or nearly so.

The next thing we need to consider is the notion of information, as applied within the context of information theory. Information is a mathematical abstraction associated with the principle of uncertainty; in simple parlance information is something which serves to reduce uncertainty. In this sense, information can be measured by using a formula to calculate how many 'bits' of information a particular message contains. The term 'bit' is a shortened form for Binary Information Unit, and, for the technically minded, the information contained in a message is the binary logarithm of the number of choices necessary to define the message unambiguously, with each choice being termed a 'bit'. As with many things, what seems scientifically obscure is in fact conceptually very simple. Suppose I am confronted with two patterns, both consisting of a series of squares. The squares which form the patterns can be of two types, black or white. Two such patterns are shown below. The pattern in fig. 14 (a)

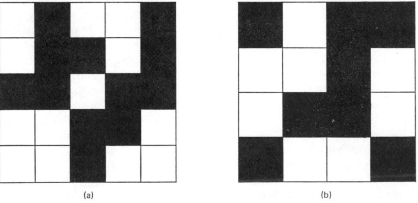

(a)   (b)

Fig. 14.   Information contained in two pattern diagrams

consists of a 5 × 5 matrix, whilst the pattern in fig. 14 (b) consists of a 4 × 4 matrix.

If I wished to define pattern (a) unambiguously, so that someone else could correctly reproduce it, I would have to provide him with information about the blackness or whiteness of twenty-five different squares. On the other hand, to specify pattern (b) he would require information about only sixteen squares. Another way of describing the situation is to say that I need more 'bits' of information in order to specify pattern (a) than I do for pattern (b). Alternatively, since information is something which serves to reduce uncertainty, and since I am trying to reduce my uncertainty about both patterns to zero, I can say that (a) contains more information than does (b). Unfortunately, most painters do not confine themselves to creating patterns of black and white squares, or other highly regular structures. If all pictures were like Mondrian's *Composition with Lines* (1917) the visual arts would be the information theorist's paradise. Most paintings, however, contain many objects of irregular outline and different degrees of detail, using a vast array of different shades of colour, and a variety of textures, so that the task of calculating how much information is present, whilst theoretically possible, becomes extremely complicated, and also rather arbitrary.

The square patterns given above are intended to be illustrations of the way in which an event (in this case a black square) or a number of events (several black squares) can occur within a space comprising a larger number of squares. Furthermore, the pattern diagrams represent a very simplified situation, since nothing has been said about the probability that particular events will occur. Normally, the probability of different events occurring is variable, and has to be taken into account in working out the information content. Thus we might see a piece of music as consisting of a number of events (the note or notes the composer selected), occurring within a space consisting of a finite number of possible events (the notes the composer might have chosen). More specifically, we might for example try to discover how much information is contained in a particular piece of music, in terms of note length, and interval, i.e. the duration of notes and the pitch intervals. To start with, we notice that notes are of different lengths, namely breve, semibreve, minim, crotchet, quaver, semi-quaver, demi-semiquaver, and hemi-demi-semiquaver. (Alternatively, we may call these whole, half, quarter, 1/8, 1/16, 1/32, 1/64 and 1/128 notes.) For the present argument, we are assuming that other durations, dotted notes, etc., are made up from combinations of the above. Next, we notice that within the musical area we are concerned with (Western classical music, popular music, or the works of a particular composer, or whatever we wish to specify), not all these note lengths occur with the same regularity. We notice that breves and hemi-demi-semiquavers are rather rare, whilst crotchets and minims are very common. In other words, certain durations of notes have a greater probability of occurrence than others. We can make a note of the probabilities. Following on from this, we start to examine intervals, and again we find that different intervals have different probabilities of occurrence. For example, a study of a Mozart bassoon concerto by Zipf (1949) showed that the probability of different intervals occurring was approximately inversely proportional to the size of the interval; that is, the bigger an interval, the less often it occurs. We might find it convenient to adopt such a rule and use it in our analysis. Now, we can use the probabilities we have obtained in Shannon's formula to find out how much information is contained within the particular tune in question. There is an actual worked example of this process in Moles (1968), in which the computations are set out. He calculates that a simple hypothetical piece of melody, from a classical composition, which contains twenty notes and lasts for some twenty seconds, produces fifty-six bits of information, or 2·8 bits per note, in terms of duration. In terms of musical intervals, the same tune yields fifty-one bits, or 2·55 bits per interval. The total information rate is thus 2·8 + 2·55 bits per second.

Basically, all we have done is to find out how often the possible different note durations and intervals occur (i.e., how likely they are), and then used this information to find out whether a particular tune contains more 'likely' or more 'unlikely' notes. Obviously, the way in which we derive our initial probability estimates is of some importance. If we used Western classical music in general as our basis for this calculation, we might find that the 'Horn concerto' written for Barry Tuckwell by Thea Musgrave, which was described to the author by a professional classical musician who had just performed it as 'just plain daft', contained a great many unlikely notes. Although the calculations have not been performed, one would guess that this would not be the case if we derived our probability estimates from other works by the same composer. In other words, the information contained, according to our calculations, will depend on where our initial probability statements come from. As we shall see later, this means that the 'Horn concerto' in question contains a great deal of information, possibly too much for many people to cope with, when compared with 'conventional' music; it probably contains only an average amount of information when compared with other similar works or works by the same composer. To put this another way, it is only unlikely by comparison with pieces which are more likely, and not when compared with other unlikely pieces.

The last point we need to make with regard to the theory of information theory concerns the relationship between information content and the probability of events. Though it may not seem always obvious, more information is contained in events which are unlikely than in those which have a high probability of occurring. This fact can be more readily understood in terms of a few simple examples:

The most probable events are those events which I know are going to happen. For instance, suppose I am talking to a friend and he tells me, 'I dropped a cup and saucer this morning', and I ask 'Which way did it fall?' His reply, that it fell 'down', and did not fall 'up', in fact tells me nothing, since I know with reasonable certainty that dropped objects fall down. In other words, his reply has such a high degree of probability it tells me nothing I did not know already. And someone telling me things I already know is not telling me anything new or original, i.e. he is not giving me any information. Suppose, however, that his response was not the highly probable 'down', but the highly improbable 'nowhere'. This could only mean that the event took place in some very strange environment where the normal forces of gravity do not operate, i.e. in a space-ship or an aircraft performing zero-G manoeuvres. My friend is thus an astronaut or something similar. His unlikely response, 'nowhere', is thus highly informa-tive, since it tells me something I did not already know. This principle, that information is greater for events that are not foreseeable, can also be illustrated quite well in music by the chromatic scale, an ascending or descending sequence of tones, all separated by a semitone. Once I have heard the first few notes of such a scale I very rapidly realize what its overall structure is, and come to anticipate (foresee) what future events are going to take place. It follows, therefore, that once I reach the state of knowing what is going to take place, the actual tonal events become redundant. Their occurrence becomes, for me, so probable that they in fact fail to provide any information. By contrast, suppose that after about twenty consecutive ascending chromatic notes, the twenty-first suddenly makes a great leap to a different part of the pitch range. I did not foresee this event, in fact it seemed quite improbable on the basis of what had gone before, and consequently it provides me with a great deal of information. In summary, then, something which I can readily foresee yields little or no information. And the most information is provided by something I cannot foresee at all.

We can thus define information as *originality*, since original events are ones that have not occurred before and which therefore have, theoretically, zero probability. An event which is highly redundant (i.e. which has a high probability of occurring), has only a low information content. Now, if we apply this notion to music, we must conclude that compositions which deviate from the normal style will be less probable, and more original, and hence will have a higher information content. On the other hand, a piece of music which is so closely based on particular stylistic norms that I am able to make pretty good predic-tions about how it is likely to go, will for me comprise high probability events, be unoriginal, and hence contain little information.

Now we come to the critical point, which is how the observer actually reacts to, selects, and finally prefers, particular pieces of music. On the whole, if a person finds that a tune is, for him, extremely predictable, it will contain little information. Since he knows what is going to happen most of the time, the notes he hears will do little to reduce his uncertainty since he is already certain. In other words it will contain little or no information for him. On the other hand, a person less versed in the particular musical style, or norms, in question will be less certain about what is probably going to happen, so that for him there will be more information. It is likely that, other things being equal, an observer who perceives a tune as predictable will rapidly become bored with it. He will, however, perceive it as a tune, but as one which is extremely naïve. On the whole, he is likely to turn away from such a tune towards one which has more originality (information) for him. He is likely to prefer a tune about which he has a variety of expectations, or hypotheses, about the probability of different events occur-ring. When a particular event takes place, his uncertainty is then reduced in a real sense. The final case to be discussed concerns the situation where events are so original that there is too much information for him to absorb. Where this is the case, the person may find the note sequence so apparently unrelated that his uncertainty is total, i.e. no event seems more likely to occur than any other. In such a case, the notes will seem random and each subsequent note will not serve to reduce his uncertainty about what is likely to happen next. We have already noted that uncertainty is maximized where any one of a number of possible outcomes seems to be (or, subjectively, *is*) equally likely to occur. Where the relationship between notes seems to have no Gestalt or pattern, each individual note gives no guide as to what is likely to come next and everything seems to be completely unforeseeable. In such a case, the occurrence of a tone will not subjectively serve to reduce uncertainty. In other words, where events are totally unforeseeable for a particular individual, the information content is so great as to effectively yield no information. Although notes are occurring all the time, he is no more certain now about what is likely to occur than he was at the beginning.

Therefore, if we were to ask the question, 'What kinds of music do people like, and what kinds do they dislike?' we might be able to couch an answer in terms of information theory along the following lines. On the whole, people will like pieces of music which provide them with information, and which consequently reduce their uncertainty about events. However, they will not like tunes which, either because of insufficient, or too much, information, do not reduce their uncertainty about events. We would predict, therefore, that people will prefer pieces of music which, for them, contain an intermediate amount of information, i.e. neither too much nor too little.

What evidence exists to suggest that the above hypothesis is true? To begin with, the differing amounts of information present in different tunes cause people to perceive them as being of varying degrees of (subjective) complexity. If I hear a tune which has, for me, a high information content, I am likely to think that it is a fairly complex tune; similarly, tunes which contain very little information for me, and which consequently contain many redundant notes, will appear to be uncomplex. Berlyne and co-workers (1968) have demonstrated just such a relationship, namely that judged (subjective) complexity is related to information content. Since extremely high and extremely low levels of information are alike in failing to reduce uncertainty, tunes which a person judges to be either extremely complex or extremely uncomplex ought to appear either meaningless or banal. The implication, therefore, is that people prefer to listen to tunes with moderate degrees of complexity, and avoid highly redundant pieces or highly complex ones. The situation we are describing can be summarized graphically in the form of a curve, known as an inverted U-curve, such as given below in fig. 15. The curve shows how people's preferences are for tunes which occupy an intermediate position between highly complex and highly uncomplex. Although the experimental findings are by no means unanimous, there is much evidence to suggest that people's preferences follow the pattern described (Vitz 1966, Walker 1973). This U-shaped function has even been found to obtain for simple stimulus dimensions like frequency and intensity (Vitz 1972).

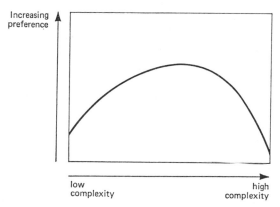

Fig. 15. Hypothesized relationship between preference and complexity level

There is evidence to suggest that data collected from groups can sometimes obscure the precise nature of this function. This is because individuals have different preferred complexity levels (i.e. the high-point of the curve occurs at different points for different individuals), and these differences are sometimes blurred when data is presented for groups. Thus Aitken (1974) found group judgements to comprise a variety of individual functions, as a consequence of differences between the 'peaks' of different subjects.

Most of the research in this area has not concerned itself just with preferences but goes further in attempting to find out what the components of preference might be. In so doing, the two components of 'interestingness' and 'pleasingness' have come under close scrutiny. There is a possible implication that, although 'pleasingness' follows the form of the inverted U-curve as shown above, 'interestingness' might behave in a different way. For instance, it is possible that people find increases in complexity to be progressively more interesting long after they have ceased to find them pleasing. For example, a concert-going companion of the author's once remarked, commenting upon a particular jazz concert by the Chris McGregor band, 'It's a row, but there's an awful lot going on.' She was saying, in other words, that she found it interesting but not pleasing.

Much of the work on the relationship between pleasingness and complexity has centred around visual patterns or figures, in which some variable like the number of sides or turns contained in a particular figure is increased or decreased to manipulate the complexity (Munsinger and Kessen 1964). On the whole, subjects do appear to rate those with a greater number of sides or turns as being more complex than those with less; as a general rule, complexity ratings are higher for figures which contain a greater number of elements, and less for those where redundant elements are present (Houston, Garskof and Silber 1965). There is also a certain amount of similar material using tones (Berlyne *et al.* 1967) and tonal sequences (Mindus 1968). Although the results are not unanimous, there is sufficient evidence to make the hypothesis, that people prefer sequences which provide them with an intermediate amount of information, seem a most promising one, and also to suggest that subjective complexity increases as a function of information content (Berlyne 1971). In such experiments, there are, however, certain problems which are specific to musical materials, and it would appear that not all the experimental work takes these problems into account.

Two pieces of work by Vitz (1964, 1966) are of interest, because they illustrate how completely opposed findings can result from a failure to take into account the nature of musical material. In the 1964 paper, Vitz investigated people's preferences for tonal sequences, which presented varying degrees of information. He failed to find the inverted U-shaped curve described above, and instead found that as he increased the information content of the sequences, people's preferences just kept on rising. In other words, the more complex the tunes, the more they liked it. The finding is clearly in opposition to our own common-sense observation, and in effect predicts that everyone should prefer Schoenberg to the Beatles. The explanation for these strange results has something to do with the nature of the 'simple tunes' used in the study. To construct the tunes, the experimenter joined together various different segments of tape, each piece of which bore a recording of a particular tone taken from the major scale. Altogether there were sixteen tones, traversing two octaves plus one note extra. By selecting his tones in various ways, the author produced sequences of differing information content, ranging from (according to Vitz) nil information in which a sequence contained mere repetitions of the same note, through to what he describes as 'completely random' sequences with a very high information rate. The musician will quickly realize that there is a fundamental error here, since the 'space' from which Vitz drew his 'completely random' sequences is in fact a musical scale. Given a sequence of notes all from a particular key or mode, the subjective probability that future notes will also come from amongst a group of notes occurring in the same key is very high indeed. The experimenter thus makes the fundamental error of assuming that because he selected his notes randomly from amongst those available, they will appear to be random sequences to the people who listen to them. This is patently not the case. If I pick, at random, a group of animals from a pen which contains only pigs, I do not end up with a random selection of animals. The truth of the matter is, that people are so much exposed to music in which tones are consistently chosen in terms of a particular key that they have very strong expectancies that the notes occurring will be so chosen as to preserve the tonality of the piece. The sequences which were supposedly random, and therefore contained a great deal of information, were in fact subjectively extremely non-random, and thus did not contain nearly so much information as was supposed. Accordingly, people's preferences simply went on increasing because none of the tunes was so unpredictable as to provide an overload of information with which subjects could not deal.

From the above, we can reason that if we choose our tones from amongst an array without any particular tonal or modal consistency, so that the subject is really unable to predict what is likely to come next, then we should obtain our inverted U-shaped function. Fortunately for us, Vitz repeated his experiment two years later in a modified form and found the inverted U-relationship we have described. Although the author blamed an inadequacy of the information theory formula for his earlier failure, his replication study was such that the tones he used in constructing his sequences were now no longer drawn from any particular key or mode, but were selected purely in terms of their mathematical relationships. Using tones drawn from such a space, the random sequences really contain a much higher information rate than those with higher probability relationships. In other words, they are not merely selected randomly, but they appear random because the subject does not have years of experience of this type of tonal array on which to base his expectancies, and consequently they have a very high information content.

These two pieces of work by Vitz now bring us to a very important point. The information content, or, in subjective terms, the subjective complexity, of a piece of music is not determined solely by the notes we choose, but upon a system of probabilities which is a function of the listener. A person who, as a result of his past musical experience, is able to predict to a large extent what is going to happen will find a piece of music less complex than does his neighbour who cannot predict so well. Furthermore, since musical experience is something which is a continuous process for most people, pieces which an individual finds highly complex at first may become less complex with the passage of time and the acquisition of new musical experiences. Pieces of music which, at one point in time, contained too much information for an individual to cope with may later come to represent the preferred level of complexity for that individual as he comes to learn what to expect. Many readers will have had the experience of buying a record and, after a couple of playings, consigning it to the darkest recesses of the record cabinet because they 'don't like it', only to find out about a year later, when they put it on again for whatever reason, that it now appears, like wine, to have improved with storage. Obviously, unlike the wine, the record has not changed, so the person has. As a result of his continuing musical experience, his preferred level of complexity has undergone a steady rise in the intervening period, and what previously contained too much information for him to handle now contains a more manageable (preferred) amount.

Certain other things follow from the above. The more we listen to a particular piece of music, the more we are able to anticipate, or expect, what is going to happen. In other words, the subjective complexity level for any given piece of music must decline the more times it is played to the same observer. We therefore predict that the more often a person hears that tune, the more rapidly is its information content, or complexity, going to decline towards a point where the subject no longer likes it because it no longer provides him with any information. (For example, Dember, Earl and Paradise [1952] showed that rats which had become accustomed to simple patterns began to seek out patterns of a more complex nature.) Furthermore, tunes which have a low information content will reach a level at which they are no longer preferred more rapidly than those with a high information content. If we accept the premise, therefore, that much pop music (though not all of it by any means) is highly redundant, in the sense of being easily predictable, and if we accept the fact that, for most young people pop tunes are the most frequently heard type of music, then we predict that pop tunes will rapidly decline in popularity, since their initially fairly low information content is rapidly exhausted as a result of intense exposure.

The above argument is not entirely satisfactory, since it implies the existence of some absolute standard in terms of which to judge information content, and we have previously argued that such an absolute standard does not have much meaning in music. None the less, there may be something to be said for the idea that certain pieces of music offer scope for increases in complexity with repeated hearings so that the reduction in complexity to a non-preferred level does not take place or is delayed, whereas other pieces of music offer no such opportunities for this type of elaboration. This process, which allows some things to become more complex with repetition, whilst others become less complex, is discussed by Walker (1973). As an example of the former process, he gives the game of chess. Once one has gained an initial knowledge of the moves, the game might seem fairly straightforward, but with successive games the player comes to discover additional levels of complexity of which he was unaware at the start. By contrast, the game of noughts and crosses very rapidly becomes non-complex once one has discovered the unbeatable strategy of preventing your opponent from claiming any three squares with sides in common (which means that he has 'got you two ways'), or three corners (which has the same effect). The complexity of chess thus increases, whilst that of noughts and crosses declines very rapidly, and we may note that there are many chess fanatics, but relatively few noughts and crosses devotees.

There are a great many complexities involved in studying people's preferences for pieces of music, and especially in finding out what happens when a piece is heard a great many times. A study by Heyduk (1972) illustrates these. At risk of over-generalizing, we might venture the following summary. With repeated exposure to the same piece of music, a person is likely to experience a subjective reduction in the complexity of that piece. In instances where the initial complexity level was too high, the reduction will be accompanied by an increase in liking since it will now move to a position closer to the subject's optimum complexity level. Where the initial complexity level was too low, the further reduction in complexity will be accompanied by a reduction in the liking for that piece, since it will move further away from the optimum complexity level. (Both these processes are implied by the nature of the inverted U-shaped preference/ complexity curve.) These conclusions are also supported by experimental evidence from Berlyne (1970), who concludes that the 'hedonic' value of complex stimuli increases with familiarity, whilst the opposite is true for simple stimuli. Finally, in the long term, all other things being equal, repeated exposure must ultimately lead to a reduction in complexity to a non-preferred level in all cases, though it appears that, for some people, several different levels of complexity may emerge during this process so that, initially, complexity and preference might increase.

Given the above, we can see possible reasons why some people like a piece of music more after they have heard it a few times, and why others like it less. But what of the person who finds a piece very complex and never comes to like it? The above predicts that, however high the initial level of complexity, it must in time reduce to an optimal level at which it will be liked. As a criticism of this view, it has been suggested that it logically implies that any unpredictable noise will eventually be liked if we listen to it enough. This is not the case. It is important not to confuse subjective predictability with randomness. A new piece of music may appear unpredictable to one person but it is not unpredictable to others who know it. In time, that person also may learn to predict. This is not the case with a random noise of the type which no one can predict, and where the noise is in fact not capable of prediction. On the other hand, if the noise is patterned in some way, then whether it will be liked or not should depend on the complexity of the pattern. The author has, on many occasions, seen people standing near to a compressor, tapping their feet and apparently enjoying the simple polyrhythmic accents which some such machines emit. As stated earlier, however, the distinction between noise and music is not a simple one to make, and one person's noise may be another's music. It is likely that a person's reaction to a potentially interesting or pleasing noise will be much tempered by the knowledge that no one intends it to be music. For example, 'concerts' have been given by 'musicians' who stand on step-ladders and throw objects into a pile of broken glass; it is a tribute to the gullibility of some sections of the public that they turn up and listen to it. On the other hand, a similar 'recital' by a gang of demolition men in the street is unlikely to attract an audience of people wishing to listen to their music. Following on from the examples given above, if the actual complexity level exceeds the optimum by a very great amount, a correspondingly large number of repetitions will be necessary to bring about the necessary reduction in complexity. Since the distance between the subjective complexity level of the piece and the subject's preferred level is so great, it is a fair bet that he is going to dislike it so much that he will never play it enough times to bring about the necessary reduction. In other words, he will never come to like it.

As a final point it may be necessary to suppose that, after a period of intense exposure to a tune, as a result of which its complexity has fallen to a non-preferred level, a period of rest during which the tune is not heard will cause it to return to a higher level when next we hear it. Presumably, something like this must happen since there is a common experience of becoming completely satiated with hearing the same tune to the point at which we become 'fed up' with it. When we play it again, after a period of some months, during which it has languished in some obscure recess, we once again find it stimulating. It appears that, during the intervening period, the piece has in some way rejuvenated itself, and has climbed up to a point on the preference curve higher than that where it finished. If this is the case, it would imply, in terms of our theory, that the tune had become more complex for us and had returned to a point nearer our preferred level of complexity. Maybe the tune recaptures some of its former attraction simply due to forgetfulness on our part.

If we now return to our starting point, which was the question, 'What makes a tune?' and the suggested answer, 'People make tunes', it should be apparent that the answer is not quite the platitude it at first appears. People seek to organize tonal sequences into Gestalt patterns, and their ability to do this depends on the complexity of the materials. Furthermore, we have found that people do not simply prefer the sequences which are the most easily handled, but appear to prefer a level of difficulty somewhere between too easy and too difficult. There is also the strong implication that differences between individuals in terms of the extent or type of their musical experience will cause them to experience different levels of complexity, even though they may all be listening to the same tune; this fact will affect the extent of their liking. Since we have already defined a tune as being a sequence of tones which a person can organize, we are in effect defining, as a tune, any sequence of notes of an order of complexity which does not exceed the person's preferred complexity level. Thus, even a very simple tune like 'Twinkle, twinkle, little star' will be regarded as a tune, even though it is at a non-preferred low level of complexity for many people. The problem is not that we cannot organize it, but that we can organize it too easily. On the other hand, once we start to exceed the preferred level of complexity, we start to encounter tonal sequences which we cannot organize, and once this happens the tonal sequence loses its essential tune-like characteristics, and is therefore, for us, not a tune.

A tune is therefore a sequence of tones which contains sufficient information to place it at, or below, our own personal preferred level of complexity. Because of differences in the musical experiences of different individuals, there are differences in the levels of complexity which people prefer. In addition, the more we grow accustomed to particular kinds of music, the more we become able to assess the probabilities of certain musical events taking place, so that a piece which we found untuneful at one time may, with repetition, come to acquire more of the psychological properties of a tune and our liking will consequently increase with repeated hearings.

Within broad limits, the above account of why people have particular musical preferences makes sense. For example, people not familiar with the scales, rhythms, and other conventions of Indian music are likely to find it rather formless at first hearing. People who restrict themselves purely to the pop scene are similarly likely to find classical music rather hard going at first, because, even within the same overall culture, there are different musical subcultures, with different norms. Any person familiar only with the norms of particular types of music will find difficulty with other types, though clearly some kinds of music have more things in common than do others. In theory, however, if we can only arrive at some estimate of a person's preferred level of complexity within a particular musical style, we should be able to predict the kinds of things he will like, and the things he will dislike within this area. Experiments along these lines have in fact been carried out, with both visual and musical material, and, in general, the results are confirmatory so long as the patterns or tunes used in the initial assessment of preferred level are of the same type as those in the later tests. Unfortunately, as with most work in this area, the experiments use rather artificial, statistically constructed material (such as the square patterns used previously, or random polygons with a prescribable number of 'turns', or statistically generated music, etc.) rather than patterns or tunes of real artistic merit. Using patterns of filled and unfilled squares similar to those shown previously, Dorfman and McKenna (1966) have shown consistent preferences for patterns of a particular degree of uncertainty, as measured in terms of matrix grain. (The term matrix grain refers to a process of varying the information content by manipulating the number of small squares in the matrix from 144 squares (or bits) in the 'fine grain' condition to four in the 'coarse grain' condition.) In Heyduk's experiments, mentioned earlier, in which subjects made judgements about statistically generated tunes, it was again possible to predict preferences from data obtained about the judged complexity of the different tunes.

As a postscript to this topic, it seems likely that there may be changes in an individual's preferred complexity level with the passage of time. For example, we have argued above that a piece of music which is initially too complex for an individual to like, may, with repeated playings, move down to a lower complexity level at which liking may begin to emerge. There is the possibility, however, that if a person repeatedly exposes himself to tunes of this type, a reciprocal movement might take place, along the following lines. If he listens to music of a type which he initially finds hard to anticipate, it is possible that repeated exposure to music of this type will, in time, cause him to anticipate rather better. In other words, his own subjective preference level might move upwards, so that music which was of a type judged too complex in the past might, in time, come to occupy the position of preferred complexity level. Thus we have not merely a mechanism by means of which a particular tune can move from a non-preferred to a preferred level, but also a possible means by which a person's preference can evolve, and in so doing lead to a liking for types of music which were disliked in the past. One might imagine a situation, for example, in which one hears a performance of a new, modern composition, and due to one's lack of familiarity with this type of music, one finds it untuneful and unpleasant at first. With repeated playings of the piece, however, liking begins to grow. Finally, when we have heard it several times, we find that we have changed our minds about it, and that we now like it. Once this stage is reached, it is quite likely that we will also find other similar pieces pleasing, even though we have not heard them before. In other words, it is not merely the initial piece which moves nearer to our preferred complexity level with repeated playings but also our preferred complexity level moves, so that other similar pieces of music, which we would previously have disliked, are now viewed favourably. Or, to put this another way, in moving towards our preferred complexity level, the first piece, unbeknown to us, brings other pieces with it. It does not much matter whether we conceive of the situation as one in which tunes move towards our preferred level, or one in which we move towards the tunes. The essence of the matter is that our musical taste has changed; as a consequence, the range of things which we now, in a psychological sense, find tuneful, will have been extended.

As a footnote, it is worth while noting that some workers have postulated mechanisms which make the above seem plausible. Berlyne, for example, speaks of the 'arousal jag', and Dember and Earl talk about 'pacer stimuli'. In a sense both these terms describe the interesting observation that, although people have a preferred level of complexity in that they find a particular complexity level most pleasing, they will in fact pay more attention to stimuli of a slightly more complex nature. In other words, the things that elicit the most attention are slightly more complex than the things we find most pleasing. It is almost as though these slightly over-complex stimuli lead us on to the next level of complexity, and thereby allow our preferences to evolve.

6 Some further aspects of musical perception

In the previous chapter we examined some of the ways in which various concepts, such as 'information', 'complexity' and 'Gestalt' might apply to people's perception of tunes. This chapter simply deals with some further aspects of tunes, necessarily related to those which have gone before, but which are of interest from the point of view of perception. The basic purpose of this chapter is to complete the picture which has been presented so far. One of the main messages from the preceding chapter is that the perception of tonal sequences or tunes is essentially an active process of construction on the part of the listener; tunes are only tuneful when a listener is able to group and organize the material in a particular way. In a similar way, the chapter dealing with emotional responses to music, it may be remembered, came down heavily in favour of the idea that learning plays an important part in enabling a person to produce expectancies which may ultimately be confirmed or disconfirmed. The notion that emotional responses to music might be instinctive or innate was assigned a lesser role. However, if the reader refers to page 67, he will recall that we refused to 'put all our eggs in one basket', and the reason for so disposing our eggs is still to be explained.

In essence, this chapter serves simply to outline certain aspects of tonal sequences which might be less dependent, or indeed might not depend at all, upon the learning processes described previously. There are probably certain properties of ears and tones which make certain perceptual events inevitable in the perception of tunes, and it is these with which we are here concerned. In addition, there is evidence that young children react pleasurably to particular sounds or motions of a regular nature, such as heart-beat, or rocking movements. These rhythmic aspects, however, are dealt with separately in chapter 12.

The first aspect of tunes which we consider here concerns the intervals between the constituent tones. There are some writers who maintain that each musical interval in the musical scale, when sounded non-simultaneously, has a particular unique quality which distinguishes it from all other intervals. In other words, the interval of a major fourth (C to F in the key of C) has a quality of 'fourthness' which is different from all other intervals; all the other intervals also have a particular distinct quality. These interval qualities are maintained regardless of key. Since any tune is made up of a series of successively presented intervals, it can be argued that at least part of the perceptual quality of a tune might stem from the intervals which comprise it. This notion, that each interval has a particular quality, has been described by Mursell, and is known as the 'interval' or 'intervallic' effect. Much of the evidence on the intervallic effect is of a subjective nature, and is based on the reports of subjects who describe the different intervals in different qualitative terms. Mursell (1937a), for example, describes work by Edmonds and Smith (1923), who asked subjects to describe the effects of various simultaneously presented intervals. The octave was consistently judged to be 'smooth', the major seventh was 'astringent', the major sixth was 'luscious' and so on for the different intervals. Although this experiment used simultaneous tones, so that an explanation which takes into account consonance and dissonance effects seems in order, Mursell claims that the intervallic effect is still readily perceived when intervals occur consecutively, as in tunes, where consonance/dissonance effects are assumed not to occur. In reality, most Western music consists of melodic lines with harmony, so that both simultaneous and successive intervals occur. These both presumably have an effect in determining the perceptual quality of the piece. Revesz (1953) in his theory of intervals also makes use of the notion of intervallic quality, and makes the point that all the intervallic qualities occur within the span of an octave (in other words, the absolute pitch of the constituent tones does not determine their intervallic quality, but merely the separation between them). These qualities thus remain constant, regardless of which octave we might choose. Trotter (1967) talks about the different notes of the scale having characteristic 'flavours'.

Most of the evidence on the intervallic effect is in terms of the perceptual quality of the different intervals. In typical experiments, subjects listen to different intervals played, and simply describe their quality. A different type of result comes from a report by Davies and Barclay (1977), though the results of this are tentative. It is reported here since the method is interesting, and suggests possibilities for a more rigorous study. In this experiment subjects listened to a number of tonal sequences (different sequences contained differing numbers of tones) which were each played very rapidly. All that the subjects had to do was listen to each sequence, and count the notes. In fact, the little tunes (if such they may be called) all contained only two alternating notes; different tunes contained different pairs. For example, one tune contained only the tones doh and soh alternating rapidly; another consisted entirely of doh and me, and so forth. Altogether, sequences consisting solely of the octave, fifth, fourth, diminished sixth, third, and diminished second, were presented. The duration of each tone was only forty milliseconds; at such a speed, the task of actually counting the notes is quite difficult, although it is easy to tell that the tones are separate and not simultaneous. Now, many studies of numerosity and fusion employing rapidly presented stimuli have been carried out (e.g. John 1972; White 1963; Symmes, Chapman and Halstead 1955; Cheatham and White 1954; Kinney 1961; Miller and Taylor 1948; Miller and Heise 1950) but none of these have interpreted the results in relation to specifically musical phenomena. The results from this experiment, whilst by no means definitive, were very interesting. Subjects were more accurate at counting the number of notes in some sequences than in others. This is hardly surprising. However, common sense tells us that things which are more different should be discriminated more readily than things which are more alike. In other words, where the tone pairs had the largest frequency separation, discrimination should be best, whereas in sequences where the frequency separation was small (as in the minor second) discrimination should be poorer. This was not what happened. The octave, where the frequency separation was greatest, was the most inaccurately counted. With the diminished second, however, counting was the most accurate, even though the frequency difference was smallest. A reason for these results is probably not far to seek. In the octave, for example, the upper tone coincides with the second partial of the lower tone, whereas with the minor second there is minimal overlap of partials. Remember, however, that the tones were not simultaneous, but presented at a speed where subjects could readily tell that discrete sounds were being presented. Also, since sine-wave tones were used, any interaction between harmonics (partials) must be explained in terms of harmonics generated by the ear, since such tones have no harmonics. (These results seem to relate to findings by Allen (1967) who found by a different method that musical subjects rated octaves as 'more similar' than intervals of closer frequency-separation. It is possible that musicians are implicitly taught that octaves are 'similar', however, since non-musical subjects did not perform in this way. More difficult to explain is Divenyi and Hirsh's (1974) finding that the order of tonal sequences was more readily perceived when the tones involved were in a harmonic relationship. However, since all the subjects in the experiment had musical training, it is probable that they identified the components in the harmonically related sequences, a task which would be more difficult for less harmonically related sequences.) It emerged that the accuracy of the subject's counting was closely related to the degree of consonance or dissonance that would have been present if the tone pairs had been presented simultaneously.

Fig. 16 below shows a typical ranking of consonance/dissonance taken from previous work (see chapter 11), and a ranking of the totals reported in the present experiment. The correct total is 1215, so it is clear that subjects under-

Interval	Totals reported	Rank	Consonance/ Dissonance ranks
Octave	702	1	1
Fifth	764	2	2
Fourth	777	3	3
Diminished sixth	784	4	5
Third	828	5	4
Diminished second	842	6	6

Fig. 16. Table showing similarity between consonance and dissonance ranking

estimated the number of tones. However, it is the degree of underestimation which is of interest. (It is repeated, however, that this study needs verification. Not all individual subjects displayed the nice tidy pattern described.)

In the column headed 'Totals reported' we see the total numbers reported by fifteen subjects (who performed 108 trials each), using sequences containing from two to seven notes. It can be readily seen how these numbers grow larger as we move from the consonant to the dissonant intervals. The main point of the experiment is, therefore, that with intervals presented in this way, and presented in the form of separate (non-simultaneous) tones, there is a measurable and quantifiable difference, demonstrating that people really do perceive them differently. It is the hypothesis that intervals which have been described previously in qualitative terms such as 'smooth', or as 'astringent', differ in terms of some discriminative dimension related to their frequency ratio, as do the consonance and dissonance phenomena. Further, it might be that every time we hear a change from one note to another, there is a very brief and fleeting effect similar to consonance or dissonance which occurs just at the moment of transition, and which gives every successively presented interval its own special quality. It seems likely, in the light of these results, that consonance and dissonance are not unique to simultaneous notes. An effect almost identical, but of more fleeting duration, occurs whenever we change from one note to another. Thus, when we listen to a tune, its overall quality may in some way be a function of the constituent intervals contained in the tune, each one of which creates its own very fleeting but unique sensory quality; that quality looks in some ways similar to consonance/dissonance. Although young children below the age of six or seven do not respond reliably to consonance and dissonance (Gesell and Ilg 1946), and although preferences for particular tone combinations do not simply reflect consonance/dissonance effects but are much more likely to be influenced by learning (Guernsey 1928), the above experiment shows how certain qualitative aspects of a tune might be independent of learning. It might be that the nature of the sound stimulus, and the way it affects the auditory apparatus, are such that particular notes following other particular notes always have a certain quality which is independent of the listener's musical experience or training. After all, although musicians are the ones who produce music, they are not the only ones who listen to it.

This hypothesis should not be misconstrued, however. Many music writers have made claims that minor intervals, such as from C to E flat, have a distinct quality of sadness and melancholy. On the other hand, major keys are said to lack this quality and to have instead a feeling of brightness and gaiety. There is a very strong chance, however, that the associations between these keys with their characteristic intervals, and the mood states mentioned, are simply learned in the way described in chapter 4. Solemn music, in our culture, is very often written in a minor mode, whilst bright and happy music occurs mainly in major keys. This being so, we simply learn that conventionally minor modes will be sad, and major modes will be happy.

In a similar way, the use of flatted sevenths and thirds in jazz or Negro blues music seems, on the face of it, to have an essential 'blueness', an intrinsic quality which seems to be produced as an inevitable consequence of the notes. (The word 'flatted' may be repugnant to purists, who might prefer 'flattened'. To dance band musicians and jazzers, however, the word flattened has different connotations: people, and not notes, get flattened.) However, it is difficult to say whether the response occurs naturally, or whether it is learned, though the author prefers an explanation placing more emphasis on the latter. After all, it might be that 'blueness' is merely an alternative word for the presence of certain notes. (The fact that a twelve-bar blues can be in a major key is irrelevant, since the flatted intervals still occur, and seem perhaps even 'bluer' as a consequence.) 'Blueness', in fact, is probably a learned association to certain notes, which regularly occur in certain kinds of songs, dating from the era of slave labour in the USA. The fact that it is learned, however, does not make it any less real.

On this very topic Valentine (1962) gives an overview of some research findings, and tends to the view that the sad effect of minor keys is in no way due to intrinsic effects of the intervals. In experiments, large proportions of subjects give happy responses to minor keys and sad responses to major ones, responses in fact that would be impossible if there was something intrinsically happy or sad about the perception of these modes. Valentine also points out that, in certain countries, the opposite relationship often obtains, with major keys frequently used for sad tones, and minor keys for cheerful ones. Within our own musical culture we do not have to look very far to find similar exceptions to the rule. For example, the hymn tune 'For those in peril on the sea', and the extremely miserable song 'Eurydice', are both set in major keys. On the other hand, 'The dance of the little swans' and 'Anitra's dance', which are both energetic and happy tunes, are written in minor keys. By way of anecdote, Delius's 'A song of summer', through association with the Ken Russell film about that composer, now produces almost suicidal misery in the author's wife, despite its being in a major key. Finally, it is interesting that our own major mode is based on the Greek Lydian mode, which, according to the Greeks, expressed sadness and melancholy (Revesz 1953).

It appears, therefore, that the minor/sad and major/happy dichotomy is probably a false one, since major and minor chords in themselves fail to elicit supportive responses. Furthermore, Heinlein (1928) states that the responses of both musically trained and untrained subjects are variable and inconsistent when they are asked to make judgements about entire pieces written in the different modes. It would seem likely, therefore, that isolated chords in major or minor modes elicit very little in the way of mood connotations, and that even within the context of a piece of music the major/minor difference is not of paramount importance in determining these mood connotations. On the contrary, there are so many other variables in a piece of music (e.g. fast or slow tempo, loud or soft dynamics, words) and so many associations which might be learned, that to make the major/minor distinction the crux of the whole argument is unjustified. It might be argued that the major/minor effect exists, but is merely swamped by associations and other factors. However, the work with isolated chords, which are free of obvious associations, makes this seem unlikely.

An experiment has already been described which appears to demonstrate that, when one note follows another, a particular quality of sensations is produced which is more or less unique to that pitch relationship. This quality is not a sad or a happy quality in itself, but merely a quality specific to the notes involved, and different from that produced by other notes. This idea, that certain stimuli have particular intrinsic qualities, bears some further examination. (Remember, however, that the other factors dealt with in previous chapters are probably of more importance in determining the nature of the final experience.) There is a fascinating phenomenon known as 'physiognomic perception', as a result of which certain states or conditions of both human and non-human objects seem inherently to express particular qualities, because they possess the same kind of structure. A weeping willow tree thus looks sad because it resembles, in physical terms, a person who looks sad, in so far as the tree, and a sad person, both have a passive, droopy appearance. The notion is that this very appearance of the tree automatically conveys the notion of sadness, and we do not therefore have to learn a specifically sad connotation for willow trees. That this type of perception exists is not an established fact, but an hypothesis, and without too much difficulty we can think of exceptions. For example, Arnheim (1954) has argued that the sad quality of a willow tree comes from its expression of 'passive hanging' but a string of sausages in a butcher's shop also seems to hang in a fairly convincingly passive manner, but does not to most people convey a feeling of great sadness, so that there is probably more to it than is contained in the description. Given these inadequacies, however, there are still some interesting phenomena which seem to support the notion of some sort of physiognomic-style perception. A number of experiments have been performed, in which people are asked to choose a name for a particular geometric shape; they appear to choose particular names for particular shapes with great reliability. For example, in fig. 17 below, two shapes are drawn. One consists of very rounded elements, and the other is very angular. (It is tempting

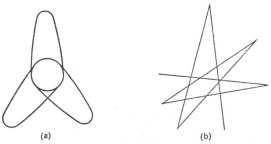

(a)   (b)

Fig. 17.   The label 'uloomu' is normally attached to (a) and 'takete' to (b)

to describe one as rough or harsh, and the other as smooth or soft, words which in themselves seem to support the physiognomic hypothesis.) If one were given the information that one shape was called 'uloomu' and the other 'takete', the tendency with most people is to attach the 'uloomu' label to the left-hand figure, and 'takete' to the right-hand one. The tendency to attach the nonsense labels in this way appears to be, to a large extent, cross-cultural, i.e. people from many different cultures and backgrounds make the same choice (Davies 1961).

In the same study, Davis also describes a tendency for 'matchstick figures' with square heads to be described as 'men', whereas similar figures with round heads are described as 'women'. Although the findings here are open to certain alternative explanations, the possibility that there is something natural about the pairing of angularity and masculinity, and of roundness and femininity, still exists, though the reader is probably best left to his own speculations at this point.

If this type of perception exists for visual stimuli of various kinds, might there not be particular tonal configurations which have similar properties?

One of the most striking ways in which this might occur concerns the sense of 'up' or 'down' and of 'high' and 'low' which tones seem to convey. This is most baffling, since, in the sense in which these words are used (i.e. to describe the pitches of different sounds), they are completely inappropriate and mis-applied because the properties of the sounds we are describing are not in any way spatial. Why does it seem so natural to describe a tone in the upper (again, why 'upper'?) register as high, and its opposite as low? Whatever the reason, we are left with the certain fact that, as we listen to a piece of music, we are unable to do so without experiencing changes in highness and lowness, attributes which are in no *a priori* fashion attributable solely to the notes themselves. In the very first chapter of this book, an effect was also described which causes high notes to sound small and thin whilst low notes sound big and fat. This was explained in terms of the number of overtones present in high and low tones. These attributes, again, are not dependent upon some kind of musical interpretation or some extra degree of learning, but are simply a function of the way human beings experience sounds. Why else should the 'Dance of the sugar plum fairy' (presumably, a small and thin fairy, rather than a big fat one) be played on a celeste, at the top end of the register; and why should the Elephant from the 'Carnival des animaux' be played way down at the bottom on a double bass? It might be argued that, through constant exposure to a particular set of norms, we have learned that elephants are normally portrayed as rumbling around in the depths of the orchestra, whilst fairies tinkle about at the top. This is no doubt true; it does not belie the fact that, played in isolation, high tones sound small and thin, qualities which are normal attributes of fairies, and low notes sound big and fat, like elephants.

The succession of tones in a piece of music does not therefore simply appear to differ in frequency, but appears to rise and fall as though it had spatial characteristics. Since the notion behind physiognomic perception means that the object perceived (in this case, music) intrinsically expresses certain states or qualities, music will also have certain qualities which are normally associated with 'upness' or 'downness' in other fields. For example, since what goes up must come down, we might speculate that objects which are 'up' are in a high-energy state, and that the normal rest position is 'down'. Within broad limits, we also find that music uses high notes and general upward movement for the expression of tense or energetic states, and the tension is released when the tune comes back 'down' again to a rest position. There are, of course, exceptions to this, since the effects of rising or falling tones do not normally occur in isolation. There may be accompanying changes of tempo, or changes in the loudness, which may either serve to accentuate or attenuate the effects of changes in other parameters. Conventionally, however, fast tunes usually have energetic connotations, and slow tunes more leisurely connotations. This seems perfectly reasonable, since a state in which events occur rapidly is usually more energy-consuming than one in which they take place slowly; this applies to rapidly changing tones as well as to anything else. It is sometimes pointed out that there are many exceptions to this type of tentative rule. For example, certain African tribes express their grief at the death of one of their number by playing and dancing to extremely energetic music, as contrasted to our own more sedate approach. However, it can justifiably be argued that this does not show that two quite different types of music have the same kind of depressive/miserable connotations. It merely shows that funerals in different cultures are surrounded by different conventions, which dictate that different types of behaviour are appropriate. The criticism would therefore only have force if we could pick out a society where people spontaneously whirled like Dervishes to the strains of the 'Death march', or where they sat transfixed by gloom whilst Glen Miller played 'American patrol'.

Changes in loudness are also worth a brief comment. Again, the properties of loudness are fairly apparent. Any loud noise, not just music, alerts us or wakes us up; under normal circumstances we take our repose at times when loudness levels are on the whole rather low. Consequently, loudness or softness in music has some of the same properties. In general terms, these common-sense interpretations of the effects of different musical parameters accord fairly well with previous work, though, as Valentine points out on several occasions, a piece of music can only be viewed as a whole, and its ultimate character for a particular person is a result of a complex interaction between the various factors.

In summary, the above paragraphs are intended merely to ask the question whether there might not be certain aspects of music which produce a particular quality of experience, perhaps even a particular emotional reaction, simply because of the physiognomic properties of the music itself, and quite independently of any musical learning or knowledge on the part of the listener. If this is indeed the case, and it would appear to be a reasonable hypothesis, then any account of musical experience which fails to take it into account must be incomplete.

7 Musical ability and musical aptitude: the problem of definition

At first glance, the term 'musical ability' seems fairly straightforward. In the course of our normal everyday activities, we find little difficulty in deciding who is musical and who is not. When we see a performer on the television, or at a concert, we might describe him as being very musical, or alternatively, as having no musical talent, depending on how we feel about his music. Most of us probably have at least one friend whom we describe as being musical, and some of us describe ourselves as being unmusical or deaf to music. As long as we use these terms to imply nothing more than a completely subjective judgement, they can serve a useful purpose. However, if we imply, by using them, the existence of some external objective criterion then the situation becomes far more complex.

Under normal circumstances there is little difficulty because we only apply terms like these in an *a posteriori* manner. We wait for a person to do something which is clearly and patently musical, such as playing 'Für Elise' more or less accurately, or singing 'O for the wings of a dove' more or less in tune, and then say that he or she is musical or has musical ability. Such a use of the term is clearly circular; people who perform certain acts are musical, and a musical person is one who performs such acts. Where a more precise and scientific use of the term is required, the above is of little value. For example, if we use performance as our only criterion, then the question, 'Does Julian Bream have musical ability when he is not playing the guitar?', becomes a difficult one to answer. The immediate and obvious response is, 'Yes, of course he does', but in the absence of any actual musical performance it is impossible to produce any evidence in support of this answer.

This circularity is extremely difficult, if not impossible, to escape from, and the problem of definition is one that has exercised many previous workers. Bentley, for example (1966a), suggests that musical ability is 'that characteristic, or those characteristics, which distinguish "musical" persons from "unmusical" persons', but he goes on to point out that the difficulty of defining 'musical' and 'unmusical' still exists. Seashore (1938) offers an alternative attempt to resolve the dilemma with the following elaborate definition: 'Musical talent is not one but a hierarchy of talents, branching out along certain trunk lines into the rich arborization, foliage, and fruitage of the tree, which we call the musical mind.' Apart from the insistence on hierarchical organization, the definition in the end is fundamentally the same as Bentley's, though it perhaps has the disadvantage of being more exotic than helpful. For example, what is the precise meaning of 'arborization', 'foliage' and 'fruitage'?

Other workers have given definitions completely in terms of the kinds of operations performed by people who are said to be musical. For example, Herbert Wing (1948a) tackles the problem in the following manner: 'Many restrict the first term [musical ability : author] to the ability to play some musical instrument. But the teacher of music uses it in a wider sense that includes speed in learning to play, ability to perform the "aural" tests . . . and ability to carry out such musical activities as composing.' The problem with a definition of this type is that an inexhaustible list of different tasks can be compiled, all of which might be manifestations of musical ability in some shape or form; yet overall there is still no clue as to what the common component is in these tasks. We are still no nearer to a definition of the central construct. Nevertheless, an examination of the various forms which musical ability can take is not entirely unfruitful, because a pattern emerges which suggests that there are three basic types of situations in which musical ability can manifest itself, namely, in performance, in composition and in listening. This latter is very important, since if a mere listener can be musical, we are forced into a situation in which we need a new definition of musical ability which does not rely solely on the production of music as its criterion.

The difficulty of definition is not unique to musical ability, but is a common one which recurs every time we try to define a concept which has no material existence. The classic illustration of this is intelligence. A casual glimpse at this area might lead the unsuspecting layman to conclude that there are almost as many definitions of intelligence as there are psychologists. The problems here are in many ways similar to those outlined above. In the first instance, our observation of people's behaviour leads us to infer the presence of some intangible entity like musical ability or intelligence, and often, in the case of psychologists, this is accompanied by a desire to find ways of objectively measuring the inferred capacity. Unfortunately, the dangers of reification often lie precisely in this direction; that is, there is a tendency to begin to think of the concept as though it were an object having physical properties and characteristics. Whilst workers in the field of intelligence have long since become aware of this problem, the same is not always true in the field of musicality or musical ability, where a certain amount of reification has been going on happily for years. A recent paper by Gillham (1974) outlines some of the arguments that have been levelled at traditional views of intelligence, and in particular points out that the idea that intelligence tests (or musical ability tests, for that matter) measure pure potential, but not attainment, is naïve. He quotes from Vernon (1968) '. . . we must give up the notion of intelligence as some mysterious power or faculty of the mind which everyone, regardless of race or culture, possesses in varying amounts, and which determines the potentiality for achievement'. The same could be said about the notion of 'musicality', since it appears to be a similar type of concept. On the other hand, intelligence tests are often the best predictors of scholastic success available (Elliott 1974), which makes the problem rather more complicated. In fact, the resolution of the conflict possibly lies in a more precise distinction between the concept of intelligence, which has no concrete existence, and intelligence tests (and people's scores on them) which do exist. The fact that the tests predict can then be seen for what it is: a purely empirical finding which does not necessarily have anything to do with intelligence as a concept.

The search for tests and measures of intelligence has led to a different type of definition, in terms of the tests themselves, which in turn leads to a different set of problems. As an introduction, we may take note of a statement from Guilford (1967) to the effect that any definition which is to satisfy the needs of 'univocal communication' must contain referents which exist in the real world, or point clearly to something else which itself has clear referents in the real world. Now intelligence tests exist in the real world, and, as early as 1923, Boring suggested that intelligence could be defined adequately as the ability to do well in intelligence tests. Such a definition overcomes some of the difficulties associated with the types of definition discussed previously, but clearly it is critically dependent on the nature of the tests themselves. What if we discover that the degree of association (correlation) between different intelligence tests is quite low, implying that different intelligence tests in fact measure different things? It is precisely this state of affairs that has led to the formulation of a number of models of intelligence which comprise a number of different capacities with differing degrees of interrelationship.

In a manner analogous to the above, there probably exist at the present time sufficient tests of musical ability/aptitude for us to suggest a definition in terms of the tests themselves. Thus, the musical person is one who gains high scores on such tests. We are therefore able to move away from a definition which is couched solely in terms of musical performance. This does however have the disadvantage of placing the responsibility for definition on the shoulders of the test constructors and their tests. It appears that a proper distinction between ability, and the more specific notion of aptitude, is not always made by test constructors. The problem will be dealt with later in this chapter. Again it is a debatable point whether different tests do in fact measure the same thing. There are also certain less specific objections to an approach which defines things in terms of test performance, to the exclusion of all else. It is legitimate to criticize such an approach on the grounds that it is too blinkered by empiricism; thus, if there are no intelligence tests, no one is intelligent. Even more absurd, it could be argued that Beethoven possessed no musical ability or aptitude because there were no appropriate tests around at that time. There is clearly a very large discrepancy between the definition in terms of tests, and the common-sense way in which people use terms like intelligence and ability. Referring back to our question about Julian Bream, and whether he has musical ability when he is not playing, we may remember that the immediate and obvious answer was in the affirmative. Why does this answer seem so obvious? Logically, if a person can perform a certain feat at one particular point in time, and can repeat the performance again later, there must be some enduring state existing within that person, between the two points in time, which makes the repetition possible. It is this unseen but enduring state which we refer to as musical ability, or intelligence, or whatever. Logically, it appears that such an enduring state must really exist. Unfortunately, the state is physiological in its critical aspects, and the present state of knowledge does not permit us to describe what the physiological correlates of intelligence, or musical ability, are. Therefore, the present argument, that a definition in terms of the tests themselves is preferable, is purely a pragmatic measure. When the time comes that we understand the precise physiological states that accompany intelligence or musical acts, and can describe the permanent physiological correlates of these acts, then we can talk about intelligence or musical ability in a more sensible manner. If we assert that there are qualitatively different types of intelligence, then we must seek support in qualitatively different types of physiological states; if we state that Fred is more musical than Jim, we will be able to show how Fred has more of a particular type of physiological attribute than has Jim. At present this is not possible, so that we need to have recourse to a different kind of definition.

Unfortunately, the definition chosen here is not completely satisfactory. It is, however, a good starting point, since it makes no assumptions about the properties of states which are not understood. There is a further advantage in using the tests as our yardstick. The types of measures used by various authors often reflect the kinds of views they hold on the nature of musical ability or aptitude. Since much of the theory of musical ability is derived in the first instance from observation of subjects' performance on various tests, it will be seen that the topics of testing and of musical ability are virtually inseparable. Theories about the nature of musical ability tend to have their roots in data obtained from different tests and measures of musical abilities. Thus, as far as the theories go, a definition of musical ability in terms of 'what the tests measure' seems to have been accepted. However, when it comes to validating individual tests, there is often a shift of criterion from the tests themselves to a performance criterion. Thus, when an author wishes to find out if his test works, the procedure characteristically involves the comparison of musical and non-musical groups, with the musical groups selected in the first instance on the basis of performance in some musical task. If a test fails to pick out the musical from the non-musical subjects, it is usually assumed that the test is a poor one, though logically it could equally well be that the definition in terms of performance is a poor one. One of the main reasons for constructing tests is that performance is unsatisfactory as an index of talent, or musicality. Yet this is always where we turn for a final decision about whether a test is a good one or a poor one. The remainder of this chapter is largely given over to discussing certain aspects of this relationship between the theories and the tests.

The topic of musical ability has probably been more discussed in the psychological literature than any other aspect of music. Hand in hand with the development of theories of musical ability has gone the search for adequate tests and measures of different types of musical performance and musical potential. A great deal of energy has been directed towards the construction of tests based on different approaches to musical ability, and as a result there are probably upwards of a dozen test batteries which are well known in musical testing circles, another dozen or so which are less well known, and no doubt several more which have barely or never seen the light of day. In the subjective experience of the author, these tests and measures have always appeared to be of more interest to musical theorists (in a psychological sense) than to musicians. Even music teachers often seem to be aware of only one or two of these test batteries, though there are of course exceptions. The reason why this should be so is perhaps a matter for speculation. However, it is not unreasonable to say that in general terms the impact of psychological testing upon music and musicians has not been very great. In addition, recent years have seen a swing away from the obsession with test production, and perhaps even a certain disenchantment with the area. In a recent article, Swanwick (1973) states that, in music, 'the field of experimentation is littered with "ability" tests and their evaluation', with the implication that this has been of somewhat limited value, and that other avenues might be pursued with equal or greater profit.

Perhaps one of the main difficulties which has dogged the footsteps of musical ability testing arises from differences of opinion about the role of a learned musical culture in the development of musical ability. As a result, the types of items used in tests range from those which are perceptual in the strict sense of the word, do not involve real music, and which demand judgements about pitch, intensity, temporal separation and so on, through to those which make no such psychophysical demands but use real musical material and require value judgements to be made. It is argued here that neither of these approaches is satisfactory, though they both clearly have something to do with musical ability. To understand how two such different approaches have evolved in response to a common set of circumstances, it is necessary to look more closely at the different ways in which musical ability is viewed.

In the normal course of events, the term 'ability' is used to describe a particular level of performance at a particular point in time. For example, the skill of a Yehudi Menuhin or a Louis Armstrong can be thought of as the expression of their particular ability or abilities. In this sense the ability has been acquired over a period of time, and has involved a learning (environmental) component, and an aptitude (innate) component. People learn from their interactions with particular environments; the absence of suitable environments reduces the likelihood that a particular ability will develop, or even prohibits it altogether if appropriate environmental influences are absent. On the other hand, if there is little aptitude, the effects of environmental influences, no matter how optimal these may be for the particular task in hand, will be limited and a high degree of ability will not be attained. For the highest degrees of ability, therefore, both the learned and the innate components must be favourable. An example may serve to illustrate this. A man who is constitutionally very thin, has a height of five feet three inches, and weighs nine stone, is unlikely to become heavyweight boxing champion of the world. We could send him to the finest gymnasiums and these could improve his physique, but they would be unable to transform his constitutionally wispy frame into that of a Muhammad Ali. In other words, his genetic endowment in terms of physique, his basic blueprint, prevents him developing the physical characteristics necessary for a heavyweight champion. By contrast, now consider the situation of a large-framed, burly farm worker, six-feet-six in his socks, and weighing seventeen stone. He has at least the physical equipment to enable him to be a heavyweight boxer, but, unless he is firstly attracted by such a prospect, then given gymnasium facilities, and actually put into a boxing ring, he too will never become the champion. In the first instance, the innate component is prohibitive. In the second, the environmental component is prohibitive, though there is probably much more to boxing than mere physique. Both components, innate and environmental, must be favourable to produce a Muhammad Ali. Perhaps one of the most striking examples of the interplay of environmental and hereditary factors is the way in which children learn to speak a language. Certain innate structures are required for language to be acquired, but the exact language which is learned depends solely on the language spoken during the child's formative years.

Unfortunately, although we can measure a man's height, or his weight, in fairly objective and reliable terms, we cannot measure abstractions like aptitude in anything like so satisfactory a manner. Music, as we shall see, is primarily a mental activity, and when speaking of an innate component or aptitude the same problem is immediately encountered. We cannot yet measure mental aptitudes with a ruler or a pair of scales, but only with test batteries which yield results in terms of scale units which lack a physical basis. It is probably this fact which is at the root of most disagreements about the nature of musical ability. Basically, there is disagreement about the place of aptitude in this scheme of things. For example, it can be argued that aptitude for music exists, independent of any environmental influences, and that it can be meaningfully measured. Contrary to this is the notion that either aptitude does not exist independently of environment, or that if it does so exist it is of little practical consequence. In so far as the debate centres on the relative contributions of innate versus learned factors, it is analogous to the fiery arguments raging in the so-called Jensen controversy. This latter debate centres around the relative importance of hereditary and environmental factors in intelligence. Arthur Jensen (1969) argues that there are differences in intelligence between different racial groups, due to innate factors; the counter-argument is that the apparent differences are due to differences in environment (social class, education, opportunity, etc.) between different racial groups. Unfortunately, the arguments in the music field appear to be less well formed than those in the Jensen controversy, which itself is a highly equivocal debate.

In the field of music, for example, two more or less polarized positions appear. One view is that musicians, especially great musicians, are born and not made. Yehudi Menuhin is reportedly a supporter of such a view; he started the Menuhin schools which seek to nourish exceptional musical talent. By way of criticism, one might point out that musicians are, obviously, born; but then so is everybody else. It is also clear, however, that musicians, like everybody else, are also made. Otherwise, schools designed to provide a favourable musical environment, like the Menuhin schools, would not be necessary. Evidence for the importance of the genetic contribution often comes from extensive studies of musical talent amongst members of particular families, or musical dynasties such as the Bach or Couperin families. Again, however, it is difficult, if not impossible, to say how far musical ability is transmitted genetically and how far environmentally. Shuter (1968) devotes a short chapter to this topic (pp. 129–36) but arrives at no firm conclusion, other than that the genetic case is not proven. One interesting study cited in Shuter (p. 132, Reser 1935) apparently shows the transmission of musicality in a Mendelian fashion as a dominant trait, but the study has a number of rather serious shortcomings. The importance of innate factors cannot be simply dismissed, however.

An opposite view places much greater emphasis on social, environmental and learning factors. The extreme version of this view might be, 'musicians are made and not born'. The evidence on this point largely consists of reports of the improvements made in various types of musical performance as a result of learning, and also sometimes, rather illogically, of musical persons being born of non-musical parents and vice versa. In an extreme form, both views are surely equally untenable, since musicians are both born and made. Factor analytic studies are reported in Shuter, which represent attempts to assess the relative strength of these two sets of factors.

The musical problem is different from the intelligence problem since the main concern is not to identify differences between groups, but simply between individuals. Despite this distinction there are certain things which might be learned from the Jensen arguments. Firstly, the discussion on intelligence centres on the relative importance of the genetic and environmental factors. Jensen proposes that genetic factors may be strongly implicated in the differences in measured intelligence between racial groups. The evidence, he says, indicates that such a hypothesis 'seems not unreasonable'. Those opposed to Jensen's thesis place larger values on the environmental influences, and smaller on the genetic. However, so far, not many people have proposed that there is no genetic contribution whatsoever.

In a similar way, any aspect of musical performance develops as a result of the co-action between innate and environmental factors. From a purely logical standpoint, it is impossible to conceive of an ability which has developed in the absence of those innate characteristics which make the task performance possible. There are no boxers without arms. Similarly, there is no pitch discrimination without the inheritance of a mechanism which permits it to develop.

However, not all workers in the field of music ability are entirely happy with this seemingly unchallengeable proposition. It is argued here that no fundamental disagreement exists in fact, but that the appearance of such a state of affairs arises from differences in the usage of certain terms and attendant lack of specification. This may be best illustrated with a specific example.

There is much evidence demonstrating that pitch discrimination improves as a result of practice. Shuter (1968) provides a chapter on 'Aids to learning' in her comprehensive book, including examples of methods of improving pitch discrimination. The conclusion from these and other experiments is accurately summed up by Sergeant (1970) who writes, '. . . the presence of a strong learning component in pitch discrimination cannot be ignored, and it is unreasonable to attribute a high level of discriminatory ability solely to favourable endowment'. So far, there is little disagreement possible, except perhaps as to the relative importance of 'endowment' and 'learning'. Continuing his argument, Sergeant writes, 'the implications for methods of psychological measurement of musical abilities are that if we seek to measure musical skills then the stimuli used in the process of measurement must be compatible with the context in which the musical learning which provides the basis for the discriminatory behaviour took place'. It is at this point that real difficulties begin to emerge and there seem to be two main sources. The first comes from the use of the word 'compatible'. Compatible does not mean 'the same as'. The common practice in psychological testing procedures is to select items for a test on the basis of how well they predict the criterion. In her book which has virtually become a standard text, Anastasi (1961) writes, '. . . test items need not resemble closely the behaviour the test is to predict. It is only necessary that an empirical correspondence be demonstrated between the two.' To put this in the present context, if we can show a certain degree of statistical association (correlation) between test items and some criterion of musical ability, then the items are, to use Sergeant's terminology, 'compatible'. Compatibility, therefore, does not mean that we subjectively judge the test items and the behaviour to be alike. It means that we have used a statistical criterion; it is a matter of empirical fact rather than subjective judgement. It is conceivable, albeit highly unlikely, that the ability to suck eggs correlates highly with (i.e. predicts) the ability to play the accordion. If such a relationship is shown to exist, then sucking eggs is a first-class test of accordion playing, and no arguments about subjective compatibility are relevant. It might be nice to have musical ability tests that comprise items which themselves sound musical or tuneful, but this should not blind us to the fact that such a bias on our part is not a satisfactory guide as to what the best test materials will be.

The second source of apparent disagreement concerns ability and aptitude. If we wish to measure ability, we are trying to assess a level of attainment. Since Western music is a cultural phenomenon, it follows that assessment of ability will take place in the light of attainment within this system of cultural musical norms. Tests of musical ability might, therefore, make use of material which is in itself musical. Since we are interested in the totality of the musical skills which a person has developed, our test will not try to rule out environmental or cultural contamination, since in this instance it is not contamination at all. It would appear, however, that the above argument has been over-enthusiastically interpreted to mean that all tests that have something to do with music should contain musical material. Again, a rough comparison with intelligence can serve a useful purpose here.

Different workers, notably Cattell (1963) and Jensen (1970), have found it useful to conceive of intelligence as having two components. Cattell has distinguished between 'fluid' and 'crystallized' intelligence, and Jensen talks of 'Level I' and 'Level II' abilities. According to Jensen, both these Levels have a genetic basis. Cattell, however, sees 'crystallized 'intelligence as being far more subject to environmental influence than 'fluid' intelligence. It is far beyond the scope of this book to go into the details of what these distinctions are said to involve. However, one aspect is of relevance here, notably the idea that intelligence might be conceived of as comprising two parts, one of which depends on environmental influence in order to develop, and the other which is, relatively, less affected by such environmental influence. Depending on which type we wish to measure, a different testing approach will be appropriate (though Jensen points out that with one or two exceptions, tests seem to contain both types of items jumbled up together). Now, Jensen's argument, that there are genetic differences between racial groups in terms of intelligence, is often disputed on the basis that the tests and measures used are not 'culture fair'. The term 'culture fair' means that the materials and items used in the tests give certain groups an advantage over others, because they are more familiar to some groups than to others. To give an obvious example, any pencil and paper type test would bestow an advantage on a group of children from Wigan when compared with a group of children from the Kalahari Bush who are not acquainted with pencils and paper. This is an extremely crude example, and most of the cultural bias in the tests is of a more subtle nature. It should be fairly obvious, however, that any test which tries to measure aptitudes ought to be so constructed as to eliminate any cultural components which give an advantage to one group over another. If, however, our aim is to find out what has been attained or how much has been learned, then we will clearly not be concerned to take out those aspects dependent on learning, in so far as these are the areas we wish to measure. Essentially this is the basis for school and university examinations (or the examinations of the Associated Boards of the Royal Schools of Music).

In the same kind of way, we might usefully conceive of musical ability as being in some respects analogous to the above. On the one hand, if we simply want to know how good a person is at musical tasks, how well he has responded to his music lessons, in other words how far he has progressed in a particular musical culture, our tests might well involve material which is musical and which reflects the musical culture of the place where the testing is taking place. On the other hand, if our aim is to try and predict for example how well a particular individual will respond to music lessons (i.e. how good he might become or what his potential is), then any aspects of the test which might build in a cultural bias ought to be eliminated. As mentioned earlier, inherent in this approach is the danger that we begin to see musical aptitude as a 'thing', whose two chief properties are (a) to determine potential and (b) to predict future musical behaviour. In fact, all we have is a test which requires particular forms of behaviour for its completion. These behaviours might correlate to a greater or lesser extent with other behaviours. The tendency is, however, to invert this situation and see tests not as a means of sampling particular types of behaviour, but as measures of inferred properties of individuals, i.e. we think we have measured some entity that exists inside the subject's head. This assumption is implicit in the titles which test constructors give to their tests, such as 'Standardised tests of musical intelligence' (Wing 1948), 'Measures of musical abilities' (Bentley 1966), and 'New tests of musical aptitude' (Davies 1971), all of which suggest that the intention is to measure the dimensions of a concept.

Provided, however, that we do not begin to invest our concepts with properties or characteristics, and provided that we have a clear view of what we require our test to do, then tests can be meaningfully devised. Thus, if we want a test to mirror what a person has learned, we can select items appropriately; if we wish our test to predict how well a person might do in the future, as far as possible ignoring what he has learned in the present, we again select our items with this in mind. If we thus construe the words 'ability' and 'aptitude' to be nothing more than convenient, if misleading, labels to describe the purpose of a particular test, the situation should be clarified. In fact, however, some of the tests in existence confuse these two functions.

There are tests which are unambiguous, for example the very comprehensive MAT (Musical Achievement Tests) tests of Colwell (1970) which are thorough-going tests of what has been learned from a particular musical environment, and which require judgements to be made about extracts of real Western music, performed on real musical instruments. On the other hand, the tests of Carl Emil Seashore (1919, 1939) attempt to measure aspects of peripheral functioning in a culture-fair manner and as a result no musical material is involved. (It appears that Seashore in fact chose to measure the wrong things by concentrating too much on peripheral functions, and this is borne out by the somewhat variable data on the predictive validity of these tests. This is a separate argument, and in no way detracts from the soundness of the attempt to take out certain aspects of cultural bias in an effort to measure aptitude rather than attainment.) Other test batteries, however, contain items which confound these two aspects to an unnecessary degree.

In simple terms, there are two opposing views about the nature of musical ability, which place emphasis on its 'unitary' and its 'atomistic' nature respectively. The former, it is argued (Gordon 1971), has its origin in the Gestalt psychology of the 1940s, which placed emphasis on the importance of overall configuration in perception. By contrast, the atomistic school of thought, having its chief protagonist in Seashore in the USA, placed emphasis on the analysis of separate components of musical ability. The unitary theory implies that any attempt to measure musical aptitude or ability (the terms seem often to be used interchangeably) is in error if it attempts to isolate separate component parts, but should rather attempt an assessment of all the parts (if indeed there are parts) in totality. By contrast, the atomistic school seeks to break the overall trait (if indeed there is an overall trait) down to separate components and evaluate these independently. Thus, in terms of the unitary theory, a person is either musical or not musical to a greater or lesser extent; in terms of the atomistic theory a person might be musical in some ways but not in others.

Because of the crucial nature of this distinction, it is not surprising that the tests devised by different authors tend to contain items which reflect their adherence to either one or the other of these two alternative points of view. This can be clearly seen in the following extracts. The first one is from Mursell (1937a), a formidable proponent of the unitary theory, who wrote, 'Only the observations of the subject in various musical situations are a guide to the degree to which talent is present.' Compare this with Anastasi's previous comment, which placed most of the emphasis on prediction of subsequent performance, rather than *a priori* assertion. In a similar vein Lowery (1932) wrote, 'If it is required to test for the presence of innate musical tendencies, the entire isolation of constituent factors in music is not likely to be of great service; rather ought a factor which is considered sufficiently worthy of special attention be brought into prominence with a musical background, the conditions of testing being therefore analogous to those occurring in musical performance.' Before proceeding to the opposite point of view, it is worth noting that Lowery's tests required subjects to make judgements about virtually intact musical structures, with no attempt being made to isolate separate component abilities. Also, it is interesting to note that Mursell uses the word 'talent', and Lowery uses the term 'innate musical tendencies'. The way in which these terms are used suggests that the authors had in mind something much more like aptitude than attainment.

On the other side of the fence, perhaps the main protagonist is Seashore. Commenting on Mursell's statement Seashore writes, 'It is my humble opinion that no creditable test of musical talent can be built on that theory', and also, 'In testing, we ask specifically, "How good a sense of pitch, of intensity, of time, of rhythm, of consonance, of immediate tonal memory has this child?" The measurements are stated in terms of centile rank and may well be the first and most basic items in a musical profile which may have scores on other factors, quite independent and equally measurable.' Even Spearman (1927) briefly joined the debate, saying on the topic of a single-factor (unitary) theory of music, 'Most of all, perhaps it might have been expected in the sphere of music, where not only innate instinct, but also environmental encouragement are incomparably more favourable for some individuals than others. And yet just here the expected broad factor has been convincingly disproved; the abilities to appreciate, for instance, the relation of pitch, loudness and rhythm have extremely low intercorrelations; no more, in fact, than must be attributed to G alone.' (For a detailed explanation of G, which is a general factor, see Spearman and Jones (1950).) One might quibble with the rather strange term 'innate instinct', or dispute the phrase 'convincingly disproved', but our main concern is the type of views expressed rather than their evaluation, which will come later.

It is clear that, in defending these respective positions, at least some of the protagonists have interpreted the arguments as having implications which are not always self-evident, and in the end it might be this fact that makes a resolution of the conflict possible. For example, it is sometimes inferred from the unitary approach that all tests, whether of aptitude (talent) or ability, must measure something *in toto*, and that this can necessarily only be done in a musical context. This might at first glance appear to follow on an intuitive basis, but in fact the logical basis for the supposition is less clear. The converse also deserves consideration. If one takes the atomistic viewpoint, one is committed to examining separate components; this fact alone does not imply that only non-musical sounds may be used. Whether we decide to use musical materials or not is a separate argument, and will depend on how important it is for us to remove any cultural bias when measuring aptitude(s), or how essential it is for us to evaluate performance in a given cultural framework as when measuring attainment. On the whole, the use of musical materials has come to be associated with the unitary theory, whilst the atomistic approach has come to imply the use of non-musical noises. What appears to have happened, as a result, is that the aptitude tests associated with the unitary approach often seem to have some of the characteristics of attainment tests.

One might speculate, however, that the villain of the piece is the tendency to see musical ability as an analogue of music. It is too easy to slip into the error of thinking that musical ability, which is something that is 'inside' a person, is synonymous with music which is 'out there'. Suppose that a person has great ability as a motor mechanic. If I take a unitary view of this ability, it does not imply that he can only fix cars which are assembled. Conversely, if I take an atomistic view, it does not follow that I have to take the car to bits before he can fix it. Similarly, I do not prove that musical ability is atomistic by taking music apart and measuring the performance on the parts; nor do I demonstrate the truth of the unitary assertion by looking at people's judgements of complete musical extracts. In this sense, the supposed nature of the ability cannot be naïvely assumed to have a simple direct correspondence to the nature of the test material. Again, it is correlations between tests of different types which provide the most important evidence on this point, rather than speculation about what tests ought to be like. Finally, on the point of atomistic versus unitary theories, it could be that strict adherence to one to the virtual exclusion of the other might be rather incautious. Shuter (1968), in her book on the psychology of musical ability, gives a comprehensive coverage of studies using the technique of factor analysis, and makes the point that all such analyses of musical ability tests reveal an initial common factor, though the size and importance of this common factor is variable between tests. (For the record, factor analysis involves describing subjects' answers to a large variety of test items in terms of a smaller number of dimensions or factors. Thus, evidence that a single factor underlay a series of different types of test items would imply that these items were measuring the same thing to some degree. It is quite possible, however, for items to measure the same thing, and different things, at the same time. For example, a person's answers to the questions, 'What make of car do you drive?', and 'How many bedrooms has your house?', might at the same time be influenced by the common factor of income, whilst at the same time yielding specific facts about cars and bedrooms. (At the same time, the correlations between sub-tests of certain test batteries are frequently only moderate, suggesting that there is also a degree of specificity about some of the types of test material produced. Such findings are hardly surprising.)

Earlier in this chapter, attention was drawn to the distinction between aptitude, as some sort of innate potential, and attainment, which is the actual level of performance at some point in time. The point was made that aptitude tests should be so constructed as to minimize any effect of cultural contamination since failure to do this confers an advantage on those people more familiar with the material. However, this distinction is perhaps less clear than it might appear to be at first sight, since innate characteristics and environmental effects are not independent. It can be argued that any attempt to measure a specifically genetic predisposition is doomed to failure if the genes responsible require a particular set of environmental circumstances in order to manifest themselves. In other words, if you take away those environmental conditions necessary for the expression of a particular genetic trait (in this case, musical aptitude) there will be nothing left. The problem is, therefore, that if we do in fact succeed in taking out the environmental influences from an aptitude test battery, as seems to be the aim, then we will end up measuring nothing. From such a standpoint, the construction of aptitude tests might seem futile.

In fact, however, the problem is really non-existent, since the task of constructing a test in which there is no environmental (i.e. learning) component is all but impossible. In constructing tests of aptitude, the aim is not to remove wholesale all environmental effects, but only to remove what are known as specific environmental effects. In practice, this involves the attempt to remove all materials which have specific relevance to a particular musical culture or subculture, and which are not common to all. Clearly, therefore, any test which made use of Western classical music in its construction, or something analogous to classical music, would favour those people familiar with this form, and would discriminate unfairly against a majority of people brought up on a diet of rock-'n'-roll and beat music. The converse, obviously, is also true. A test of musical aptitude therefore should not contain any material which has a particular stylistic bias, is specific to a particular type of musical culture, or demands a knowledge or awareness of any specific set of musical conventions. It should be constructed so as to permit any individual, whose musical aptitude has resulted from a particular genetic expression in a particular environment, to tackle the items on as nearly equal a footing as possible, regardless of the type of musical background to which he belongs. It is important to realize that taking specific environmental effects out of the test battery is not the same thing as taking environmental effects out of people. The environment in which a genetic trait of musicality has expressed itself in a particular person is not removed simply because I try to take specific environmental effects out of my test. The search is thus for a type of material which allows musical aptitude to manifest itself, regardless of the precise conditions under which the genetic component has been expressed. It is argued on this basis, therefore, that any test which contains formal musical material will be unsatisfactory as an aptitude measure, since it will invariably be an example of music in a particular style, and not equally familiar to all. The idea that the test constructor penalizes the musician by deleting formal musical material is completely erroneous, since it assumes that musicians only occur within a particular musical style. On the contrary, all we are doing is refusing to give certain types of musician a head start in a race they are already winning.

The main points concerning atomistic and unitary theories, and the problems arising when we wish to measure aptitude as opposed to ability, have been dealt with in some detail. The arguments should become plainer, and perhaps come to life a little more, if we direct our attention to various aspects of musical ability or aptitude tests, and try to find some illustrations for the different points by looking at specific examples.

8 Problems of measurement

Tests and measures of human abilities exist in almost every area of human performance, and amongst these are a number of music tests of various types. In general terms, such tests fall into two broad categories, attainment and aptitude. The attainment tests are usually designed to answer questions about the extent to which individuals or groups have learned particular tasks, often from some syllabus. Aptitude tests on the other hand are supposed to measure what is sometimes referred to as natural ability, i.e. the extent to which an individual has potential in a particular area. The actual form taken by such tests is variable, but, in the main, they take the form of pre-recorded tapes or phonograph records, on which are recorded a series of tasks of different kinds, accompanied usually by verbal instructions. The subject or subjects to be tested fill in their answers on a standard answer form, as the tape or record is played. Such a mode of test administration has the advantages of ensuring a high degree of procedural standardization, and also of being a convenient way in which to administer the test items to large numbers or groups of subjects.

Characteristically, the items contained in tests consist of short presentations of some musical or non-musical sound about which a specific type of judgement is required. The MAT tests, for example, are thoroughgoing attainment tests, and comprise short extracts of musical material performed on musical instruments. Subjects must perform a number of tasks, including making comparisons between an extract of written music displayed on the answer form and an extract heard on the record, identifying musical instruments on the basis of the sounds they make, locating the position of a melody embedded in a harmonized extract, and many others. Many of the tests, including some of those given above, clearly demand a degree of formal musical knowledge for their performance, and this is consistent with the description of the tests as Musical Achievement Tests (Colwell 1970). On the other hand, aptitude tests tend to demand less in the way of formal musical knowledge or learning, though it can be argued that this is not always the case. The classical example here is probably the Seashore tests, which require subjects to listen to various kinds of non-musical stimuli, such as pure tones, clicks, buzzes, and artificially synthesized complex tones. Subjects must, typically, discriminate between the higher and lower of two tones, estimate time intervals between clicks, or state which of two buzzes is the louder. In so far as these tasks do not demand any appreciable degree of formal musical knowledge, the approach is consistent with an attempt to measure aptitude.

However, not all tests are as unambiguous as the two examples given. The tests of Herbert Wing (1948b), for example, comprise aptitude items and also appreciation items involving music of a formal nature from a variety of sources, including nursery songs, folk tunes, and extracts from Bach chorales. In all the items which involve real music, subjects are asked to make judgements of a purely aesthetic nature. They are presented with two versions of each extract, which may differ in phrasing, harmony, intensity (dynamics), or rhythmic accent, and they are asked to choose which of the two versions they think is the better. In fact, the test constructor has already determined which of the two versions is the 'right' one, a procedure which implies that aesthetic preference is of two kinds, namely correct and incorrect. Other test constructors have made the same assumption.

The Meier art judgement test (1940), for example, involves exactly the same principle. The subject is instructed to indicate which of two pictures he prefers. His preferences are then scored on a 'right/wrong' basis depending on whether or not they accord with the opinions of experts. The whole basis on which an individual's preferences are scored as right or wrong is worthy of some semantic scrutiny. This point is also made by Pickford (1972) in relation to the Meier–Seashore art judgement tests which are simply an earlier version of the Meier tests referred to above. He raises the whole issue of using 'agreement with the experts' as a criterion, and points out that, as far as artistic innovation is concerned, disagreement with experts might be more important than agreement. He questions the supposition that disagreement with experts is necessarily wrong, and gives as evidence the finding that a group of Fine Art students in Edinburgh obtained higher scores on the Meier–Seashore tests before attending a lecture course. On subsequent testing, their scores were lower, showing that they now agreed less with experts than they had done previously.

If you ask a person which of two things he prefers, his answer is by definition correct, provided he is not lying. On the other hand, however, it cannot be argued that asking a person 'which he prefers' is just the same as asking him 'which is the better'. In an experiment conducted by the author (1965), subjects were requested, amongst other things, to say which of four records they preferred. One of the records was a modern jazz record, one pop, one folk-singing, and one classical music. (The author made the incorrect assumption that in a test situation subjects would vote for the type of music they preferred, even though they might not like the particular example.) One subject, who was awaiting the results of his examination for the degree of Ph.D in music, and who was an extremely fine pianist, was amongst a minority who chose the Beatles record ('I want to hold your hand') when asked to say which they preferred. When questioned later about this, he said the Beatles record was in some respects reminiscent of Ravel, whereas the classical piece chosen (Haydn's 'Trumpet concerto in E flat major') was for him uninteresting. As a consequence of this, post-experimental discussions were held with this subject, and with others. It became apparent that some subjects found themselves in a dilemma. They wanted to vote for the Beatles (the one they actually preferred) but they had an uneasy feeling that if they chose the more highbrow classical or jazz examples they would do better on the test. (In fact, the experiment was purely concerned with preference, and there were no right or wrong answers.) The piece which was actually preferred was thus in many cases different from the one which subjects thought they ought to choose in order to do well. This problem is likely to be even more acute where subjects are asked to choose 'which is the better'. Does the question mean, 'Choose which is the better for *me*' (i.e. which one do I prefer), or does it mean, 'Choose the one the experimenter thinks is the better' (i.e. the one I will receive most marks for)? Furthermore, in many cases, the subsequent choice of the classical record was based on a knowledge of the musical bias and prejudice sometimes shown by test constructors and experimenters.

That such musical bias exists cannot be denied, though perhaps it is becoming less widespread. Wing, for example, wrote, 'From the psychological point of view, although acquired knowledge is often an indication of interest and ability, any music test which is considerably affected by it is better avoided, owing to the very unequal opportunities which exist in musical instruction.' The reader may like to try and reconcile this admirable sentiment with a subsequent test involving Bach chorales in an original and mutilated form. Subjects are asked which they think is better (not 'Which one do you think is the original') and then given a mark if they choose the original. One might surmise that a sample of people who know the originals will do better than a sample who do not. The same author also wrote, 'Jazz music was not included, as this would be unlikely to yield examples of really good harmony, would be likely to prejudice the authorities against the tests, and would waste the children's time if they were listening to poor music.' The sentence contains a number of misconceptions and pre-conceptions. Popular music, which, like it or not, is the staple musical diet of most people, never receives a mention, though admittedly in 1948 it was hardly the same phenomenon as today. It appears, however, that this approach to any music which is not, as the Americans say, 'strictly legit', is still to some degree present. One still occasionally encounters the school music teacher who pretends not to have heard of the 'top ten', or takes actual pride in not knowing what the latest 'hits' are. It is the author's view that there is good music and bad music in all spheres, and that the difference does not coincide with the distinction between classical music and everything else. Suffice to say, any test constructor so motivated could produce a test containing original and mutilated jazz extracts, or pop extracts, requiring subjects to state which is better (i.e. which is the original version) which would leave any ivory tower musician with a score of zero. And again, such a result would tell us very little about the person's musicality. It would be unfair, however, to proceed further without taking note of a study by McLeish (1968), in which three test batteries were compared. The tests in question were the Wing tests, which comprise mainly musical material and require a variety of tests to be performed; the tests of Hevner and Landsbury (1935), in which an original version of a melody, and a distorted version, are compared, and subjects must say which they prefer (i.e. which is the original) and in what way the versions differ; and the tests of Seashore, which are psychophysical in nature and have usually been regarded more as measures of auditory acuity. The findings from this study are baffling. Using the technique of factor analysis, McLeish found that these three tests, one of which is highly divergent from the others in character, were essentially measures of the same thing. (McLeish gave it the name 'musical cognition'.) Furthermore, closer examination showed that one could not account for scores on the tests in terms of the factor of intelligence, since this accounted for only a small percentage of the variance. These findings are difficult to understand, though one or two comments are in order. Firstly, the results were obtained from a sample of 100 postgraduate and undergraduate students, described by McLeish as highly intelligent. The fact that the Wing tests and the Seashore tests yielded scores which were only to a very slight extent a function of intelligence (differences in intelligence, as measured by the Cattell IIIA, accounted for only 7·75 per cent and 3·6 per cent of the variance on the two tests respectively) is thus hardly surprising. In terms of intelligence test scores, students represent a more homogeneous group than the population at large, since they fall towards the upper end of the scale, and none of them fall at the bottom. It is not unexpected, therefore, that differences in scores on the music tests do not reflect differences in intelligence, since in a student group intelligence scores are very much more homogeneous, and, relative to the population at large, there is much less variation. Had the experiment been conducted on a sample covering the normal range of intelligence test scores, then intelligence scores would most probably have emerged as more important. As it is, we may note that the intelligence test scores account for about twice as much variance on the Wing tests as on the Seashore tests. However, the finding that all three tests produced high loadings on the same factor is more puzzling. The tests with the highest loadings on the musical cognition factor (as in all factor analyses, the name given to the factor is purely a matter of choice) are the Hevner and Landsbury 'nature of change' tests, the Seashore 'memory' test, the Wing 'pitch change' and 'memory' tests, and the Hevner and Landsbury 'appreciation' tests. All these tests require subjects to listen to two presentations of some tonal material, and make some judgement about the difference between the two. The musical cognition factor thus might have something to do with the ability to perform tests of this type. In a later chapter, more will be made of the point that, despite some obvious differences, certain of the tests used by different authors have much in common; we might to some extent account for the high loadings in McLeish's study in terms of the above similarities. The only difficulty lies in the high loading on the Hevner and Landsbury appreciation test, since much has been made previously of the problems associated with asking people to express a preference which is then scored right or wrong. From the point of view of this argument, it would have been preferable if this test had a rather lower loading. No explanation seems apparent, though the finding is in some ways anomalous. For example, the Wing appreciation tests (of which there are four different types) involve exactly the same type of psychological operations, i.e. listening to a correct and a distorted version of a melody and saying which is preferable; yet these four tests on the whole have much more moderate factor loadings than Wing's other tests. And none of them approaches the high loading obtained by the Hevner and Landsbury appreciation test, despite the fact that they are almost identical. Finally, the results of this study indicate that, in general terms, the subjects who did well on the more musically oriented tests of Wing and Hevner and Landsbury, also did well on the less musical tests of Seashore. One would like to see the study extended to a broader sample comprising not just 'willing, able and intelligent subjects' as used by McLeish, but including those who are perhaps less willing, less able and less successful on intelligence tests. Certainly, the very different results that have been obtained from the Seashore and the Wing tests, when these have been subjected to validity checks, suggest that the tests do not actually perform in the same kind of way. A comprehensive coverage of factor-analytic studies of music tests, and details of test content, reliability and validity, is contained in Shuter (1968). In many instances, the factors revealed by the factor analyses are difficult to interpret.

However, despite McLeish's results, it should be apparent that the use of musical materials in tests which are not simply measures of attainment presents certain problems. Once the decision to use musical material has been made, it is difficult not to be biased in favour of music of a particular type. Even within our Western culture, exposure to all kinds of music is not uniform through all sections of society (a process of 'musical' acculturation has been demonstrated by Zenatti 1973) and questions involving classical music will hardly be the same for the pop fan as for the classical concert-goer. It does not follow that the former is automatically less talented than the latter, and one simply cannot assume that a high level of ability always stimulates an interest in classical music, rather than in jazz, pop or Pibroch. Unfortunately, the situation is further complicated by the belief of some test constructors that any test battery which does not include tests of appreciation is likely to be of limited value. The argument against this is simply that appreciation cannot take place in a vacuum, and demands a background knowledge of music similar to that used in the test, against which evaluation or appreciation can take place. The person encountering Hindu music for the first time is unable to appreciate the music, since he has no frame of reference and no expectancies, so he could not tell a 'right' Raga from a 'wrong' one. It would appear therefore that the use of actual music in tests presents difficulties, and that these difficulties are compounded when the task itself is one of appreciation. The notion that test batteries should include appreciation tests, however, should not be simply dismissed, as we may thereby throw out the baby with the bath water. The reason why some tests fall down on this issue is because they ask the question in the wrong form. Instead of asking, as is the usual case, 'Tell me how well you appreciate particular aspects of this piece of music which the test constructor has decided is good', test constructors should adopt the more open-ended technique of asking, 'Tell me something about the kinds of music you appreciate.' The problem of how to score the answers to such a question is a very tricky one, but is a problem for the test constructor; it is probably not a good strategy to reduce the constructor's problems by creating difficulties for the people who are to attempt the tests. By adopting such an open-ended approach, people should be able to start on a more equal footing, regardless of whether they come from South Kensington, or South Africa.

In the sections to come, some concrete suggestions for testing methods will be given. However, it may be apparent that a central crucial issue has been completely missed out, and this must be dealt with before the more specific points are gone into in detail.

The first, and possibly most important, question to be asked in this area is, 'Why should anyone want to test musical ability or musical aptitude?' In general terms there are two replies to this question. The first reason is entirely pragmatic and is based on the claim that properly constructed aptitude tests are valuable as a teaching tool. The aim of testing, it is stated, is not simply to pick out the promising ones, and weed out the bad ones. The intention is not to select some sort of musical elite to whom will be awarded all the advantages of a good musical education, whilst denying any such facility to those who do not do well on the tests. On the contrary, the tests are supposed to provide a guide to the natural ability of individuals (usually children in schools), so that each and every one can receive the type of musical training that will best allow him or her to express fully whatever natural and creative gifts they may have. The theory is thus a Utopian one, where every child has the opportunity to achieve self-expression in music as far as natural capacities will permit. (An amplification of this position is given in 'The child's bill of rights', Nickson 1966.) In fact, the distinction between the tyranny and the Utopia stems to some extent from the mere words we choose to describe the one or the other; the actual difference between the two is perhaps not as great as we would like to think.

Secondly, testing procedures can have value as scientific tools, in so far as they can be used to find out more about the processes involved in musical activity. Musical ability is primarily a mental ability, so that studies of people's performance with musical materials or quasi-musical materials of various kinds can at least help to define the things that people can and cannot do, and perhaps even throw some light on the nature of the processes involved. The extent to which this second goal can be attained is dependent upon the nature of the tests used, and the context in which they are employed. The simple administration of a battery of standardized tests to classes of schoolchildren is unlikely to yield anything appropriate to this second set of goals. In fact, it must be admitted that experimental methods are generally much better suited as research tools to this class of goals, and that investigations which seek to find out what sort of things children can or cannot do with various test materials are likely to be more fruitful than those which simply seek to place children in some sort of order of merit according to a table of established norms. An open-ended approach to testing would thus appear to be more appropriate here. It is not surprising therefore that one of the most interesting aspects of existing tests and measures is the rationale behind the test construction, and the implications of the methods adopted, rather than the *de facto* production of the standardized test in its final form.

Although the present chapter is concerned to look at various aspects of existing tests and measures, it is hoped to discuss matters which are appropriate to both the types of aims described above, since the act of test construction automatically relates to notions about perceptual and cognitive processes.

From the outset, any constructor of musical aptitude or attainment tests finds himself between two stools. On the one hand, he wants to produce something that will be acceptable to musicians, so that they will be well disposed towards it. On the other hand, the demands of test construction sometimes suggest that particular strategies be adopted which are not likely to be well received by musicians. The use of musical material in tests has already been discussed, and the importance of eliminating cultural bias has been stressed. Unfortunately, another set of considerations impinges on this issue, namely that there is evidence to suggest that many musicians regard in a very unfavourable light any type of test material which is not music, or which does not have musical value. Sometimes, even the very notion of taking scientific measurements of something as essentially visceral as music is seen as some sort of corruption. For example, the registrar of one of the country's leading music colleges, in correspondence with the author in 1967, wrote, 'I must confess that the idea of a "battery of tests" mentioned in your first letter, is to me rather frightening.' He went on to say in no uncertain terms that such a notion did not meet with his approval. More recently, a paper by de Troch (received 1974) puts this type of view very strongly. The paper consists of an evaluation of the Musical Aptitude Profile (MAP) devised by Gordon (1965), and has the following to say (translation by author): 'One can well see how much the author of the *Musical Aptitude Profile* fails to understand music. The tests consist of tunes written as solos or duets for the violin or 'cello. But the author knows nothing whatever about the art of melody, counterpoint and string technique.' (Professor Gordon is, in fact, Professor of Music and Education at the University of Iowa.) The article by de Troch contains a scathing, perhaps over-passionate, attack upon the very notion of psychophysical measurement, and concludes, 'The musician feels great anxiety at the thought of seeing musical education entrusted to producers and users of such tests. This fear completely justifies an evaluation which only the uninformed would think too severe. That is why many of them consider the *Musical Aptitude Profile* to be a normal step in scientific progress. In fact, the Gordon tests constitute a damaging weapon, to psychology as much as to music, which sees the two of them brought together into a dangerous and vain confrontation.' In fact, like other test batteries, the Gordon tests are not ideal; but de Troch's criticisms tend to be emotional and opinionated rather than scientific, and fail to point out several areas where legitimate criticism can be made. The notion that anyone who disagrees with him does so out of ignorance, is an argument which is barely worth comment. However, one of the themes running through the article is that the tests are not really musical (*'On va bien que la situation n'est vraiment pas musicale.'*) and, as indicated earlier, there is no important reason why they should be. They are tests, not works of art. The problem seems to be that, in the field of psychological music testing, many workers put far too much faith in the face validity of test items, i.e. they believe that any test which is a measure of some musical ability ought to be plainly seen to have something to do with music. The notion of face validity is one of the 'plausible *a priori* considerations' which make various kinds of evasion possible in the area of test validation, according to Campbell (1960).

It is the view of the author, however, that any attempt to produce test material under the constraint that it must please musicians is likely to be seriously handicapped. As far as test constructors are concerned, it appears that, on this issue, 'you pays your money and you takes your choice'. A great many note-worthy test constructors have indeed taken as axiomatic the view that all test material should meet with the approval of musicians. On the other hand, the author takes the view that, if the aim is to produce the best possible test items, no such constraints should be permitted. After all, provided a test is shown to be valid, and it discriminates between musicians and non-musicians, what does it matter if the musicians do not approve or like the type of material used? A more cogent argument in favour of the use of musical material is that musicians are unlikely to make use of tests of which they do not approve. This could well be true, although one would need to consider seriously just how much use is made of psychological test batteries by musicians, and also if it is desirable for them to use tests which might be suspect as a result of the constructor's desire to please. (Certainly musicians who are not engaged in education seem to have a very limited knowledge of the existing test batteries.) In the end a preference for one approach or the other might well be a matter of personal taste. It is interesting to speculate, however, that the more a test constructor considers himself to be a musician, the more likely he is to have an entrenched bias in favour of musical test material.

9 Test material: pitch

There are clearly a great many issues involved in test construction, and the preceding chapter should serve at least to outline some of the more contentious. Bearing these in mind, we can now proceed to look in more detail at the types of tasks involved in some of the existing tests. Descriptions of all the major test batteries have been given in Shuter (1968), and more recently in Gordon (1971), so that little purpose is served by a similar exhaustive coverage here, more so since such a coverage is not germane to the present discussion. In fig. 18 below, an outline is given of some of the types of test material which have been widely used, in similar ways, by different authors.

Pitch tests	Mainwaring, Seashore, Kwalwasser/Dykema, Bentley, Gaston, Wing
Chord analysis tests	Wing, Bentley
Tonal memory* tests (a)	Wing, Bentley, Seashore, Kwalwasser/Dykema, Gaston, Whistler and Thorpe
Tonal memory tests (b)	Drake, Kwalwasser
Interval tests	Madison, Lundin
Rhythm tests (involving tones)	Seashore, Bentley, Kwalwasser/Dykema, Whistler and Thorpe, Thackray
Rhythm tests (involving no tones)	Thackray, Drake, Seashore (1919)

Fig. 18. Table showing summary of existing tests and measures

*Note that the word 'memory' is used by some workers in connection with particular abilities (i.e melodic memory) but not always with others (i.e. pitch discrimination). In fact memory is of central concern for all the tests discussed, since some form of memory or storage is a prerequisite for the performance of all the tasks involved. It would be erroneous to infer that memory was specific to certain types of tests, and not required for the others.

It can be seen that, of the tests involving tonal material, the two aspects of pitch and tonal memory (sometimes referred to as melodic memory) are the most widely used. Chord analysis and interval tests have also been used, the latter sometimes in combination with tonal memory in transposition tests where the subject has to recognize, or detect differences between, renditions of short tunes in different keys (e.g. Drake 1933, Lundin 1949). Most test batteries also include a rhythm test of some kind, though there is a considerable range of types offered, ranging from tasks involving a psychophysical-style estimation of duration (Seashore 1919, 1939) through to fully fledged appreciation tests (Wing 1948b) which latter fail to qualify as rhythm tests in any meaningful sense, on account of the strong appreciation component involved.

Fig. 18 includes only tests which, taken at face value, appear to require little formal training or musical knowledge for their completion. Tests of appreciation, such as those occurring in the second half of the Wing battery, or the Oregon (1935) musical appreciation tests, are not included. Tests of attainment (e.g. Colwell's MAT tests) are similarly not listed. (The problem of aesthetic judgement, or appreciation, is dealt with separately in chapter 8.)

There is general agreement that a sense of pitch is a central component in musical ability. This capacity is so fundamental to musical performance in the West that it is almost impossible to conceive of musical ability in its absence. That test constructors tend to agree on this point is evidenced by the widespread use of some type of pitch test in most batteries. As a complete digression here, it is of interest that musicians themselves rated a good pitch sense as the most important attribute from a list including 'musical memory', 'sense of time and rhythm', 'sensitivity to intensity change', and 'good muscular co-ordination'. This finding was obtained from a questionnaire survey of musicians on the staff of four leading music colleges, and is of interest since the respondents were asked only to indicate those capacities which they felt were more important to the playing of their own musical instrument than to any other. In other words, there was a tendency for everyone to feel that their own musical task demanded a higher degree of pitch sense than anybody else's. Other abilities listed as of lesser importance included 'intelligence', 'musical taste', 'creative imagination', 'emotional response to music', and others. (One delightful answer was received from a well-known female bass player, who, in response to the question, 'Are there any abilities which you think help in the performance of your musical task, which have not been included in the questionnaire so far?' replied, 'Sense of humour' (Davies 1969).)

The actual ways in which pitch abilities have been tested in psychological test batteries tend to be surprisingly uniform, and the most prevalent method clearly owes something to a classical psychophysical procedure known as the 'method of constant stimuli' (Corso 1970). In essence, this involves presenting subjects with a pair of consecutively sounded tones, and asking them to make judgements about the pitch of the two tones. This may involve either the simple judgement of whether the tones are the same or different, or, more usually, indicating whether the second tone is higher or lower than the first. A problem has sometimes been encountered with the instructions in this type of task, particularly with young children. The subject must remember to say whether the second tone is higher or lower than the first, a task which is easily confused with that of saying whether the first tone is higher or lower than the second. In the latter case, a subject's answers will all be reversed, so that all the items he answers correctly will be wrong, and all the wrong ones will be right. This confusion has even been observed amongst university students performing similar types of task. The pitch test involves a number of such trials, using different tone pairs. Within this simple system, it is possible to devise items which range from very easy discriminations (involving tones with large pitch differences) through to extremely difficult ones (in which very small pitch differences, perhaps only fractions of a semitone, are involved). The test batteries of Bentley and of Seashore, for example, both utilize smaller-than-semitone differences. By contrast, workers like Wing and Mursell have argued that such fine pitch discriminations are never actually required in musical performance and that therefore their inclusion in tests is suspect. (As argued previously, this type of purely intuitive criticism is unsatisfactory unless backed up by data; the arguments for or against the inclusion of a particular type of material are to a considerable degree statistical. It could well be, after all, that the ability to make very fine pitch discriminations usefully predicts the ability to make less fine pitch discriminations.) It has sometimes been argued that this difference between the two approaches is a crucial one, in so far as making judgements about tones which do not occur in a musical scale is a non-musical task, whereas the use of musical pitch differences elevates the task to the level of a musical one. The use of notes of a musical scale is said to make the task a more complicated and dynamic process, and to require a grasp of tonal relationships not present in, for example, the Seashore tests, which demand discriminations as fine as one two-hundredth of a tone. Although this may be the case, it is certainly not a parsimonious assumption, and one which we are not justified in making. From the scientific viewpoint, there is only one difference between the tasks, and that is in the order of difficulty. (Note that in the tests of Herbert Wing, the two notes involved in the pitch change are both embedded in a chord. The other notes of the chord remain constant, and act as masking tones, the effect of which is simply to raise the threshold of audibility for the tones involved in the pitch change, i.e. they make them more difficult to hear.) A discrimination of a semitone is more easily made than a discrimination of less than a semitone. In other words, the difference between the two types of task would appear to be merely quantitative rather than qualitative.

Although pitch tests by and large have been amongst the most successful test tools, both in terms of prediction and in terms of overall importance (as suggested by factor analytic studies of musical ability which almost invariably yield high loadings for pitch), it is still pertinent to ask whether the standard format for pitch tests, regardless of the pitch differences used, is the ideal one. Do musicians normally regulate their intonation by referring every note back to the previous one? Do listeners spend their time thinking higher or lower, same or different? There is evidence to suggest that they do not. It could well be that there are other ways of measuring pitch abilities which might satisfy statistical requirements, and have even greater predictive validity for musical behaviour. It is even conceivable that there are different kinds of pitch abilities, and that the relatively simple task involved in the typical pitch test is only one of these, and possibly not the most important. For example, it would appear that one of the more important pitch abilities essential to a musician involves *not* the comparison of successive tones, but the comparison of tones with some kind of internal standard. The traditional pitch test asks for judgements about two tones which are presented as physical stimuli, and therefore requires only the short-term storage of the first stimulus, and comparison of the stored tonal image with the subsequent stimulus tone. Teplov (1966) has pointed out that change of pitch is also accompanied by a subjective change in timbre and in loudness, so that there are several cues to pitch change other than simple pitch *per se*. He also presents evidence to the effect that the ability to detect simple pitch change is so elementary that it does not correlate highly with other 'musically meaningful' tasks, though there are alternative views on this point. However, the main point is that the performance of the traditional pitch test involves comparison of two external stimuli, but does not involve any kind of internal standard. That such internal standards exist cannot be disputed, the ultimate classical illustration being the person who possesses perfect pitch. A person with this ability seems to carry round with him some sort of internal representation of a tone, or tones, such that at any time he can reproduce or recognize them. This capacity is fairly rare, and most musicians have to make do (which they do quite adequately) with relative pitch. A person with good relative pitch is able to reproduce or recognize tones, but only after he has been given a named starting point. The difference between perfect and relative pitch may be illustrated in the following way: the person possessing perfect pitch can recognize a note anywhere and anytime. For example, the pupil with perfect pitch comes into the teacher's room from the busy street outside. The teacher strikes a note on the piano and asks, 'What note is that?' 'It's an A,' he replies.

By contrast, the person with relative pitch can recognize a note, provided we first present him with another note and tell him its name. For example, the pupil with good relative pitch enters the teacher's room. The teacher strikes a note on the piano and announces, 'That's a D sharp.' The teacher then strikes another note, and demands, 'What note is that?' The pupil, by using his sense of relative pitch, is able to reply, 'It's an A.' In the past, perfect pitch has tended to be viewed with a certain degree of reverence. Nowadays, however, there is less interest, and it is generally accepted that a sense of relative pitch is crucial to musical performance, whilst perfect pitch is little more than an unusual curiosity which confers little or no musical advantages on its possessor. The interest in perfect pitch is epitomized by the great debate between Bachem (1948) and Neu (1947, 1948) in the pages of the *Psychological Bulletin* in the

1940s, in which the two authors disagreed about the nature of perfect pitch. The argument centred around whether perfect pitch could be learned, or whether the capacity was innate. The debate eventually boiled down to a fundamental disagreement about definitions. Despite protestations to the contrary, there is fairly convincing evidence that learning can play some part in the development of perfect pitch (though Neu would argue that, by definition, this is then no longer perfect pitch), and Sergeant (1967) has shown that early training has a considerable bearing on the development of perfect pitch. The author has personally found that during periods of intensive musical activity there is a period of increasing perfect pitch accuracy, often specific to the note A to which instruments are customarily tuned. This decays again during less active periods. It is possible that this phenomenon is more widely experienced, though there is no scientific data on this aspect.

Not everyone, however, would think that the disagreement between Bachem and Neu was entirely semantic. In its extreme form, perfect pitch can be so startling as to appear a unique phenomenon. Some persons possessing this faculty to a high degree can name instantly any note played. They appear not to work it out from some more or less permanent standard, but to actually recognize the note *per se*. In other cases, it is sometimes claimed that the sense of perfect pitch is so strong that a piece played in a key different from that in which it was originally written sounds quite wrong. On the basis of such evidence it is sometimes suggested that this type of perfect pitch is quite distinct from lesser manifestations. However, a position at least equally tenable is that the difference is one of degree rather than type. Ward (1970) argues that all that is necessary is that the relative pitch grid possessed by the person has an anchor point which is not movable. (There may, of course, be more than one anchor point.) Ward attempts to de-mystify perfect pitch by pointing out that absolute judgements made by ordinary people in other sensory modalities pass without comment. We can recognize the colour crimson, the taste of salt, the smell of camphor, and so on, without the need to first sample some known anchor point. Looked at in this way, Ward expresses surprise, not that some people have perfect pitch, but that so many do not. He suggests that, with tunes, transposition is the rule since we hear the same tune in many different keys, so that absolute judgements are trained out of us at an early age, and we learn merely to attend to the relative aspects of pitch. Ward's view on this point may be a little oversimplified, however. Firstly, people's judgements in other modalities are not as unfailingly accurate as Ward suggests, but are also influenced by other stimuli present in the same modality. (For example, the perceived colour of an object depends to some extent on the colour of the background; the taste of something depends to some extent on what you just ate previously.) Secondly, the analogy between hearing and other modalities, as put by Ward, is not especially good. Perfect pitch and relative pitch both refer to only one type of auditory stimulus, namely those that have a definite periodicity, and hence a pitch, i.e. tones. There are other types of auditory stimuli, however. It would therefore be senseless to try and determine if a person had a good sense of relative pitch by playing him the sound of a motor-bike, saying to him, 'That's a motor-bike', and then asking him to name the pitch of some tone. The motor-bike and the tone are different types of auditory stimulus. The normal person can, in any case, identify a motor-bike as a motor-bike, and also a tone as a tone, without need for a reference point. Now, in the case of recognizing camphor by smell, Ward is speaking only of recognizing that type of smell from other types of smells, and the analogy with perfect pitch is thus invalid. To demonstrate 'perfect smell' a person would have not merely to recognize camphor but would have to recognize a precise concentration. A comprehensive review of the literature on absolute pitch is given in Ward (1963 a and b), though certain issues remain unresolved. This account, however, is possibly one of the most comprehensive, and most readable, available. The main conclusions seem to be that perfect pitch abilities are not separate from other pitch abilities, but merely the extreme end of a continuous distribution. Although training in later life can cause improvement in perfect pitch judgements, these may be of short duration; Ward suggests that only training during early childhood can produce lasting perfect pitch, though it is not absolutely clear why this should be so. In addition, Ward gives accounts of perfect pitch in animals, including rats, dogs, and the case of a parrot that always whistled the first four bars of Beethoven's 'Fifth' in the correct key. Ward also makes the point that perfect pitch does not guarantee musicality, as is sometimes assumed. He quotes from an article by Abraham (1901): 'If . . . the musician sings a song off key or even merely wavers because the accompaniment has been transposed, . . . especially when he has been given the starting pitch, – or if such transposition causes him to louse up a selection with which he is familiar, he is, – I must put it bluntly – eminently *un*musical, no matter if his perfect pitch sense is so acute that he could demonstrate it before an International Congress of Psychology. . . .' (Earlier in his article, Ward states that one can often tell whether an author has perfect pitch or not, by whether he describes perfect pitch as an innate ability or 'gift' bestowed on only the chosen few, or as a rather less-than-magical learned ability. In view of Ward's conclusions, we must assume that he does not have perfect pitch.)

The point is that the distinction between perfect pitch and relative pitch may be less clear than has been supposed in many cases. It is as though the person with perfect pitch carries round his internal standard with him from day to day, whereas the person with relative pitch carries the standard around with him for shorter periods and needs to renew it from time to time because it has been lost or has decayed. It may well be that people are placed on a continuum with respect to the durability of this internal standard, rather than a bi-modal distribution (Maltzew 1928). Certainly, people with perfect pitch *do* make errors (but they make very many less than people who are said not to possess this faculty). Furthermore, the reason why perfect pitch confers so little musical advantage on the possessor is that once the possessor of relative pitch has obtained his standard (as he invariably does in musical performance) there is no difference between them. In musical performance the musician establishes a standard, usually in the context of a particular key, and all his efforts are then evaluated in terms of that particular key. This sense of tonality or key will underlie all his manipulations, and serve as the basis for his pitch judgements. If, as suggested by existing pitch tests, each note serves as a comparison for the next one, we have a system which is inherently unstable, in so far as any deviations from 'in-tuneness' will proliferate through subsequent notes, and produce massive deviations from the tonal basis of the piece being played. In fact, a solo instrumentalist may play one particular note out of tune, but play the subsequent ones correctly, an act which is impossible if every note serves as a standard for the next one. For this reason, we may strongly suspect that there are other ways of testing pitch abilities than those used in test batteries which place the emphasis on the musically rather trivial comparison of pairs of successive tones.

One possible alternative is a type of 'pitch location' task, in which the subject hears a standard tone, and is asked to locate this tone in one of a series of 'sweep-frequency' tones (Davies 1969, 1971). A sweep-frequency tone is one in which there is a continuous frequency change, either in an upward or a downward direction; for example, the traditional wolf whistle, used to show appreciation of an elegant pair of female legs, consists chiefly of an upward sweep-frequency tone followed by a downward one. Since, in sweep-frequency tones, there is no steady-state tone against which to match or compare a standard, the subject must use alternative cues to find the sweep-frequency tone which starts below the standard and finishes above it, or vice versa. On p. 136, in fig. 19, are given schematic representations of the tasks performed by subjects in the traditional pitch test, and in the pitch location task just described.

In the pitch location task the simple comparison of two tones or tonal images is impossible. Furthermore, comparisons of a same/different type are ruled out, since the sweep-frequency tone which contains the standard is almost as different as any of the others. In theory, since there is a steady change of frequency in the sweep-frequency tone, there is never present a tone of any particular frequency. The reports of subjects who perform well on the task reveal that they experience a feeling of approach ('It's getting nearer') and of recession ('It's getting farther away'), when hearing the sweep-frequency tone which is the 'right' one, whereas the 'wrong' ones merely either approach or recede.

At first sight, such a task seems rather an odd way of going about things. However, the development of the task is quite logical and stems from a series of psychophysical experiments in which people had to tune an audio-oscillator to a previously heard standard. This task involves storing a tonal image of the standard, and then turning the frequency-selection control on the oscillator so that the frequency of the tone it produces approaches, and finally matches (or, in the case of an unsuccessful trial, passes through and recedes from) that of the standard. This procedure was thought to be an approximation to what

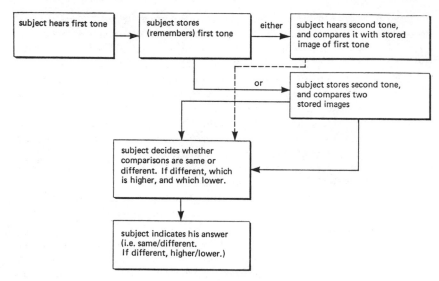

Fig. 19a. *Process involved in traditional style pitch tests as used by Bentley, Wing, Seashore et al.*

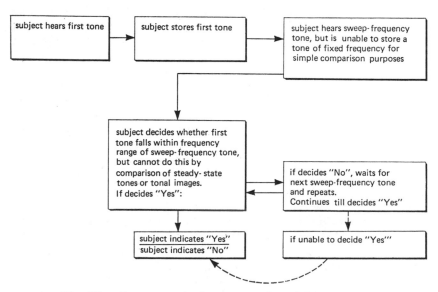

Fig. 19b. *Process involved in suggested 'pitch location' task*

happens when a musician tunes his instrument: the tuning process involves the comparison of a standard tone or tonal image with a sweep-frequency tone. The suggestion for the pitch location task thus arises in a straightforward fashion from the attempt to build a tuning task into a test battery that could be used in the classroom. As such, the task is rather different from that involved in the more usual same/different or higher/lower tasks described previously, and also circumnavigates to some extent the argument about whether to employ musical intervals or smaller-than-semitone differences. One or two additional observations are in order, however, since the task does raise certain issues. In the first instance, the use of more than one comparison stimulus raises a problem of interference. Briefly, interference leads people to forget things more rapidly than they otherwise would. For example, if I present a subject with a list of words, using a tape-recorder, and after an interval of time ask him to remember as many words from the list as he can, he will remember a certain number. However, if in the interval between hearing the list and asking him to reproduce the items from memory, I interject other material or perhaps even a supplementary task, this will cause him to remember less of the original material. The interjected material will have interfered with his memory of the list. In a similar way, a new and different list will interfere with his learning of the first list. The general effect is illustrated by Ceraso (1967), who gives an amusing anecdote about a professor of ichthyology who, every time he learned the name of a new student, forgot the name of a fish. Now, in any music test which presents a subject with a standard of some sort to be remembered, followed by several comparison stimuli out of which the correct answer is to be chosen, there will be an interference effect of differing magnitude every time the correct answer is other than the first comparison stimulus. This is illustrated in fig. 20 below.

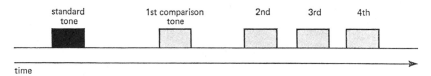

Fig. 20. Interfering effect of successive comparison tones

If the first comparison tone is the correct answer in terms of the judgement required about the standard, there is no interference, and the only effect of the gap between the two might be some decay of the tonal image due to the straightforward passage of time. However, if the second comparison tone is the correct answer, there will be an additional interfering effect due to the first one (Wickelgren 1966). Similarly, if the third comparison tone is the correct one, the interference effect will encompass both the first and second comparison tones, and so on. Thus, it will be more difficult to perform an item where the correct answer is the second comparison tone than where it is the first; each subsequent comparison tone will likewise be more difficult, because there will be more interference, and more time will have elapsed.

In addition, there is evidence to suggest that the interfering effect of interpolated material is affected to some extent by the similarity of the interference to the material involved in the memory task. Briefly, the more similar the interference is to the material to be remembered, the more interfering it will be (Wickelgren 1965). If such findings have some application to our music test situation, and there is no reason why they should not, we may conclude that a sweep-frequency tone which is the wrong answer is a similar type of stimulus to a sweep-frequency tone which is the right answer; also, the standard and comparison stimuli are similar, both being tones. The interference thus resembles both the preceding and anteceding stimuli. In other words, the similarity in the types of sounds used in such a test makes the task more difficult than it would be were they less similar. (By way of illustration, sounds which are dissimilar might be, for example, the bark of a dog, the squeal of brakes, the spoken word 'hello', the crack of a gun, and so on. In the above test, all the elements are similar in being types of tone.) So far as the pitch location task is concerned, we might now hazard a guess that the task involves the ability of the subject to preserve a stable tonal image (a temporary internal standard which is set up in the first instance by the standard tone) under varying conditions of interference. Furthermore, we might also hazard a guess that the ability to preserve a standard in the face of interfering similar stimuli is an ability required of the musician, who must maintain accurate intonation in the face of a crowd of other people striving to do the same thing, but all producing highly similar yet different stimuli, namely different notes. The suggestion here, then, is that such a pitch test is more pertinent to musical performance than those utilizing the more traditional format of same/different or higher/lower comparisons. More important, results from the use of pitch location are encouraging, and show that a test along these lines can discriminate between musical and non-musical groups to a high degree, with relatively little overlap (Davies 1969).

This type of pitch test has been criticized on the grounds that the level of discrimination called for is insufficiently fine. After all, one has the entire frequency range swept by a comparison tone to choose from, which would appear to give a great deal of leeway. Although there are difficulties with this test (as with all tests) this objection is the least pertinent, for three reasons. Firstly, the test does discriminate between musical and non-musical groups, and gives a good range and distribution of scores. If there were any substance in the criticism, this would not be the case, as everyone should be able to do the test. Secondly, the task is not a pitch discrimination task at all in the sense that other traditional pitch tests are. The nature of the task has already been outlined above. Thirdly, it is possible to regulate the difficulty of an item, not merely by varying which comparison tone is right, but also by varying the position of the standard within the appropriate sweep-frequency tone, as illustrated in fig. 21.

The situation represented above comprises two sweep-frequency tones,

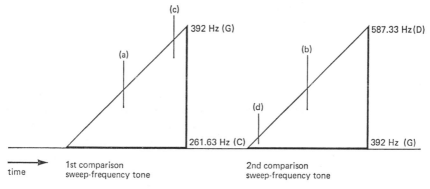

Fig. 21. *Representation of task involving sweep-frequency tones*

which are represented graphically. It is assumed that the standard has already been presented. The first tone traverses a musical interval of a fifth (there is no *a priori* reason why one must use a musical interval) from middle C to G. The second tone also traverses a fifth in the same time interval, from G up to D. Suppose now that the standard tone was of frequency 326·81 Hz. This would locate it, for comparison purposes, right in the middle of the first comparison tone, at position (a). If, however, the standard had a frequency of 489·66 Hz, it would be located right in the middle of the second comparison tone, at position (b). (Note, however, that this will be more difficult than the first example due to the interfering effect of the first comparison tone.) There is no reason, however, why we should always pick our standard tones so as to fall exactly in the centre of one of the sweep-frequency tones. Suppose we choose a standard of 385 Hz, this would then occur at position (c). Any tendency for the subject's tonal image of the standard to stray slightly in an upward direction will result in the subject wrongly choosing the second comparison tone for his answer. Conversely, by choosing a standard of 400 Hz, we detect any tendency for the subject's tonal image to stray slightly in a downward direction. Such a tone would occur at position (d), and a downward fluctuation in the standard could again easily cause the subject to slip over into the wrong comparison tone. It will be seen, then, that the test can provide not merely information about correct or incorrect responses, but might also be used as a tool for investigating how wrong answers come about. If a subject made about equal numbers of errors on items of type (c) and (d), we could infer that his internal standard varied unsystematically, if he indeed was able to form such a standard. (This latter point could be resolved by examining his responses to items of type (a) and (b).) However, a consistent tendency to obtain correct scores on type (c) but not on type (d) items, or vice versa, would imply a systematic tendency for the tonal image to stray in a particular manner.

The above comments merely illustrate the possibilities of an alternative way of looking at pitch (and there may well be other, perhaps better, approaches). It should be apparent that the types of pitch tests used in the past have tended to be rather stereotyped. It is possible to think of alternatives which are both more pertinent to musical performance, and also capable of yielding more information. In considering these comments on pitch tests, the reader might like to refer back to chapter 7, and the argument about the use of musical material in test batteries. One argument was that non-musical tests concern themselves with basic sensory functions, e.g. Seashore, and that these have little to do with musical aptitude or ability. Note that the test suggested here contains no musical material, but rather a series of odd electronic noises. However, there can be no doubt that the task involves higher central processes and not merely basic peripheral (sensory) ones. The simple sensory storage of a tonal image, by means of a mechanism such as the postulated Precategorical Acoustic Storage (Crowder and Morton 1969; Morton, Crowder and Prussin 1971; Crowder 1973), could play little part, if any, in the task since every subsequent sound wipes out the previously stored material. In essence, the postulated PAS system is one which stores a representation of the last sound a person has received. The stored image resembles the last stimulus in all its physical detail. This might manifest itself as a tendency to 'hear inside one's head' a sound which has just been heard in reality. The stored image is in terms of the physical, rather than the symbolic or associative characteristics of the sound. Further, the PAS system is said to have a property, such that it is wiped clean or erased by the presentation of any subsequent sound, which then replaces the original image in the Precategorical Acoustic Store. In the pitch location task, any material in PAS would thus be erased by a sweep-frequency tone or a part of one, so that simple PAS material cannot help in the task. In the traditional pitch test, however, the second comparison tone might be compared with the sensory-type PAS image on a same/different or higher/lower basis. The PAS type of sensory storage is probably of limited relevance to musical performance when compared with a longer term type of storage which has the property of being more resistant to interference.

To sum up, it is possible, therefore, to test musically relevant capacities without using musical material; the use of non-musical material does not confine one to testing simple sensory processes.

10 Test material: memory for tonal sequences

After pitch tests, the most frequently occurring of the other musical tasks are those involving tonal memory or melodic memory. Both these terms refer to the ability to remember a tune. Usually, the task confronting the subject involves listening to two versions of a short fragment of melody, which may be either the same or different. He is usually asked to make a statement about whether the two versions are the same or different, and to qualify his answer in some way. Referring to fig. 18, those tests labelled (a) employ differences between the two versions which involve a change in the pitch of notes. In other tests, such as those labelled (b), the difference between the two versions might involve some other dimension than pitch, such as rhythm or key. (It goes without saying that changes in pitch constitute a very different task from changes in rhythm or key.) This section is mainly concerned with tests of type (a), since these are most often in current use. In tests where there is a change in one of the notes in the second version, the subject is usually asked to indicate which note was different, i.e. the first, second, eighth, etc.

The first question to be asked in relation to many of the tests described is, 'How far does the introduction of a change to an isolated element or note result in a tune which can justifiably be called different?' It can be argued, for example, that changing a single note may amount to little more than tinkering about with a tune which remains basically the same. This argument stems in the first instance from some consideration of a couple of bad analogies. For instance, suppose we go to a performance of a particular concerto, and take along a copy of the score, identical to that being played. During the performance we note a discrepancy between a note heard and a note in the score. Do we conclude that the soloist is playing a different tune? Or do we simply conclude that he played a wrong note? For the purposes of the illustration, it is assumed that the score contains no misprint. Similarly, if the soloist happens at the time to be playing from memory, that is, without music, as is the usual case with piano concertos, do we conclude that he cannot remember the concerto on the basis of his one discrepant note? One swallow does not a summer make; nor does one changed note make a different tune.

In deciding what does make a different tune, we clearly have to take into account the *number* of elements which are changed in relation to the number which remain the same; and in addition, the *extent* of the changes involved. If the distinctive features of a tune remain unaltered, there can be a fair number of alterations to other elements in spite of which the tune will remain psychologically the same. The differences become mathematical curiosities rather than substantive alterations. An example is given below in fig. 22, which shows brief extracts from two excellent tunes, written out here in the same key. The top line shows the concluding bars of the tune 'Misty', composed by jazz pianist Errol Garner, and widely used as a vehicle for jazz improvisation. The lower line shows the concluding bars of the ballad 'A Nightingale Sang in Berkeley Square'. In terms of their distinctive features, there is reason for saying that the two extracts are fundamentally similar. This is not to say that any deliberate copying has taken place; but rather that there are probably limits to the number of acceptable combinations of notes within any extant musical culture, which makes the occurrence of similar ways of resolving similar problems almost inevitable. In the present examples, the problem is to find a 'logical' (in Western musical terms) way of producing a concluding phrase for a ballad, the penultimate phrase of which ends on the dominant (5th) note. Although there are clear differences between the two short extracts in terms of the exact notes used, there is justification for the suggestion that they contain the same distinctive features, and that the two composers have solved the problem in the same way. The phrases are, in other words, effectively the same. The extracts have the following distinctive features in common. First, a descent from the 5th which terminates the previous phrase, to the major third, which commences the concluding phrase shown. Next, three notes of the major scale rising to the 5th, followed by a descent to the root. There are still two bars to go, and both tunes now shift from the root to the 2nd note of the scale, implying a dominant 7th chord in the accompaniment; before finally returning to the root. Three bars from the end, 'Misty' is more complicated than 'A Nightingale Sang', involving as it does some passing chords. None the less, the solution arrived at by the two composers is fundamentally the same.

"A Nightingale Sang in Berkeley Square"

Fig. 22.   Tunes with similar distinctive features

In the above two extracts, the distinctive features which occur in both are as follows:

1 descending link from previous phrase which terminates on 5th
2 three rising notes (3rd, 4th and 5th)
3 descent from 5th to root
4 2nd, implying dominant 7th chord.
5 return to root for two final bars*
These features are indicated by arrows in fig. 22.

The intention in the above paragraph is not to suggest that any form of deliberate plagiarism has taken place; the extracts after all are not identical in terms of notation. The aim is merely to illustrate a fairly common occurrence in music; namely that different composers produce phrases, and occasionally longer extracts, which are psychologically and functionally identical. Clearly, there is more to writing a new tune than merely altering one note, which is what the majority of test constructors appear to do; and it is this practice against which the argument is directed. Even so, examples like the above must produce interesting copyright problems from time to time, in so far as a 'new' tune could contain a number of deviations from an existing tune, and yet because these differences involve non-distinctive features the two can still be 'obviously' the same.

The above paragraphs illustrate the main point by reference to completely subjective and intuitive arguments. There is other evidence of a more scientific type. Teplov (1966) has distinguished between two components in the *oreille mélodique* (literally, 'ear for melody'). One of these components is the ability to recognize and reproduce the intervals between tones correctly. There is also a component which he terms the *courbe mélodique*, which concerns only the overall shape of a tune, that is the manner in which the pattern of pitch changes rises and falls over time (i.e. the direction of the pitch changes, but not their magnitude). Several studies cited by Teplov illustrate this difference between an interval sense and a sense for the *courbe mélodique*. Since the general context is concerned with the development of abilities, many of the studies cited show the emergence of a capacity to remember the melodic contour (*courbe mélodique*) of a tune at some stage before there is accurate recognition or recall of the precise intervallic distances involved. More recently, and in a context which is less developmentally orientated, Dowling and Fujitani (1971) have demonstrated the difference between the pitch/interval, and contour aspects of memory for tunes, and present a nice way of representing this difference. In fig. 23, for example, is given the tune for the first eight bars of the modern waltz, 'The loveliest night of the year'.

It is possible to extract the contour (Teplov's *courbe mélodique*) from the tune by looking at the changes which occur from note to note, and denoting a change to a note of higher pitch by the sign (+), and a shift to a note of lower

*The fact that, in original versions, the two tunes might be in different keys, is irrelevant, since as we shall see a tune is distinguished not by its absolute pitch, but by the pitch ratios it employs.

Fig. 23. *'The loveliest night of the year'*

pitch by the sign (−). Viewed from this aspect, the melodic contour of the tune would appear thus:

$$- \ + \ + \ + \ - \ + \ + \ - \ - \ + \ - \ + \ +$$

The signs indicate the properties of the melody only in terms of whether successive notes rise and fall. The completely accurate treatment of the melody can only occur, however, when the magnitude of the pitch differences, as well as their direction, is correctly noted. The magnitude of pitch differences might be measured in several ways (e.g. frequency, mels, etc.), but the most convenient here is to use the semitone as the unit. A semitone is the difference between any two consecutive notes regardless of colour, on the piano, and involves a frequency ratio of 1·059/1. In terms of the magnitude of the pitch differences, the same tune would thus appear:

$$1 \ 1 \ 3 \ 5 \ 1 \ 1 \ 2 \ 2 \ 1 \ 1 \ 8 \ 3 \ 4$$

A description of the tune in terms of both magnitude of pitch differences, and the direction of pitch differences, would therefore yield the result:

$$-1 \ +1 \ +3 \ +5 \ -1 \ +1 \ +2 \ -2 \ -1 \ +1 \ -8 \ +3 \ +4$$

The main point is that, although memory for the magnitude of pitch differences appears to be associated with the ability to remember the direction of the pitch changes, the reverse is not always true, i.e. melodic contour can serve as a cue to the recognition of a tonal sequence even when the actual pitch differences are altered from the original. In one experiment, Dowling and Fujitani used passages of computer-generated tunes, which subjects were subsequently asked to recognize. When the comparison (recognition) sequences were transposed (i.e., the comparison tune started on a different note, but preserved exactly the same pitch differences) the transposed version was almost completely confused with versions having the same contour but altered pitch differences.

In a second experiment involving long-term memory, subjects were asked to try and recognize versions of well-known folk tunes which were more or less distorted in particular ways. The tunes included, for example, 'Twinkle, twinkle, little star', 'Yankee Doodle', 'Oh, Susanna', 'Good King Wenceslaus' and similarly widely known tunes. The subjects in the experiment were able to recognize the tunes at a better-than-chance level when they heard versions which preserved only the melodic contour; they performed slightly better on versions which preserved the relative (not the absolute) magnitude of the pitch differences as well as the melodic contour. Relative pitch differences are preserved when the actual magnitude of the distance between adjacent tones is altered, but their relationships in terms of 'greater than' or 'smaller than' are unaltered. Dowling and Fujitani distinguish between absolute and relative interval size.

Since, in a control condition, subjects' recognition of 'undistorted' versions was virtually perfect, the authors concluded that they must recognize more than just contour or relative magnitude of pitch differences (in fact these versions were rhythmically distorted, in the interests of experimental rigour, to ensure comparability). The authors also noted that subjects appeared to have 'good long-term memory for exact interval sizes in the context of familiar tunes'.

The results of this experiment have important implications for tests of melodic memory. For example, in the original version of the Wing memory tests, the altered versions differed from the standard only in terms of the pitch of a particular note and involved no changes in melodic contour. This is also true of virtually all items in the revised (1962) version. Again, in the more recent Bentley (1966) tests, all the changes involve alterations to the pitch of one tone, which means that only the magnitude of the pitch differences is altered, since melodic contour again remains identical. There is no theoretical reason why the failure to employ tests of melodic contour should be viewed with suspicion, provided one accepts that the format of many melodic memory tests examines only the specific aspect of melody concerned with pitch and pitch differences. On the other hand, it would be erroneous on the basis of the above evidence to conclude that this is the only attribute of a tune which has any importance for melodic memory, when there are clearly other important factors at work. The implication for melodic memory tests is that a different approach might be adopted which does not place all the emphasis upon a change of a single note, and which might more precisely indicate those aspects of a tune which a subject is able or unable to deal with, namely, relative pitch differences, absolute pitch differences, and melodic contour.

Before moving on to other issues, it is important to consider the findings from Dowling and Fujitani's second experiment referred to above, in the light of two more recent experiments conducted by the author (Davies and Jennings 1977, Davies and Yelland 1977). It will be remembered that Dowling and Fujitani found that when the intervals of well-known melodies were distorted, they were less well recognized. However, with undistorted melodies, where the intervals were not mutilated, recognition was much better. Since variations in contour were experimentally controlled throughout, the authors concluded that subjects had good long-term memory for absolute interval size. There is reason to suppose that this conclusion is not logical when derived, as it was, from the recognition paradigm. When the intervals were undistorted, subjects recognized the tune, not necessarily the interval magnitudes *per se*. It is suggested here that people have an internal representation or template of the tunes that they know, and a tune is recognized when it is sufficiently similar to this template. Distorted versions do not match, and hence are different. Such a process need involve no storage at all of information about actual interval magnitudes in any direct sense. The danger with the recognition paradigm is that, if interval magnitudes are manipulated, and this affects recognition, one can erroneously conclude that subjects store information about interval magnitudes. In fact, it is only necessary that the method used by the subject to perform the recognition task be compatible with the experimenter's manipulations. They need not be the same. To support this interpretation, Davies and Jennings performed an experiment in which subjects (non-musicians, and members of a professional symphony orchestra) drew contours of well-known tunes, and also estimated the magnitude of intervals from memory. Although all these subjects recognized the tunes when these were played at the end of the experiment, neither the non-musicians nor the musicians made accurate magnitude estimates of interval sizes. Since musicians can remember tunes, it is apparent that they do not do so in terms of the magnitudes of intervals. (As pointed out elsewhere, such a system which compared each note to one immediately preceding would be inherently unstable, since one pitch error would proliferate through subsequent notes.) Davies and Jennings hypothesized instead that subjects compared external tones to an internal representation of the tune.

In a second experiment, Davies and Yelland indicated the importance of such an internal representation. Three groups of subjects were asked to listen to statistically generated tonal sequences, and to remember them. After hearing each sequence there was a short pause; then they were asked to draw the contour of each sequence (in terms of a rising and falling line, to represent the rising and falling pitches) from memory. Each group then received a different training procedure. One group spent fifteen minutes on an irrelevant task; a second group listened to tonal sequences and drew contours as these were played, with feedback about whether they were right or wrong; and a third group heard nothing, but were asked to think of a tune and draw its contour, again with feedback about how well they were doing. When the first part of the experiment was repeated (i.e. subjects again listened to novel tonal sequences, and after a short pause drew the contour from memory), only the third group improved. This group, it will be remembered, only received training in thinking about tunes (i.e. in forming the internal representation). On the other hand, the group which actually heard material and drew contours at the same time, during the training task, showed no improvement in their subsequent memory for tonal sequences. The group given the irrelevant task actually got worse. Taken together, these two experiments thus suggest that (a) well-known tunes are not coded in memory in terms of the differences between the pitches of tones, and in particular they are not recognized in this way; and (b) the ability to remember tunes is related to the ability to produce an internal representation, with which external musical events are compared.

There is another reason why investigation of different ways of measuring the ability to remember tunes might prove fruitful. Examination of studies of musical aptitude tests using the technique of factor analysis, such as are reported by Shuter (1968), repeatedly show a high degree of association between the conventional pitch tests and the conventional tests of melodic memory, in terms of a general factor. This association between these two types of test can be construed either as an indication of the nature of the structure of musical abilities, as it were, in abstract, or a reflection of the fact that certain tests which are supposed to measure different aspects of aptitude are, in fact, redundant to some extent. The notion that pitch tests and melodic memory tests are to a considerable extent measuring pitch abilities is worth some consideration. Consider what happens in the normal pitch test, when a subject hears two tones presented and makes a same/different judgement perhaps followed by a higher/ lower judgement as previously discussed. Fig. 24 gives a representation of the situation, in which a subject is asked to make judgements about a pair of tones comprising first the presentation of the note B flat, followed by the presentation of the note B natural.

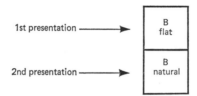

Fig. 24. Pitch test

The subject hears the first tone presented, and, after a pause, the second, and bases his judgement on the comparison of the second with the tonal image of the first.

Consider now what happens in the conventional melodic memory test where the subject hears presentations of two short extracts of tune one after the other, and is asked to locate the position of a note which is changed in the second version. An example of this situation is given below in fig. 25.

s	s	s	s	s	D	s	s	s	s
B	F sharp	G sharp	E flat	F sharp	B flat	D sharp	B flat	G sharp	F sharp
B	F sharp	G sharp	E flat	F sharp	B natural	D sharp	B flat	G sharp	F sharp
1st note	2nd	3rd	4th	5th	6th	7th	8th	9th	10th

Fig. 25. Melodic memory test

In fig. 25 the top row of boxes represents the first tune presented, and the bottom row shows the second, different version, the difference lying in the two cells which occur 6th in each of the two little tunes. All cells, other than the

6th, are marked (s) since they are the 'same' in both versions. The 6th, however, is marked (D) for 'different'. To perform the task correctly, the subject has to detect the difference between the two notes which occur in 6th place in both tunes. It will be immediately noticed that the situation described, which involves the two 'different' cells, is identical to the situation illustrated in fig. 24, which describes a pitch test. Because of this similarity, the findings of high degrees of association between pitch and memory abilities no longer appears as some semi-mysterious consequence of the underlying unitary structure of musical ability, but rather as a perfectly logical result of asking very similar questions in slightly different ways. Dowling and Fujitani concluded, in their study, that in short-term memory for melodies, subjects solved the problem of recognizing 'same' comparisons by using pitch recognition whenever melodies were not transposed. The comparison of untransposed melodies is exactly what is called for in the traditional musical memory task, so we may conclude that the primary faculty demanded here is pitch recognition. Needless to say, this is also what is required in the traditional pitch tests. In concluding this point, it is useful to bear in mind the previous comments on interference. The attentive reader will realize that the major difference between pitch and memory tests of the type described above will be in terms of difficulty. On the whole, we would expect the memory task to be harder, since there is more interfering, similar material surrounding the two comparison tones which would lead us to expect a greater interfering effect with this task. A subject who could successfully perform a particular item in a pitch test would not necessarily be able to perform the same item when embedded in an interfering tune as in the memory test. The difference in performance, however, is due only to a difference in the difficulty of the task and not to its type, which involves pitch discrimination in both cases.

The tests of type (b), listed in fig. 18, i.e. memory tests in which the difference between two versions of a tune might involve some musical aspect other than pitch (such as key, phrasing, loudness, or rhythm), can now also be seen in a clearer light. Tests such as those devised by Drake (1933) and Kwalwasser (1953) use items which differ in several dimensions, and so we might expect them to be measuring not one, but several, abilities. It would be naïve to assume that people are equally sensitive to changes in different physical parameters, so that total scores on these types of tests must be regarded as a compound measure within which several different abilities are intermingled. In other words, the 'ability to spot a change, and to describe it' is dependent upon the nature of the change. Finally, from the point of view of the present discussion, the memory tests of Lundin (1949), described as 'melodic transposition' tasks, are of special interest. In these tests, the second of two versions may or may not have an altered note, but the second version is always in a different key (in other words, the second version preserves not the actual notes, but the absolute pitch differences, of the first). This test is thus in some ways very similar to the tasks used by Dowling and Fujitani and we would expect these tests to be measures of something more than simple pitch discrimination. Where transposition is involved, the evidence suggests that melodic contour will be much more important as an aid in recognition, and where an item involves a change in the absolute pitch differences but *not* in the melodic contour we might expect the task to be correspondingly difficult. The tests thus have the advantage of not being preponderantly a type of pitch discrimination task, as many of the others are. Ideally, however, one would like some method of separating subjects' scores into two components, one of which would provide a measure of subjects' ability to deal with absolute pitch differences, or intervals, and one to give a measure of melodic contour abilities.

Returning now to the starting point of this section, that one altered note does not make a new tune, we might see some new possibilities for ways of testing melodic memory. The ideal test will, firstly, not place all its emphasis upon the detection of a pitch change in one note, but will deal in larger units; secondly, it will make possible the independent measurement of ability to recognize absolute pitch differences and ability to recognize melodic contour. The first of these ideals is more easily met than the second, and one way of doing so is described below.

It is not difficult to devise a task in which subjects are asked to recognize entire fragments of tune. In a task devised by the author (1969), a high level of discrimination between musical and non-musical samples was achieved in a task calling for the recognition of a short, entire, melodic sequence, presented in the context of a longer melodic sequence. The arguments against the use of material of a formally musical nature have already been given. In the experiment discussed here, all the melodic sequences were constructed by a statistical procedure, and are statistical approximations so devised as to eliminate any stylistic bias. The way in which this was done has already been discussed in chapter 4. In retrospect, however, it is difficult to see any reason why the melodic sequences should necessarily involve musical intervals; it would be interesting to produce tests of this type based on an interval system which does not exist within any musical culture (i.e. a purely synthetic mode), with the aim of reducing the culture-specific component still further. Subjects in the experiment were first presented with a short sequence of notes which they were asked to remember. This was followed by a longer sequence of notes which might or might not contain the entire fragment heard at first. Subjects merely had to state whether the short tune heard at first was contained in the longer sequence of notes, answering 'Yes' or 'No'. A representation of this task is given in fig. 26. This type of task has been used in studies of 'field articulation', in which the recognition of hidden tunes is seen as an auditory equivalent of the embedded figures test, e.g. White (1954). Witkin *et al.* (1971) describes such a task as an 'auditory translation of the visual embedded figures test'. In the opinion of the author, however, the resemblance is almost entirely superficial. The notion that a sequence of tones automatically forms a 'figure', and that surrounding tones form a 'context', is simplistic (see chapter 5). Also, the temporal nature of auditory phenomena, as opposed to the spatial nature of the visual mode,

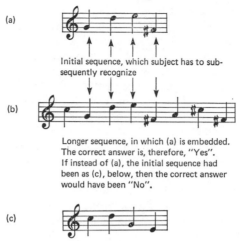

(a)

Initial sequence, which subject has to subsequently recognize

(b)

Longer sequence, in which (a) is embedded.
The correct answer is, therefore, "Yes".
If instead of (a), the initial sequence had
been as (c), below, then the correct answer
would have been "No".

(c)

*Fig. 26.   Recognition of embedded tonal sequence (N.B. notes were presented at
the rate of two per second)*

ensures that the so-called figure and context never actually coexist at the same
point in time, thereby placing far greater emphasis on memory. (The correla-
tional evidence is also not convincing.) As part of the task described, subjects
were also asked to count how many notes were 'left over' after the termination
of the short sequence on every occasion when they answered 'Yes'. The effect
of this additional measure was to discover whether they had accurately located
the short sequence within the longer one, serving as a check on people who
merely guessed 'Yes' or 'No'. (It was hypothesized that in order for subjects to
recognize the short extract within the longer, they would have to know where-
abouts it occurred. In retrospect, this hypothesis does not necessarily have to
be true, though it appeared that in the context of this experiment it was valid.)
The task was successfully completed by subjects down to the age of seven years
old, despite its apparent complexity.

The above task removes the emphasis upon single tonal elements within a
tune, but is still unsatisfactory in so far as it fails to distinguish between abilities
concerning pitch differences and those concerning melodic contour. To achieve
this latter aim, however, is a very complex problem, for the following reasons.
Preserving the absolute pitch differences automatically preserves the melodic
contour, unless we change the direction of the pitch differences which then
automatically inverts the contour. We cannot therefore manipulate contour
independently of pitch differences; but if we *do* change direction of pitch differences, melodic contour becomes completely inverted and intervals which the
subject has learned as ascending will become descending, and vice versa. This
is illustrated by a *reductio ad absurdum*, where one preserves *all* absolute pitch
differences, but reverses their direction to produce an inverted contour. The

result is virtually 'upside-down music' as illustrated in fig. 27. The point is that to change the melodic contour by turning the absolute pitch differences upside-down is to completely invert the melodic contour out of all recognition when viewed in the context of a previously presented standard tune. (For example, the call of a cuckoo becomes 'oo-cuck'.) Deutsch (1969) has even suggested that there may be a mechanism through which certain neurones respond only to ascending intervals, and others to descending ones, when successive intervals are presented. A comparison tune which altered the direction of the intervals as presented in the standard version would thus involve a different type of neural activity. However, since in non-inverted versions of tunes, in different keys, subjects made interval discriminations at about the same level as when tunes were inverted, a process which also changed the key, we might conclude that pitch differences are always less accurately judged whenever there is a change of key. The conclusion that ascending and descending intervals are equivalent might thus be specific to tasks in which intervals are always less salient than contour, i.e. tasks involving transposition. This interpretation is more in line with the findings of Dowling and Fujitani (1971). On the other hand, however, Dowling (1971) performed experiments with inverted tunes and interpreted his results as showing that the main source of difficulty in recognizing inversions lies in the contour rather than the intervals. He argues that the listener loses his memory representation of the non-inverted contour in the process of trying to invert it.

Fig. 27 shows what can happen when four notes are taken and their pitch differences preserved in magnitude but reversed in direction, in order to give a different contour.

Fig. 27. Effect of preserving magnitude, but reversing direction, of pitch differences

In (a), we have four tones that might be taken for the beginning of the tune, 'Christians awake'. In (b), however, we have altered the contour, whilst preserving pitch differences by reversing them. The result is the first four notes of 'Abide with me', but in a totally different key. It would seem, on *a priori* grounds, unlikely that a subject would recognize very much sameness between two melodic extracts differing in notes, contour and key. Because of this, it is probably non-productive to consider as test material anything which attempts to preserve the absolute pitch differences whilst manipulating melodic contour.

It would, however, be possible to present a 'standard' tune, followed by a comparison which preserved the relative pitch differences of the standard without altering the melodic contour. Subjects reporting the two as different would then be using pitch differences as their cue for discrimination; those reporting 'same' would be using melodic contour to identify the similarity, assuming that they were not simply guessing. Unfortunately, the results from such a test would undoubtedly be very much dependent upon which aspects of the stimulus material the subject was attending to, and his opinion about how salient those aspects were. For this reason, results might be critically dependent upon the instructions given to subjects.

The chief problem in this area, then, is that it is impossible to vary melodic contour whilst preserving either absolute or relative pitch differences (unless we resort to inversions), so that there is inevitably some confounding of variables. The best that can be done is to isolate the following five types of items:

1 Items which involve preservation of relative pitch differences and melodic contour (the version to be recognized preserves the direction of pitch differences, and their relative magnitudes).
2 Items which involve preservation of absolute pitch differences and melodic contour (the version to be recognized is transposed into a different key, that is, it starts on a different note but is still the same tune).
3 Items which preserve absolute pitch differences, melodic contour, and overall pitch (the version to be recognized is identical in every melodic respect to the standard).
4 Items which preserve the melodic contour, but do not preserve absolute or relative pitch differences (the version to be recognized merely has the same pattern of 'ups' and 'downs' as the standard).
5 Items which do not preserve melodic contour, and therefore, also involve changes in the absolute and/or relative magnitude of pitch differences, or their direction (the version to be recognized differs in every important melodic respect from the standard).

In terms of subjects' responses to items of the above types, we expect that items of type 5 will evoke a 'different' response most of the time, since in truth there is little basis for a 'same' response. More importantly, by comparing types 4 and 1, and using the former as base line data, we might be able to separate subjects into two groups depending on whether melodic contour or relative pitch differences form the basis for their judgements. Logically, however, we cannot assign subjects who make correct identifications on both types of item to one of two exclusive groups. They might have used contour as their cue in both types of item, or they might have used contour in type 4 items and relative pitch differences in type 1 items. There is no easy way to disentangle this, as noted above. We would expect type 3 items to be the most easily recognized, other things being equal, and type 2 items to be slightly harder since they call for an encoding of pitch differences, and offer no useful clues in terms of actual pitches heard.

If the task were set up in the first instance so that subjects were looking for the various different aspects of similarity, it is interesting to speculate whether musical or non-musical groups would be more sensitive to melodic contour. There is evidence to show that melodic contour is the most primitive, in a developmental sense, of the melodic abilities (Teplov 1966, Gesell and Ilg 1943).

If musicians come to rely on more sophisticated interval or pitch-difference criteria it might be that sensitivity to melodic contour remains relatively unused. The non-musical person, however, might develop his melodic contour abilities further if they are the only ones he has. In other words, might not the non-musician detect similarities between tunes involving distorted melodic contours more readily than the musician? (In terms of decision theory, they might have different criteria for the same/different response, e.g. Egan, Schulman and Greenberg 1959.) In recognition tasks of the type illustrated in fig. 25, the observed tendency for some non-musical subjects to label items, which are in fact different, as 'same' calls for more sympathetic treatment than the simple attaching of a 'wrong' label. It might be that the difference between the musical and non-musical subjects lies not in terms of a right/wrong dimension, but rather it indicates a different type of answer, using different criteria.

Precisely such an effect is demonstrated in a paper by Allen (1967) who indicated that musical subjects consistently rated tones occurring in an octave relationship as more similar to a standard than did non-musical subjects. The author points out the possibility that his results are due to differences between the groups in terms of their construing of the word 'similar', though he does not favour this explanation. The possibility cannot be ruled out that musicians learn, or are implicitly taught, that octave relationships are similar, however. (Also of interest is a demonstration of the octave-generalization effect by Blackwell and Schlosberg (1943) using rats as subjects. Does this mean the rats were musical?)

This section would not be complete without a few general comments on tests of melodic memory which involve recognition of 'embedded' sequences. The reader will probably have realized that certain other variables need to be taken into account in constructing such tasks, namely the overall effect of the position of the recognition tune within its framework, and the degree of organization of the fragments used, in determining the overall difficulty of items. Dealing with the first of these, we may remember that the task suggested here involved listening to a short fragment of tune, followed by a longer fragment which might or might not contain the recognition sequence. We have already noted that material interjected between the standard and comparison items of a test has an interfering effect, and that the more this interference resembles the items themselves, the more interfering it is. (The effects of acoustic similarity upon recall was shown by Baddeley (1966, 1968) using verbal material; Corcoran and Weening (1967) also showed the effects of 'redundancy' (changes in more than one stimulus dimension) in memory for tonal sequences, though a musical sample was unaffected by the presence of correlated changes in an additional dimension.)

Because of interference, items in which the recognition fragment occurs towards the end of the sequence in which they are embedded, will be more difficult than items where the recognition fragment comes earlier. There is, in fact, a correlation between this kind of melodic memory task, and the previously described pitch location task, of 0·36. This figure, obtained from a study of

2,000 Durham schoolchildren (Davies 1969), is rather lower than correlations between pitch and melodic (tonal) memory tests in other existing test batteries. In the opinion of the author, the substantive significance (several discussions of the merits of substantive as opposed to statistical significance are available, e.g. Kraus 1972, Reynolds 1968, Gold 1969) of this correlation is not very great; in so far as there is a relationship, it might arise from the need to preserve in memory various aspects of tonal material under conditions of interference, which is common to both tasks.

The second point, organization, has been dealt with in general terms in chapter 4. It was argued that the degree of organization has an effect both upon people's preferences and also upon their ability to remember the music. In tasks of the present kind, we would expect fragments with a high degree of contextual restraint to be more easily remembered than those with lesser degrees. The material used in the experiment with the Durham schoolchildren was produced by an adaptation of Miller and Selfridge's (1953) procedure for producing statistical approximations to language, as described previously. It was in fact found that the difficulty of items could be regulated by selecting material with different levels of organization.

The last two chapters have concerned themselves entirely with tests of pitch and melodic memory. These two aspects of musical performance appear to be the most frequently recurring in existing test batteries, and as such deserve a fairly detailed coverage. (Other aspects, such as harmony or rhythm, are dealt with in different chapters, though not in a test context.) In addition to describing the usual forms which these tests take, suggestions have been made for alternative methods which might offer certain advantages, although there are clearly attendant problems. The aim in making these suggestions has not been to imply that existing standardized tests are totally inadequate for their purpose, but rather to make suggestions for alternative procedures which could be adapted for use in group test batteries. It is suggested that, within the constraints of a group test, it is possible to adapt procedures so as to cast some light on how people make judgements, rather than concentrating solely on the normative aspects of 'who falls where' in terms of standard scores. It is also the belief that the pitch location and melodic memory tasks described here are tasks of a musically more meaningful nature than some others which have been devised, though, as argued earlier, this is not in itself a strong argument. By trying to devise tasks which cast light on *how* as well as *who*, musical aptitude testing may be able to evolve and improve. As it is, there is a variety of tests in existence, but there has been very little development from one to another. We have already noted how testing procedures used by Seashore (1919) (e.g. pitch tests using two tones and a same/different judgement and melodic memory tests involving changes in a single note) are still present in batteries used in the present day, in forms which are identical in every important psychological respect. The alterations have consisted of manipulations of the order of difficulty of tasks rather than their nature. What is needed is a more open-ended approach to testing, so that we can find out which tasks give the best results, thereby achieving a feeling of development and continuity in the testing field, with each new approach building directly from previous effort. By contrast, the tests existing are characterized more by stereotyped approaches and redundancy, with scarcely any deviation from the traditional forms, particularly in the fields of pitch and melodic memory. Without greater variety in these areas, it is not possible to demonstrate that any one particular approach is better than the others.

It goes without saying that any new testing methods must take their place in the market square along with the others, and stand or fall not by their complexity or novelty, nor by how musical they are, but by how well they satisfy statistical requirements. There is some evidence that the new tests suggested here can meet such requirements. There are probably several dozen other approaches equally worthy of investigation.

Amongst the tests used by different authors, the aspects of memory and pitch have been the most widely used in those tests not involving an appreciation component. This and the preceding chapter have been almost totally concerned with these two aspects. Tests of 'chord analysis', or 'harmony', and tests of 'interval' have been used by some workers (see fig. 18) and a fuller discussion of these less popular aspects is given in Davies (1969). Very briefly, in harmony tests problems arise due to cultural and developmental influences in the acquisition of an analytic listening style. With interval tests, issues are raised by the adoption of simultaneous (harmonic) *v.* successive (melodic) presentation, which are not completely resolved (Doehring 1968, 1971). Many of the comments made previously apply also to harmony and interval tests, particularly those concerned with the removal of experiential bias.

11 Consonance and dissonance

Consonance and dissonance are the two opposite poles of an effect which occurs when two or more tones of differing frequencies are heard simultaneously. (Where more than two tones are present, musical writers often prefer the terms 'concordance' and 'discordance'.) There are degrees of consonance and dissonance. The phenomenon is the subject of a certain amount of disagreement, and descriptions and/or explanations have tended to be of two types, as pointed out by Berlyne (1971, p. 239). The first type of view places emphasis on the perceptual quality of the consonance/dissonance experience, and attributes such qualities as 'pleasantness' (Guernsey 1928), 'smoothness' or 'fusion' to tone pairs which are consonant. In other words, these subjective qualities are the characteristics of consonance. By contrast, dissonant tone pairs have a perceptual quality which is 'displeasing', or 'a type of auditory friction' (Winckel 1967). Helmholtz (1885) writes: '. . . consonance causes an *agreeable* kind of gentle and uniform excitement to the ear . . . whereas the sensation caused by . . . dissonance is *distressing* and *exhausting*' (author's italics). In a similar vein, Littler (1965) writes, 'When two pure tones are sounded together and the pitch of one is gradually raised, beats appear which are not necessaily *disagreeable* but, in fact, may appear *attractive* until they become very rapid, when they are *definitely unpleasant*' (author's italics).

Yet another type of definition does not stress the perceptual attributes of consonance/dissonance, but sees the phenomenon in terms of properties of will be one which sounds dissonant (i.e. rough, unpleasant, exhausting, or what have you) to a listener. As a corollary, it follows that if a person says a particular tone pair does not sound dissonant, then it is not, notwithstanding any arguments to the contrary.

There is another type of definition which stresses not the perceptual attributes of consonance/dissonance, but sees the phenomenon in terms of properties of the tones. (The frequency ratio of two tones is simply the frequencies of the tones involved, expressed as a fraction. Thus tones of 100 and 200 Hz respectively have a frequency ratio of 1/2. So do tones of 150 Hz and 300 Hz. Similarly, a pair of tones of 150 and 450 Hz have the frequency of 1/3, and so on.) For example, tone pairs which are characterized by simple frequency ratios like 1/2 or 2/3, as in the octave or the fifth, are said to be consonant. By contrast, tones of non-simple frequency ratio such as 15/16 or 8/15, as in the minor second and the major seventh, are said to be dissonant. This is all right as far as it goes, but there is still room for discussion as to what constitutes a complex, and what a simple, frequency ratio. There are other explanations of consonance/dissonance which are also couched in non-perceptual terms, and these will be mentioned later. The main difficulty, however, lies in the less-than-perfect correspondence between the two types of definition. In other words, people may find that a particular tone combination sounds consonant, or dissonant, when the other type of theory suggests it should be the opposite. With 'mistuned consonances', for example, the intervallic character of tone pairs is preserved even though there are deviations, or errors in frequency. This degree of tolerance of the various intervals can be measured (Moran and Pratt 1926). Boring (1942) also notes that although the interval of a just tempered third has the simple frequency ratio of 4/5, the equally tempered third which occurs in the almost universally employed system of equal temperament has the very complex ratio of $1/1\cdot259921$.

This then is the problem. If we accept definitions in terms of perceptual quality, we encounter all the problems of subjective report resulting from the lack of an objective externally verifiable criterion. If, on the other hand, we couch our definition in scientific terms, such as physical properties of tones, or mechanisms of the ear, we may find ourselves in the absurd position of having explained a phenomenon which has no perceptual existence. Berlyne's statement to the effect that the term consonance/dissonance has two overlapping but different meanings must not be too loosely construed therefore.

There will be no overlap if, in searching for objective criteria for the phenomenon, we in the end forget the phenomenon itself and arrive at a definition which only exists 'by definition'. If I say that tones of a particular type will be consonant, this is only musically meaningful, as a prediction, if people say they sound consonant.

It is the purpose of this chapter to mention some of the major attempts at the elucidation of the consonance/dissonance phenomenon, and to give some musical examples of supposedly consonant or supposedly dissonant tone combinations which to a greater or lesser extent bedevil all the theories.

To start with, it is important to realize that fashions change. Tone combinations which at one epoch have been judged dissonant, and consequently avoided, become musical clichés at others (Bartholomew 1942). So long as dissonant was synonymous with 'unpleasant and to be avoided', and consonant synonymous with 'pleasant and to be used' (the definition of Helmholtz is along these lines) there is little problem. It is apparent, however, that nowadays the fact that a tone combination is dissonant does not mean its use is eschewed; conversely, consonance might be avoided for seeming too bland. This means that the actual meaning of the terms consonance and dissonance has effectively changed, and we no longer have an adequate behavioural definition. Our starting point is therefore an attempt to answer the question 'What does a person mean when he judges one tone combination to be consonant and another to be dissonant?'

The relevant experiments in this area have all been of a broadly similar type, consisting of presenting subjects with tone pairs comprising different intervals, and asking them to make judgements about various perceptual aspects of these. Some workers have directly asked subjects to produce judgements of the intervals in terms of consonance or dissonance, leaving individual subjects to decide for themselves the meaning of the terms. Others have used terms like 'beautiful/ ugly', 'euphonious/non-euphonious' (Van de Geer, Levelt and Plomp 1962), 'pleasing/displeasing' (Valentine 1914), 'blending', 'purity' or 'fusion' (Malmberg 1918), and taken subjects' answers in these terms to be an index of consonance/dissonance, on the basis of the high degree of similarity between the rankings obtained using the different terms. Significantly, however, in a more recent study, when subjects were asked to say which tone pairs they preferred, the typical consonance/dissonance order failed to emerge. Musicians in particular preferred dissonant chords to consonant ones (Frances 1958). This is clearly in opposition to the notion that dissonances are distressing and exhausting, since people do not normally prefer experiences whose chief characteristic is to distress and exhaust, to those which are pleasant. For the sake of illustration, fig. 28 below gives some examples of the typical rank orderings, in terms of consonance/dissonance, obtained for the different intervals by the above methods. Typically, there is agreement about the high degree of dissonance produced by seconds and sevenths, and the consonance of the octave and the fifth. Disagreement usually involves only the middle positions.

		1st ranking	2nd	3rd
Most consonant	Octave (C–C)	1	1	1
	5th　(C–G)	2	2	2
	4th　(C–F)	3	3	3
	3rd　(C–E)	4	5	4
	diminished 5th (C–F sharp)	4	8	7
	6th　(C–A)	6	4	5
	diminished 6th (C–G sharp)	6	7	6
	diminished 7th (C–B flat)	8	10	8
	diminished 3rd (C–E flat)	8	6	9
	2nd　(C–D)	10	8	11
Most	7th　(C–B)	11	11	10
dissonant	diminished 2nd (C–C sharp)	12	12	12

1st ranking, by Helmholtz (1885), using 'roughness' as criterion, calculated on the basis of beats
2nd ranking, by Stumpf (1898), using 'fusion' as criterion
3rd ranking, by Malmberg (1918), using 'smoothness' as criterion. A different ranking by Malmberg, using the criterion of fusion, tallies less well with Stumpf's fusion rankings.

Fig. 28.　List of consonance and dissonance rankings

A number of theories have been advanced to explain the differential effects of the different intervals. Some of these theories are of considerable antiquity, and some are relatively new, but they all have certain things to commend them. Helmholtz offered one explanation in 1862, when he suggested that intervals having the property of consonance contain upper partials or harmonics which coincide to a high degree, and therefore do not produce beats. Conversely, dissonant tones contain harmonics which do not coincide, but which occur sufficiently close together to produce 'beats', as described in chapter 3. The theory thus attributed consonance/dissonance effects to the roughness, or rapid intensity fluctuations due to interference, produced by upper partials of tones, or their absence. In other words the effect is due to beats. In passing, we may note that Helmholtz claimed that beats were heard only in the region of the octave, the unison and the fifth, so that all the associated phenomena were a consequence of beats in these regions. More recent studies, however (Cotton 1935), showed that at least nineteen beat regions could be 'readily observed' at frequencies between the unison and the octave. Expanding on this, Helmholtz stated that 'roughness' (dissonance) increased as the number of beats per second increased, up to a maximum of thirty-three beats per second, thereafter diminishing again. Certain predictions follow from this theory, however, which are in need of verification. It ought to be the case that, since dissonance arises from competition of upper partials, a particular interval played by two oboes (rich in harmonics) will sound more dissonant than the same interval played on two clarinets (with relatively fewer harmonics). It is not observed, however, that a tune pleasantly harmonized for two clarinets is rendered a sequence of dissonances when played on two oboes. Furthermore, extremely strong beats are produced by sine-wave tones, which have no upper partials at all. To preserve the theory, one would thus have to speculate about aural harmonics, that is 'partials' produced by distortion within the human ear (Bekesy 1934), and beats caused by their occurrence: phenomena not known to Helmholtz. In fact, Wegel and Lane (1924) located nineteen such harmonics produced as a result of stimulation with just two pure tones, and showed that these harmonics could produce beats with an external tone. However, complex tones presumably produce more aural harmonics than sine-wave tones, since they have more components to produce such harmonics. (If this is the case, the argument about pure tones is only half a red herring.) In addition, the statement that maximum dissonance is produced at a beat frequency of thirty-three per second, leads to some strange corollaries. Firstly, the overall degree of dissonance of particular intervals should change from octave to octave, because the beat frequency is a function of frequency differences, and this changes from octave to octave. There would also be some interesting reversals. For example, the notes middle C and the adjacent D have a frequency difference of some thirty-two cycles, and should thus be more dissonant than the C and its adjacent C sharp which has a difference of only about sixteen. Furthermore, the notes F^2 and F sharp^2, which in fact produce a howling dissonance, should be just as consonant, or even slightly more consonant, than the notes C_1 and G_1, since the former has a frequency difference of some eighty-three cycles, and the latter sixty-five cycles. The theory here predicts that a diminished second will be more consonant than a major fifth taken from another octave. This is not the case.

Finally, one would predict different consonance/dissonance effects for the just and the equal-tempered scales, since the scale of equal temperament is not mathematically correct and should produce more beats. Helmholtz actually gives different roughness scores for scales of different temperaments derived through calculation of what the beats ought to be. There is little evidence to show that these predictions have any relevance for what people actually perceive. Winckel (1967) cites evidence suggesting that the normal scale of equal temperament (which is the one adopted in the present day) has, by virtue of its slight mistuning, greater tolerance for further tuning deviation than does the theoretically correct system of just temperament, where any deviations are more disruptive.

Some twenty years later, Stumpf (1898) offered some pertinent objections to Helmholtz's theory, principally contesting the notion that consonance/dissonance effects were entirely a function of beats, and gave evidence to the effect that there could be consonances with beats, and dissonances without beats. As an alternative explanation, Stumpf advanced the slightly less-well-formed notion of 'tonal fusion'. The notion of fusion was based on the observation that, in experiments where subjects had to report whether one or two tones were sounding, they made more incorrect discriminations when tone pairs were consonant than when they were dissonant. In other words, two tones forming the inverval of an octave would be more often judged to be a single tone than would tone pairs forming, say, a minor second. It was this tendency for tone pairs forming consonances to merge into a unitary sensation which was given the title 'fusion'. Edwin Boring (1942), describing the work of Stumpf, gives a listing of the chief laws of tonal fusion, of which the main ones are summarized below:

1 Fusion is held to be a function of the frequency ratio of the components. Fusion would therefore be the same for particular intervals regardless of which octave they were taken from. Stumpf also added that slight mistuning did not affect the degree of fusion.

2 Degree of fusion is the same for intervals within the octave as for intervals beyond the octave. Thus middle C and its adjacent D will fuse to the same degree as middle C and the note one octave above the adjacent D.

3 Fusion is independent of timbre. The degree of fusion (or consonance/dissonance) will thus not be affected by a change from clarinets to oboes, for example.

4 Fusion occurs even when the two tones involved are heard in different ears provided that the ears belong to the same person. (This assertion has physiological implications. If consonance/dissonance occurs when the tones are presented to different ears, then the phenomenon cannot be explained in

terms of properties of 'the ear', or more specifically, in terms of the function of the part of the ear known as the basilar membrane.)

5 Fusion can take place not only between real tones but also between imagined tones.

The above is not a comprehensive list, but gives some idea of the basic notion of fusion. The actual experimental basis for many of Stumpf's assertions is often vague or even non-existent. Stumpf relied heavily on the method of expert introspective observation, and rather less upon results obtained in experiments with random samples of subjects. The present climate of research, at least until very recently, has very much favoured the experimental method, and consequently observations based largely or in part upon introspection have been regarded as in some way inferior. Stumpf's theory has consequently lost most of its influence 'not so much from confutation', as Boring says, 'as from disuse'. Pratt (1921), however, argued that the notion of fusion was a bad one, on the grounds that the notion was rather vague, and that the different degrees of fusion, in Stumpf's terms, could not be verified. He further argued that, apart from the octave, all intervals were about equally unitary if beats were removed with the implication that tonal fusion was nothing more than an alternative name for beats.

However, in spite of the demise of the fusion theory, it still has some aspects of interest for the present discussion. Firstly, there can be no doubt that Stumpf's original observation, that certain intervals provide a more unitary sensation than others, was perfectly valid. Anyone who has ever worked with pitch matching experiments rapidly becomes impressed by the regularity with which some subjects judge a variable tone to be the same as a sounding standard tone when there is an interval of an octave, a fifth, or less often, a fourth, between the two tones (Taylor 1965). It looks as though they are using something very like fusion in making their judgements. Where both standard and variable tones are sounding, an explanation in terms of beats would also be appropriate, but these kinds of errors also occur in tests where only one tone is permitted to sound at any one time, and where consequently there are no beats. In a similar vein, Shuter reports research by Culpepper (1961), who found that children whose ability to sing was '96–100 per cent defective' consistently sang a major sixth below the tonic, while those who were 80–90 per cent defective sang a fourth below. A group judged to be 60–70 per cent defective sang a second below true pitch, and one might argue that this group made poor pitch discrimination, whereas the other groups used 'unitariness' between sung and perceived tones as their guide. Ritsma (1966) examines the well-known phenomenon of octave confusability, using highly sophisticated methods, in a paper entitled 'The "octave deafness" of the human ear'. Extremely interesting results are reported by Hickman (1969), from experiments using children aged from eight to fourteen years. In one experiment, the children were asked to say how many notes were present when a number of simultaneous two-note stimuli, representing the different musical intervals, were presented to them. Hickman writes, 'Results showed a proclivity for the division of intervals into those evoking a relatively unitary response, and those having the opposite effect.' This sounds very similar to Stumpf's fusion. Hickman continues, 'The larger musical intervals from and including the octave down to about the augmented fourth showed a marked tendency to swing violently from an extreme unitary to an extreme multivalued response on going from one interval to the next in order. . . . This pattern contrasted strongly with the smaller intervals.' Finally, Hickman makes a point which further supports Stumpf, and which is also of importance for some of the more recent theories to be covered later. 'At first it was thought that the subjects were responding simply to interval size, but then it was found that the intervals in the range greater than the octave showed the same kind of indecision in response behaviour as for the smaller group of intervals. Secondly, it was noticed that discrimination did not gradually improve as the intervals became larger and larger, but improved quite suddenly at about the augmented fourth.' In other words, the pattern of unitariness, non-unitariness, and confusion found within the octave was repeated for intervals beyond the octave. This is exactly what Stumpf predicts in saying that the degree of fusion for particular intervals is the same beyond the octave as within it.

It is clear that some writers have seen a close analogy between the phenomena of fusion and consonance/dissonance. For example, Myers (1928) wrote, 'This blending or fusion of simultaneous tones corresponds in degree precisely with the recognized order of "consonance" or agreeableness of the intervals of music.' However, not all research supports such a notion. As mentioned on page 158, some fusion rankings seem to bear little resemblance to rankings of consonance. Brues (1927), for example, encountered much difficulty with the word 'fusion'; in a preliminary experiment he discovered from the introspections of his subjects that the notion of fusion 'bore a wholly different meaning' for each one of them. He substituted the Stumpfian word 'unitariness', but still found differences between 'unitariness' and 'pleasantness'. Also, more recent experiments have sometimes shown fusion to increase simply as a function of interval size (Van de Geer, Levelt and Plomp 1962), i.e. the further apart two notes are, the more fusion they evince. None the less, the notions of Stumpf, although they may have fallen into disuse, are still useful in a descriptive sense.

The final 'law' of Stumpf's which is of interest here asserts that fusion can take place between imagined tones as well as between real ones. This opens the door for some fascinating possibilities. For example, if there can be an inter-action between real tones, and between imagined tones, then why not between a real and an imagined tone? It would be tempting to offer an explanation of Mursell's (1937a) 'interval effect' (which causes a sequentially presented interval to have a particular unique quality which distinguishes it from other intervals) in terms of interactions between a tone sounding and a previous tone held in some brief memory store. Revesz's (1953) conclusion that melody effects cannot be explained in terms of consonance/dissonance should thus be viewed carefully. In stating that the phenomena of consonance and fusion are wholly lacking when tones are sequentially presented, he overlooks the possibility of interactions between tones and tonal images.

One of the more intriguing of the older theories comes from Lipps (1885). Lipps's theory was based on the notion that the separate impulses constituting a sound wave could in some way be 'unconsciously counted'. Coupled to this counting process was a preference for tone combinations in which the impulses making up the constituent tones coincide most frequently. For example, a tone of 100 Hz sounding together with a tone of 200 Hz would produce a high rate of coincidences, every pulse of the 100 Hz tone coinciding with every other pulse of the 200 Hz tone. Such a rate of coincidence would be preferred, and would thus constitute a consonance. In the given example, the tones would form the maximum consonance of the octave. The preference itself would have to be explained in terms of the pleasantness and unpleasantness of consonance and dissonance. It might seem at first sight that the discrimination of successive individual impulses is rather implausible (the 'volley principle' of Wever and Bray (1937) strongly suggests that neural discharge cannot take place sufficiently rapidly, and places an upper limit of about 5,000 Hz, even taking into account the rotational firing of cells) and even more implausible that these should be counted in some way. However, the word 'counting' does not necessarily have to imply a numerical ability in this context. All that is necessary is some change in perceptual quality as a consequence of changes in the proportion of simultaneous events. Without too much imagination, it is possible to see similarities between Lipps's notion, and theories based on periodicity (e.g. Licklider 1959, Schouten, Ritsma and Lopes-Cardozo 1962). Again, however, it is difficult to see how Lipps's theory accounts for mistuned consonances, i.e. the fact that consonances still sound consonant even when they are slightly out of tune, and thus have far fewer coincidences. In addition, phase relationships as outlined in chapter 1 might also have implications for consonance/dissonance according to this theory.

The discussion of theories of consonance/dissonance would not be complete without a mention of one of the more notable recent theories. This is the 'critical bandwidth' notion, which specifically relates the phenomena of consonance/dissonance to the structure and function of the basilar membrane of the inner ear. The precise mode of functioning of the basilar membrane is still not known, though it is clearly very complex. The interested reader might refer to Bekesy (1960) for further details. In essence, the basilar membrane is a strip running the length of the cochlea. Organs in its surface are capable of initiating neural discharges, and the position of these on the basilar membrane is related to the perceived pitch of sounds according to some theories. The critical bandwidth theory postulates that, when two tones are heard simultaneously, two separate areas of the basilar membrane are stimulated. If the two stimulated areas are at opposite ends of the membrane, everything is fine and there will be no overlap between the two stimulated areas. However, if the two tones are fairly close together, the two stimulated regions of the basilar membrane may overlap, and mutually interfere with each other (Plomp, Wagenaar and Mimpen 1973). The critical bandwidth is the frequency difference beyond which two stimulated regions do not overlap. Thus, for any frequency difference greater than the critical bandwidth, there will be no interference between the two stimulated areas; whereas for frequency differences less than the bandwidth, there will be a progressive increase in the mutual interference as the distance decreases. According to Plomp and Levelt (1965), consonance and dissonance effects are due to the interference between tones occurring within the critical bandwidth. For pure (sine-wave) tones, therefore (complex tones behave differently), intervals will sound consonant if they contain tones not occurring in the same critical band; on the other hand, if the two tones of an interval fall into the same critical band, they will sound dissonant. Fig. 29 below may serve as a guide in conceptualizing this basic idea, though it is not an accurate anatomical drawing.

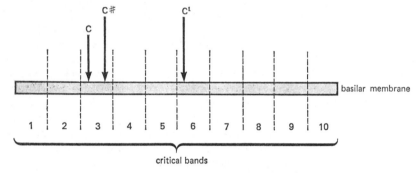

Fig. 29.   Schematic representation of critical bandwidths as applied to consonance/dissonance

In the above figure, the notes middle C and the C one octave above are shown. Since we know these to be consonant, they must, according to the theory, fall into different critical bands. The diagram shows them as falling into the bands arbitrarily labelled 3 and 6 respectively. On the other hand, the note middle C and its adjacent C♯ form a diminished second which we know to be dissonant. Accordingly, the diagram shows these as falling into the same critical band. Experiments by Plomp and Levelt suggest that maximum dissonance occurs when the interval separating two tones corresponds to 25 per cent of the bandwidth; so the diminished second, being the most dissonant of musical intervals, ought presumably to fall somewhere near this value.

The implication of this theory, for pure tones at least, is that consonance/dissonance is chiefly a function of the frequency difference between tones. In other words, maximum dissonance occurs at 25 per cent of the bandwidth, and thereafter consonance gradually increases up to 100 per cent of the critical band and is maximal outside the band. The graph shown opposite in fig. 30 illustrates this relationship, as envisaged by Plomp and Levelt.

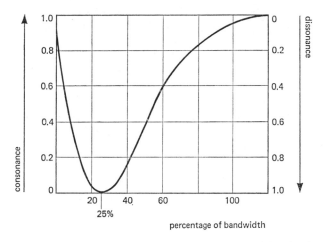

Fig. 30. Consonance/dissonance as a function of bandwidth

The main characteristic of the above graph is that it predicts that the greater the distance between two tones (over and above 25 per cent bandwidth) the more consonant they will sound. Musicians might well be sceptical about this suggestion. If the notion were true, the whole idea of orchestration would be absurd. It would be impossible to produce dissonances between instruments in different ranges, chords could not resolve from conditions of suspense to positions of rest, and there would in fact be very little point in having a range of instruments from treble to bass since, beyond the bandwidth, the choice of notes would be more or less irrelevant in the absence of any shades of consonance or dissonance. Plomp and Levelt, however, argue that the above graph only represents the state of affairs obtaining for pure tones. Since orchestral instruments do not produce pure tones, consonance/dissonance peaks occur beyond the bandwidth due to the interaction of the upper partials of the tones concerned. Thus, if two complex tones do not fall within a particular band, some of their upper partials might well fall into a higher one, and thereby produce consonance/dissonance effects of the type predicted by the old 'ratio-simplicity' theory. The fact remains, however, that, as predicted by these authors, consonance/dissonance with pure tones is simply a function of interval width. This is at variance with musicians' experience. Stumpf, for example, found consonance/dissonance relationships to hold for tones without audible harmonics. In answer to this, Plomp and Levelt claim that the musician's training leads him to identify intervals, and then to expect the same consonance/dissonance effects to occur with pure as well as with complex tones. With non-musicians as subjects, they claim, pure tones simply operate on the interval width principle.

The critical bandwidth theory is one of the more recent theories to appear on the consonance/dissonance scene, but in its original form it was not postulated as an explanation of harmonic effects. One of the principal workers in this field, Zwicker *et al.* (1957), found the bandwidth theory useful because it seemed to explain certain phenomena, especially loudness summation. Loudness summation means that when the spread of energy within a tone is increased it produces not a gradual loudness increase but a sudden one when the bandwidth is exceeded. The critical band was seen as defining the limits within which the spreading of energy leaves the loudness of a complex tone unchanged. The subsequent application of the bandwidth theory to harmonic relationships is not without problems. In the first place, the division of tones into two types, pure and complex, is a highly simplified and arbitrary decision. Almost all the tones people hear are complex and virtually none of them are pure apart from in experiments. The bandwidth theory of consonance/dissonance is thus inferred from an event that hardly ever happens, and then qualified to take into account the common event. The more usual way of proceeding is to seek an explanation for the common event, and modify it to take into account the exceptions. In other words, the theory is more interesting as an explanation of the exception than of the rule. Secondly, there are varying degrees of complexity as we have seen in previous chapters, and not just a simple dichotomy. In so far as highly complex tones have more harmonics than do less highly complex tones, they should produce more dissonances. In other words, different instruments should obey different harmonic laws. If this were the case, it is difficult to see how any consistent rank order in terms of consonance/dissonance could ever have come about. There are also some more specific problems. According to Zwicker (1961), the width of the critical bands is fixed, though their actual positions on the basilar membrane are not, but varies depending upon what we are listening to. In a sense, the tone we are listening to forms its own critical band around itself. There are thus no data to test, as far as the positions of critical bands are concerned, since this is variable. However, we do have data on the width of the critical bands, since Zwicker produced a table showing their position and width. Although the positions he gives are somewhat arbitrary, since there are a great many such lists which could be compiled (due to the changeable nature of the bandwidth position), the width of the bands is fairly constant. It is possible, therefore, to translate bandwidths into tones and semitones, and discover if the 25 per cent bandwidth position does in fact coincide closely with maximum dissonance in musical terms. Fig. 31 opposite gives a table of bandwidths as described by Zwicker. The frequencies which identify the limits of the different bands are given, along with the frequency which marks the operational centre of each one. Remember, when examining the figures given, that we are more concerned with the width of the bands than with their positions.

If we examine the column labelled 'Bandwidth Hz' we will note that, in terms of frequency, the width of the bands increases as we move towards the higher pitches. This is consistent with what we know about the relationship of frequency to pitch, i.e. to raise the pitch of a tone by one octave, the frequency is not increased by a constant, but is doubled. Taking the 'Centre frequencies' from

Number	Centre frequencies Hz	Cut-off frequencies Hz	Bandwidth Hz
1	50	20–100	80
2	150	200	100
3	250	300	100
4	350	400	100
5	450	510	110
6	570	630	120
7	700	770	140
8	840	920	150
9	1,000	1,080	160
10	1,170	1,270	190
11	1,370	1,480	210
12	1,600	1,720	. 240
13	1,850	2,000	280
14	2,150	2,320	320
15	2,500	2,700	380
16	2,900	3,150	450
17	3,400	3,700	550
18	4,000	4,400	700
19	4,800	5,300	900
20	5,800	6,400	1,100
21	7,000	7,700	1,300
22	8,500	9,500	1,800
23	10,500	12,000	2,500
24	13,500	15,500	3,500

Fig. 31. Limits and centre frequencies of bandwidths

fig. 31 to equal 50 per cent bandwith, we can work out roughly what the 25 per cent frequencies ought to be, and then turn these points into musical terms. If the theory, as applied to consonance/dissonance, is correct, we should find that these points coincide with maximum dissonances. In fact the position that emerges is rather an odd one. The musical interval which is most dissonant appears to be larger for bass intervals than for treble intervals. For example, using the figures given, bandwidth two which runs from 100 to 200 Hz approximately, produces maximum dissonance when the frequencies 100 and 125 are sounded. The nearest musical interval to this is a major third. The theory thus predicts that, within this frequency range, the notes G and B will sound more dissonant than the notes G and G sharp. By contrast, in the higher registers, the interval which corresponds to maximum dissonance becomes progressively smaller, until it is in fact much less than a semitone. Thus the interval from B flat to B natural covers something much more like 50 per cent of the bandwidth at the top of the musical range, whereas the semitone in the middle of the range is closer to 25 per cent of the bandwidth. Thus semitones played at the top end of the range should sound more consonant than those played in the middle register, since the former exceed the 25 per cent bandwidth which is said to produce the maximum dissonance. The implication is, therefore, that the harmonic relationships between notes change from octave to octave, and a chord which is harmonious when played at one point on, for example, a keyboard will be unharmonious when played at another. Transposition thus becomes not a mere change of key, but virtually a new piece of music, if we take this theory literally. By changing the key of a piece, or simply shifting it up or down an octave or so, we can perform the magical task of making consonance become dissonance; where before there was dissonance, we can produce consonance. When we superimpose the changing interrelations of the harmonics upon this state of affairs, such that sometimes they combine to produce consonance and sometimes to produce dissonance, more or less independently of the harmonic relation of the notes involved in musical terms, the picture becomes very complex indeed. Plomp and Levelt's notion that musical learning alone accounts for the consistency of judgements hardly seems adequate in the face of this type of conflict. Even more important, it seems strange, in the face of all these changing harmonic relations, that anyone should have ever have hit upon the strange notion that they might be constant.

In concluding these observations on critical bandwidth, however, we must try to avoid being blinded by our own musical preconceptions. In an interesting follow-up Plomp and Levelt performed a statistical analysis of chords contained in two pieces of music, namely 'Trio sonata for organ no. 3', by J. S. Bach, and Dvořák's 'String quartet op. 51 in E flat major'. The results are interpreted as showing that the way a composer selects the chords and intervals which he uses, bears a relationship to the degree of consonance/dissonance which would be predicted from the critical bandwidth. The theory also offers an explanation of the tendency of composers to avoid the use of close position chords in the bass register, but less so in the upper registers. This is consistent with what was argued above, namely that the interval corresponding to maximum dissonance is greater in the lower than in the upper registers. Our criticism therefore loses some of its force. None the less, the marriage of the critical bandwidth theory to consonance/dissonance is not an entirely happy one. There is a suspicion that, in this case, the argument may be circular. In the first instance, consonance/ dissonance phenomena are interpreted as being consistent with a particular theoretical model. Subsequent analysis of pieces of music then shows that the bandwidth notion fits nicely with the use of consonant and dissonant intervals. Since composers are well aware of consonance and dissonance phenomena, this does not constitute an independent validation of the theory. If we define theory X in terms of event Y, it is not surprising to find that event Y predicts theory X. The one real point of interest, however, is the prediction of wider intervals in the lower register. It is arguable, though, that close position chords in the bass sound not so much dissonant as cluttered or bottom heavy. Whatever the truth of the matter, there is no doubt that the bandwidth theory explanation of consonance and dissonance phenomena constitutes an extremely fascinating development in the scientific study of music.

If we take an overview of the theories presented so far, it will be apparent that there are differences in the types of explanation offered. The Helmholtzian explanation is based on the view that consonance/dissonance is related to the phenomenon of beats, which is a property of sound. The monaural beats described by Helmholtz consist of rapid fluctuations in intensity (i.e. amplitude modulations) brought about by interference between sound waves. The amplitude modulation is 'out there' and all that the ear does is to hear it. The ear therefore is simply a perceiver of consonance/dissonance. If we look at the fusion theory of Stumpf, it is less clear whether we are talking about fusion, and the related consonance/dissonance phenomena, as properties of sound or properties of the observer, though an explanation in terms of the physics of sound is certainly not ruled out. Lipps's theory, in which an unconscious counting, or correspondence-detection, process takes place clearly puts more emphasis on the observer as a cause; finally, Plomp and Levelt's application of critical bandwidth is quite uncompromising in making the physiological attributes of the basilar membrane of paramount importance in causing consonance and dissonance. Naïvely, we might wonder whether the premises underlying these different orientations have been adequately investigated. After all, if I throw two stones into a pond, they will each produce nice, even ripples on a circular front, until the ripples collide at a particular point. Once the ripples do encounter each other, the smooth even pattern disappears and is replaced by a choppy and turbulent area where they overlap. If you prefer, an area of roughness is produced. The fact that the rough area is produced is a property of water, falling stones, speed of impact and so on. We would scarcely expect to sensibly account for it by examining the function of the retina of the eye. Air also is an elastic medium, and the fact that explanations are offered at a physiological level should not blind us to the fact that simultaneous tones do influence and interfere with each other in a physical sense as well as at the level of the basilar membrane. An explanation in which the physical factors are ignored, and which implies that the sole cause lies within the ear of the listener, is necessarily incomplete unless the intention is to explain all behaviour at the same level. It is not possible to set up mutually exclusive categories such as 'physiology' and 'music' and then proceed to explain a specific act of perception by hopping between the two, since all sound is in the end a physiological event. Theories which emphasize physiological factors in the perception of consonance/dissonance phenomena are not, therefore, complete causal explanations, but rather explanations of why a particular physical phenomenon is perceived in a particular way. This having been said, it also appears that an entirely physical explanation is also inadequate, and fails to account for the psychological facts. For example, the beat frequency which produces the maximal sensation of dissonance does vary for different parts of the pitch range; normal amplitude modulation fails to produce the perceptual quality of dissonance, and dichotic presentation (a separate tone in each ear) of two tones close in frequency causes binaural beats or 'beats in the brain' which are different from the monaural beats which Helmholtz describes (Oster 1973). These things point to properties of the observer rather than of the physics of sound.

Suppose we had an ideal explanation of consonance/dissonance, paying due attention to the physical attributes of sound as stressed by Helmholtz, and incorporating the latest physiological knowledge. Since we have found that, in evaluative terms, consonant relationships are usually judged favourably, at least by non-musicians (e.g. smooth, pleasant, euphonious, gentle, etc.) and dissonant relationships are judged unfavourably (e.g. rough, harsh, unpleasant, etc.) we might now assume that we have the whole area nicely sewn up. We should be able to look at a particular interval, assess its degree of consonance or dissonance, and predict a person's response to it. If it is an interval that we know receives a positive evaluation, we will expect the person to like it. If it is a dissonant interval, and one which consequently receives negative evaluations, we will expect him not to like it. Our predictions, however, will still be wrong.

Although, as we have seen, physical and physiological factors are determinants of consonance and dissonance, they are not the sole determinants. As mentioned earlier, musicians produce consonance/dissonance ratings for the different intervals which are different from their preference ratings. Perhaps more importantly, our own everyday observations can leave us in no doubt that, within the context of a piece of music, even non-musicians do not simply like consonant chords and dislike dissonant ones. If we are to accept a definition of consonance/dissonance in terms of liking or not liking, we must also accept that the musical context within which an interval appears, and the musical norms which a person learns to accept within a particular culture, are also important determinants. It is difficult to throw overboard the idea that consonance/dissonance has something to do with pleasantness or unpleasantness, and equally hard to abandon the belief that people prefer the pleasant to the unpleasant. From a subjective point of view, these are the very qualities that define the phenomenon, and without such subjective qualities consonance and dissonance do not even exist as sensory phenomena but only as scientific abstractions. Above all else, consonance and dissonance are things that people hear, and react to in terms of an evaluative dimension. Fortunately, however, we do not have to abandon the subjective aspects completely, since it is manifestly obvious that intervals presented in isolation to subjects as part of an experiment are very different from intervals presented in wave after wave to an audience at a symphony concert. By presenting people with single intervals, we deprive them of all external references, and take away all the contextual clues. Their judgements are therefore made on the basis of the most meagre information. If we ask a person to make evaluations of intervals presented in isolation, the only peg on which he can hang his judgements is the consonance/dissonance effect produced by the interactions of the tones involved. Characteristically, the results from such an experiment will approximate closely to those presented previously in fig. 28. If, however, we present him with those same intervals in the context of a piece of music, his evaluations will then take into account the 'fitness' of the interval in relation to other intervals, and also its function. He will therefore produce different, and possibly variable evaluations. People do not have to be musicians in order to judge fitness or function, though non-musicians may have difficulty in explaining what they mean, and may not even have conceived of their responses in these terms. All that is necessary is that they are familiar with the musical style in question.

Whether in the end we choose to define consonance/dissonance subjectively in terms of evaluations, or whether we take the mathematically calculated number of beats or some other physical measure as our definition, is therefore of little consequence, so long as we realize that the way people feel about intervals presented in isolation is often very different from how they feel about those same intervals occurring within a tune. This conclusion is admirably summarized by Gulick (1971) who writes, 'Historically there have been two major difficulties with the treatment of consonance and dissonance. First, many writers have equated consonance with pleasantness and dissonance with unpleasantness; and second, judgements of consonance and dissonance have been made sometimes to isolated sounds and sometimes to sounds presented in a musical context. We take the view here that *consonance and dissonance are no more than polar opposites to describe the degree of tonal fusion.* Therefore, if fusion is assumed to be a discriminable attribute of complex sounds, then it seems clear that judgements of fusion can only be made satisfactorily when the matter of pleasantness is ignored and when stimuli are presented in isolation. This is an important observation to make because there is now ample evidence that when dissonance is judged along a pleasant-unpleasant dimension, it is heavily influenced by musical context and it is not always unpleasant.'

There is still one puzzling question. When we present intervals in isolation, why do subjects so consistently rate consonance as having positive attributes (e.g. smooth, gentle, pleasant, etc.) and dissonance as having negative ones (e.g. rough, harsh, unpleasant)? It would appear that, although in this situation there is very little upon which the person can base his judgement as compared with the situation in a piece of music, there is simply something about the nature of the perceptual experience which leads people to judge it in this way. This is not an explanation at all, but a truism. In the absence of any knowledge of the circumstances or the justification, a punch on the nose from a big pugilist is in some way an intrinsically unpleasant experience, because of the nature of the stimulus (the punch) and the way I am made (my nose is such that it hurts when punched). By contrast, a kiss on the mouth from a big blonde is intrinsically pleasant, again because of the nature of the stimulus and the way I am made.

If we examine almost any popular piece of music, we will find that it consists of chords which, when presented in isolation, are judged to be dissonant as well as those which are judged to be consonant. Whether people react favourably to the piece of music in question bears little relationship to their preferences for individual chords, but will be a function of their ability to make sense out of the musical whole. Within the popular music idiom, for example, people are widely exposed to, and like (if record sales are anything to go by) chords containing the major seventh, i.e. the highly dissonant pitch ratio 15/8. Although some (e.g. Mursell 1937a, p. 15) would argue that the major seventh serves a function of creating a state of tension which is resolved by moving to the tonic note of the chord (in other words, it leads into a more consonant chord, hence its alternative name of 'leading note') this is by no means always the case. Popular ballads, for example, often use a major seventh chord as a conclusion to the piece, and achieve thereby not a state of unrest, but a definite feeling of completeness or resolution. For example, if we take the well-known tune 'My funny valentine' we can imagine a variety of endings that might be used involving sevenths, seconds, or diminished fifths, or what have you, all of which would be quite acceptable alternatives. In fig. 32 the last four bars of the tune are given, together with a variety of chords of varying degrees of complexity, and involving

Each day is   Val - en - tine's   Day

The top line shows the normal line sung by the singer. The small notes indicate a variation sometimes used on the 'last time bar' by cabaret singers, culminating in a heart-rending delivery of the note D, which is the major seventh in this instance. Sometimes an F, or ninth note, might be used in preference.

Below the last note appear some chords such as might be used by an accompanist, which include a variety of dissonant notes. The first such chord shown is the normal, or doh - me - soh - doh chord which is, however, usually eschewed. The right - hand position only is shown.

Fig. 32.   Possible endings to 'My funny valentine'

various degrees of dissonance, which a night-club pianist might use to terminate the performance.

Examples (a), (b), and (c) are normal night-club positions, and represent the common devices of using sixths, sevenths, and ninths. These may be used in various combinations, but in the examples given we see positions involving the dissonant interval of a major seventh (a); a minor seventh (really a ninth or second in disguise) in combination with a major second (b); and in (c), a chord involving three simultaneous dissonances in the form of major seconds. The principal dissonances are indicated by arrows. All three examples given produce a sound which musicians would describe as sweet and slushy, or *schmaltz*. Some would go further and say they were tasteless or sickly. However, they are certainly not the type of harsh and rough dissonances described by Helmholtz; on the contrary they would nowadays be judged to be cloyingly sweet (like many of the people who sing the songs!). For comparison, two more examples, (d) and (e), might be described as more jazzy, and as arguably preferable for being less sickly though they do not always meet with approval from the lady in the spotlights. The author recalls an occasion when some rather advanced chords inserted into 'See-saw Marjory Daw' led to angry and tearful recriminations from a lady entertainer, who claimed that the open fourth positions much favoured by the pianist had caused her performing dogs to see-saw in an extremely half-hearted and unconvincing manner. A similar complaint was made by another lady who tap danced on plates, and who unexpectedly ran into a string of breakages.

The chord shown in (d) resembles chord (b) in having two strong dissonances, yet strangely enough it sounds completely different in character. Combined with an E flat triad in the left hand, it has none of the sweetness characteristic of the previous examples, the main reason for this being the A natural which is in opposition to the E flat mode being used. The same is true of example (e) which in effect combines two totally competing triads, those of E flat and D major. Each tone in the bass conflicts with at least one, and sometimes two, tones in the treble. The harmonics make the picture even more complicated. Considering only the tones indicated, the chord contains three major sevenths and a ninth. Viewing the situation overall, we can see that all the chords given contain a combination of intervals of a consonant and dissonant nature. If we imagine that all the chords are played with a simple triad in the left hand (as shown in (e)) it appears that the night-club chords contain a higher proportion of consonant to dissonant intervals than do the other examples or else they do *not* contain notes which are in octave relationships to very high order harmonics (such as the A natural in the above example, which is effectively not based on a harmonic of E flat). This might account for their greater sweetness. The way in which consonant and dissonant intervals interact, and whether they summate or cancel each other out, is a topic on which almost no work has been done.

Of course, dissonance is not just a property of popular melodies, but is also a device used widely in classical music, by means of which the composer creates tension, which he may subsequently resolve. In Debussy's 'Claire de lune', referred to in an earlier chapter, we once again encounter chords which, if judged in isolation, would be judged as rough or unpleasant (i.e. dissonant) but which, in context, serve instead to enhance the tranquil and placid mood of the piece. Although there are many examples, two only are shown below, taken from bars fifteen and thirty-eight respectively. Both examples contain, amongst other things, the minor second, which is normally considered the most

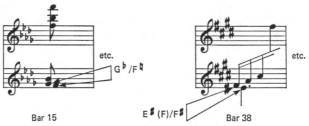

Fig. 33.   Extracts from 'Claire de lune'

dissonant interval when played in isolation. In both instances, the interval of the minor second occurs in the context of a downward progression, involving the lower note. In bar fifteen, the tension created by the F and the G flat is resolved by a movement of the F to E flat, thereby creating the more consonant interval of a diminished third. Subsequent downward movement leads to yet further increases in consonance. The diminished second shown cannot therefore be viewed in isolation, but only as part of a general movement from a state of dissonance to one of consonance, and this overall movement is pleasing. In so far as the minor second fits with this pattern, it is completely apt, and therefore pleasing. The second example is very similar, with the lower note, E sharp (in fact, this is the same as F in terms of the piano keyboard; the notes involved in the two examples are in fact identical, though they are written differently) moving in turn to E (creating a major second) to D sharp (minor third) and finally to C sharp, at which point the upper note also changes. The progression is once again from dissonance to consonance, leading to the subjective effect of decreasing tension, which is characteristic of the piece as a whole.

We have seen, in the above paragraphs, how people's judgements about the pleasantness or unpleasantness of two-note chords played in isolation show a great degree of consistency. When asked to evaluate chords in this way, there is a high degree of correspondence between their rankings, whether these be in terms of roughness, pleasantness, smoothness or whatever else. Because of the similarity in these rankings, we are justified in believing that they are all under-laid by the same effect, namely consonance/dissonance. (The fact that the rankings of musicians, who are a very atypical group, sometimes do not tally, need not concern us here.) With isolated chords, then, the effects of consonance/dissonance are reflected in the subject's judgements. In other words, the phenomenon of consonance/dissonance is synonymous with the way the person feels, either positively or negatively, towards this chord or that chord. This chord consists of the interval of a minor second, I feel negatively about it, and this means it is dissonant. On the other hand, this chord consists of the interval of a fifth, I feel positively towards it and it is consonant. Unfortunately, this treatment of intervals or chords as isolated events casts only a limited degree of illumination upon what happens in music. In a sense, it is essentially the treatment of a musical element as an event of the present, and, as we have seen previously, the heart of music lies in the fact that we treat elements as events of the past. If we are to maintain a definition in terms of subjective evaluation within a musical composition, the consonance/dissonance relationships of different tones must change from instant to instant, as a function of context; or, if we throw away this definition, consonance and dissonance is no longer an experienced phenomenon, but merely an arbitrary definition which has little experiential reality within music.

Whichever type of definition we choose is in the end going to be a matter of personal choice, and the functions the definition must serve. The point to be remembered, however, is that the apparent consistency of judgements about particular note combinations tells us nothing about how people will react to those same combinations within a musical context. This issue leads us to expect that people's reactions are therefore not solely a function of a physical stimulus, but are influenced by other variables, and, more importantly, are a function of what people interpret these variables to be. In other words, to understand harmonic relationships as they occur within pieces of music, we must take into account the culture within which the music exists, and what a person knows about the prevailing musical culture, or subculture.

12 Rhythm: tonality's poor relation

If certain experiences result whenever a human being, regardless of race, creed, or colour, encounters particular musical sounds, we might expect music from very different cultures to have certain things in common. In an interesting account, Revesz (1953) attempts to explore the origins of music, and tries to identify the basic core of music by finding common elements within the music of different cultures. He concludes that every form of music, from so-called primitive music through to the complex polyphony of the West, is characterized by three common elements. These are (a) fixed intervals, (b) transposition of intervals to different pitches, and (c) the use of such intervals in heterogeneous, rhythmically articulated tone combinations. More specifically, the use of tonal rows containing some intervals which are readily recognizable, such as seconds, seems almost universal. According to Revesz, the octave relationship is found everywhere, and some other 'framework tones' are fairly widespread. Indian music, for example, with its quarter tones, is remarkable more for the similarities it has with Western tonality than for the differences. The observer is able to hear tonic and dominant notes and may even notice that the quarter tones themselves sound more in the nature of artistic deviations, rather than an incomprehensible scale. The fact that tones occurring in 'our scale' are also to be found in the scales of other cultures is also made by Mersenne (1957), in the work *Harmonie universelle*, cited by Pikler (1966). Again, the manner in which many African and South American peoples sing chants in octaves attests to the inevitability of the octave relationship. After all, when men and women wish to sing together, and find that their voices have different ranges, the conditions are created in which the octave must naturally emerge.

It is not, surely, just a matter of chance that there are such widely distributed similarities in terms of certain framework tones. Differences between musical cultures are likely to concern particular conventions, or differences in the emphasis placed on different aspects; such differences should not lead us to overlook the fact that there are often similarities in terms of certain very basic musical events. If we return again to Revesz's definition of musical fundamentals, however, we can see that his is the type of definition likely to be offered by someone from our own musical culture. The emphasis is placed upon the tonal aspects of music, whilst the rhythmic element manifests itself almost accidentally through the organization of the tonal elements themselves. According to his definition, rhythm has no independent existence. Revesz's definition, therefore, whilst of value in highlighting certain tonal similarities, is deficient in the role it assigns to rhythm. Such a deficiency is to be expected when the basis used is our own Western classical tradition, which is tonally extremely sophisticated, but rhythmically naïve. Stravinsky's magnificent 'Rite of spring', for example, is often felt to be the height of rhythmic sophistication. Compared to much other Western classical music, this might be the case; compared to some so-called primitive music, the use of rhythmic devices is unsubtle. The author recalls a brief exchange with a tuba player, at that time playing with a well-known London symphony orchestra, and also with the Mike Gibbs orchestra which is an advanced modern jazz band. After finishing a concert with the jazz band, the player replied, in answer to a question, 'We're doing the "Rites" tomorrow. After this lot, it's like "Polly put the kettle on".'

The role assigned to rhythm, as one of the corner stones of music, therefore, needs more emphasis than we tend to give it. To begin with, we need to define what is meant by 'rhythm', in music. Many notable workers in the field of musical abilities (e.g. Bentley 1966a, Thackray 1969) have proceeded on the assumption that a rhythm is, in essence, rather like that which is left if we remove all tonality from a tune, i.e. we are left with elements which differ in intensity (accent), which have variable time intervals between them, and which themselves are of variable duration. Again we see the notion that rhythm is inextricably bound up with tonality, and has no independent existence. It is just the stuff which is left over when we take out the tonal component. Certain of the tests of rhythm which have been produced actually incorporate rhythm into a tonal framework (i.e. Thackray, Wing, Bentley). The problem centres around the idea that a rhythm is specified by intensity, time intervals, and duration. It is the opinion of this writer that the last of these three parameters, duration, is a characteristic of tones, and from a psychological point of view has nothing to do with rhythm. Rhythm is seen instead as an order which the listener imposes upon sequences of events, solely on the basis of their relative intensities, and their relative times of onset. It is argued that changing the duration of elements affects the rhythm in no way, provided accent and relative onset times do not change. After all, if we play a short tune to someone, and then ask him to clap the rhythm (when he claps, of course, all the durations become very short, and the same), provided he indicates that he has correctly perceived the relative onset times, and the accents, we say that he has produced the rhythm correctly. Rhythm, from the listeners' point of view, is thus (in part, at least) a system of temporal anticipations. It involves the ability to infer that particular events will take place, or commence, at certain specific points in time. Whether they actually do or not is another matter. On the whole, in Western classical music, they do. In jazz, and in some 'primitive' music, they frequently do not, so that the listener has to know where they ought to come.

Music in the Western classical tradition, although tonally very complex, is usually rhythmically simple. There are two possible reasons for this. Firstly, as stated earlier, the rhythm of a piece tends to be carried by the notes themselves, whereas, in rhythmically more complex music, the rhythm is to a greater extent expressed independently of any tune, perhaps by way of drums, gongs, whistles or pipes. (Indeed, a study by Vidor (see Mursell 1937a, p. 151), in which rhythms carried by tones, and rhythms carried purely by a series of taps, were compared appeared to show that the ability of subjects to reproduce the one was only marginally related to their ability to reproduce the other. In other words, if this is the case, the rhythmic abilities demanded by Western classical music might have little to do with those demanded by African music or jazz. On the other hand, the difference might be one of degree, rather than type.) Secondly, Western music has confined itself largely to the use of metres involving units of two, three, or four beats. (The term 'metre' is used here to describe the basic, underlying pulse of a piece of music, around which the different rhythms are fitted.) Even the distinction between two and four time is in a sense artificial, since what can be grouped in fours can also be grouped in twos. Pieces involving an underlying metre of five, such as Holst's 'Mars', from the well-known 'Planets' suite, are the exception rather than the rule. Until recently, the tyranny of twos and threes has also dominated jazz. Dave Brubeck, the much maligned jazz pianist, was one of the first well-known performers to try experiments with 'new times'; in fact, the Western audiences were so amazed to hear attempts at five-four time that the very moderate little tune 'Take five' became a top seller. So successful was this, that Brubeck was tempted to explore the unknown reaches of seven-four ('Unsquare dance') and nine-four ('Blue rondo à la Turk'), all of which involved an invariant underlying, repetitive riff (or repeated tonal sequence), whose only virtue was that it fitted the time sequence in question, and probably served as an anchor to prevent the musicians getting lost. The early attempts to improvise over these time sequences were rather moribund, and, in the case of 'Blue rondo', the sequence lapses into an easy four-four swing for the solos, on account of the difficulties involved in *feeling* these unaccustomed metres.

There, in a nutshell, is the problem. Fed an unvarying diet of metres involving twos or threes, the Western listener is unable to feel anything else. There is no intrinsic reason why five should be impossible to feel, but for most of us this is the case. Imagine the chaos that would be caused on the dance floor by a Boston Five-step, or by Tea-for-Seven-cha-cha-cha-cha-cha-cha-cha. Put one of the crudest examples of complex time, such as 'Take five', on your record-player and ask a friend to tap his feet to the music. More than likely he will say something like, 'It's got no rhythm.' Compare now the Western preoccupation with twos and threes, and the occasional foray into the realms of five and seven, with other forms of music, in which the basic metre might be twenty-four, with different subdivisions for the rhythm and the tune as in an Indian piece described by Meyer (1956); or an African piece described by the same author, in which rhythms of three-eight, two-four, three-sixteen and twelve-eight occur simultaneously, with the different patterns commencing from different points of the basic metre (whatever that is); or a recent composition by guitarist John Mc-

Laughlin entitled 'Binky's beam', in which improvisation takes place in a completely natural-sounding fashion over a basic metre of nineteen-eight.

When we describe music as 'primitive', therefore, we should beware. In tonal terms, the description is to some extent justifiable, perhaps, but in rhythmic terms our own music is largely primitive compared with many other cultures. Some authors have not always made this distinction. Revesz, for example, writes of some music from the Vedda tribe of Ceylon, with charming naïvety. 'The rhythm is very simple,' he writes, and, almost in the next sentence, 'the frequent change in time-outline makes it very difficult to determine the beat.' In fact, without a grasp of the basic metre, or 'time-outline', it is impossible to see the function of the rhythms which occur. Revesz's statement (p. 221) that the rhythm was very simple should thus be interpreted in the light of the later statement that he found it difficult to tell where the beat was. (It is interesting to see how transcriptions of primitive music, by Western observers, often involve the forcing of the phrases into Western-style bars of three or four beats, occasionally five; this sometimes does great violence to the piece in question.) By way of contrast, we can look at some early research by C. S. Myers (1904), carried out in Borneo. Through careful observation, Myers to a very large extent avoided the pitfalls which appear to have snared Revesz. He studied the rhythmic playing of a Sarawak Malay, who was beating a large gong-type instrument called the tawak, in the context of a normal group music-making session. Initial observation led him to believe that the tawak was not beaten in any regular or systematic fashion, but apparently randomly. To examine this impression, he substituted a Morse key for the tawak, and analysed the time intervals between strokes. The subjective impression, that the gong was beaten in no regular fashion, was confirmed; but Myers did not conclude that the apparently random irregularities stemmed from the performer's lack of rhythmic sense. It is clear from the report that initially Myers was to some extent befogged with the Western notion that if a metre is present it will manifest itself in the form of a series of equidistant, and regular, sounds or groups of sounds. This is not the case, and his final conclusion is very perceptive, more so when one considers that the research was carried out in 1904. He concluded that the musicians he heard were capable of remembering, using, and improvising upon rhythmic structures in which the main pulses were separated by different, and varying time intervals. Myers wrote, 'The faculty [i.e. the one described above] they carry to a degree which lies so far beyond the power of civilized musicians, that the latter may reasonably be sceptical as to the possibility of its occurrence among less advanced people.' Indeed, this scepticism still exists today, some seventy years later.

It is the intention later to give some example of complex rhythms, taken from tape-recordings of Bantu and pygmy music, in the possession of the author. Unfortunately, the ones given are by no means the most complex, since these latter elude the author's skill. Examples will also be given from some modern jazz. Before producing the evidence, however, there is one more topic to consider, namely 'syncopation'. There seems to be a fairly widespread belief that the major difference between jazz and classical rhythm lies in the heavy-handed use of syncopation in the former. In fact, there are two sources of error here. Firstly, syncopation is only one aspect of jazz rhythms, and possibly not the most important; and secondly, the classical view of what syncopation entails tends to be rather simplified. In addition, many musicians who do not play jazz regularly have the impression that the notes, in jazz, are made to 'swing' by the simple expedient of alternating long ones with short ones, to give a rhythmic pattern of a daa-di-daa-di-daa-di-daa or 'trochee' type. Far from adding the magic ingredient of swing, such a stilted rendition has a completely stultifying effect on the music, and has very little to do with sounding 'jazzy'. Furthermore, jazz music has its origins in the songs of the American Negro, which are in turn to a great extent influenced by musical, and particularly rhythmic, traditions coming from Africa. On the whole, syncopation is not a characteristic of African music, but merely a device given great prominence by the big bands of the swing era, like Glen Miller, Artie Shaw and Benny Goodman. Meyer (1956, p. 239) is very perceptive on this point. He writes, 'The very essence of African music is to *cross the rhythms*. This does not mean syncopation. On the whole African music is *not* based on syncopation.' This same point applies as much to jazz as it does to the culture in which jazz has its roots. Simple cross-rhythms do occur in classical music also, usually involving crossing two beats against three.

What makes the rhythmic aspects of much primitive music so difficult to comprehend, when compared with our own Western tradition? The answer lies in the deliberate crossing of metres to produce either ambiguity or apparent confusion. Suppose we take as a basic component the sound of a drum struck regularly at equal time intervals, and use this as our basic metre. We might represent this visually in terms of a number of black pegs stuck into the ground at equal intervals, thus:

Fig. 34.   Sample 'metre'

So far so good. We can readily appreciate the simple recurrence of an event at regular intervals, both in the auditory and in the visual mode. The only slight hint of uneasiness might stem from the fact that we cannot tell how they are grouped. Are they in pairs, threes, fours or what? To add to the confusion, we might suppose that the first, third and sixth strokes (or pegs) are accentuated, offering us two alternative hypotheses about grouping.

At this point a second sound joins in, again perfectly equally spaced; we might represent this sound by white pegs stuck in the ground, in the following manner:

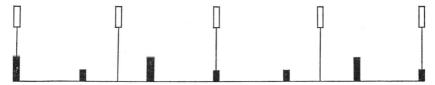

Fig. 35. Two conflicting metres

Because of the way they are spaced, the white pegs coincide with every fourth black peg. This creates an ambiguous state of affairs, in which the beat appears to alternate between a 'two feel', as indicated by the white pegs, and a more rapid three to the bar created by the accents occurring on the first, fourth and seventh beats where the pegs coincide. The ambiguity is heightened by the perverse accents on the black pegs, which offer us no help at all. This very simple two-across-three rhythm is fairly straightforward, and is often encountered in the music of Latin American countries. Our perception of it seems to alternate between twos and threes.

The two possible ways of hearing a two-across-three rhythm are given in normal notation, in fig. 36. Arrows indicate accents. In a similar way, Deutsch (1974) has made an analogy between particular auditory phenomena and the figure-ground illusion, though in a more experimental context. Apart from their

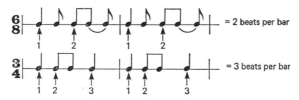

Fig. 36. Alternative ways of perceiving fig. 35. Do the black pegs or the white pegs provide the basic metre?

value as illustrations, it is not clear how good such analogies are. Exactly this device is used by Leonard Bernstein in the piece, 'I wanna be in America', from *West Side Story*. In terms of notation, the two possible ways of hearing the theme are given in fig. 37.

Again arrows are used to indicate accents. However, these accents may be subjective rather than real. Depending on how we group the notes (i.e. the way in which we dispose our subjective accents) we hear the rhythmic groups in one fashion or the other. It is almost as though, when presented with an ambiguous rhythm, we assign some type of psychological accent to particular notes, to find out how the stimuli are grouped. Unfortunately, in this case, there are two

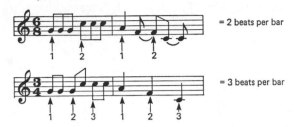

Fig. 37.   *Alternating perception. Example from* West Side Story

ways to do this, and so we are unable to come up with any conclusion as to how the elements are grouped.

Up to now, we have coped fairly well, and we understand the nature of the ambiguity. But now another percussion instrument joins in, again with equally spaced strokes, but starting, apparently, from a completely different point. The strokes are alternately heavy and light, and are represented by circular pegs

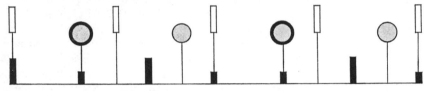

Fig. 38.   *Ambiguous metre with three instruments*

below. The circular pegs appear to be stating a pulse of two, like the white pegs, but starting from a different point. On the other hand, they also imply a further subdivision of the white pegs into triplets, by falling at a point two thirds the distance between each white peg.

The next instrument to join in plays not equidistant strokes, but in groups of

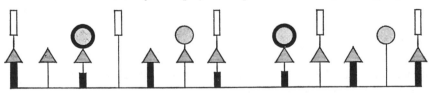

Fig. 39.   *Ambiguous metre with four instruments*

three, as indicated by triangular pegs. This now is a statement of a fast four, with the last stroke missing but played at a speed which does not fit with anything else in any obvious way. For example, the white pegs accentuate respectively the first beat in the first group of three, then the gap between groups, then the last of the third group, and the second of the last group. We can just see, from the coincidence of white pegs and triangular pegs, that this cycle is about to repeat itself, thereby threatening to make the whole thing into just one bar. Or is it really three bars of four-four? Or four bars of three-four? And just which four and which three are we talking about?

The crossing of metres, as illustrated in the above simple example, can be carried to extreme lengths, with each additional instrument implying a different grouping, some of which are barely recognizable. In addition, it is quite possible for a player to play his instrument in a purely aesthetic manner, using rhythms which accentuate first one metre, then another, so that there is in fact no underlying regularity in the strokes. (It is apparent that the distinction conventionally made in the musical literature between 'rhythm' and 'metre', in which rhythm is seen as a pattern or group superimposed on top of a basic beat or metre, is difficult to make in rhythmically advanced music. The basic metre is not always easy to find, and the superimposed rhythms may in fact serve to introduce a new, crossed metre. In addition, two metres may combine to produce rhythmic patterns not related to either. The distinction between rhythm and metre which seems so obvious when there are three beats in every bar, and a tune that fits over the top, is probably less useful when music is rhythmically more sophisticated.) In addition, particular groupings can be accentuated either in a conventional way, by playing louder, or by actual omission. To appreciate this, it is of course necessary for the listener to realize that an omission has taken place, if he is not to be deceived and lose his bearings.

So far, the argument has been illustrated with home-spun examples, and it is fitting now to turn to some instances of complex crossed rhythms taken from actual performances. The first example comes from a recording of a live concert by Miles Davis, the modern jazz trumpeter, and his band, of a tune called 'Seven steps to heaven'. The tune, transcribed below in four-four time, starts off with a fairly simple opening phrase of seven notes, presumably as a reflection of the title. This is followed by a full bar's rest, with a final repetition of the last three notes of the opening phrase. This should be apparent even to those who do not

Fig. 40. Notation, not precisely representing musical events

Fig. 41. 'Viennese waltz'

read music. The only thing of interest, with regard to these notes, concerns the encircled G. Although, in strictly temporal terms, this is part of the second beat, its real function is to accentuate the third beat of the bar. It is not part of the second beat, but the third beat brought forwards by a small amount. It is impossible to write down in notation the exact way in which this is played, without venturing into absurd fractions of a beat, but the above is as nearly correct as one can write it. The situation is analogous to the problem of the 'Viennese waltz', in which the first beat of each bar is shortened, and the second extended by a fraction. Written thus, and played in a precise fashion, the end result has none of the essential lift of the 'Viennese waltz', which is ultimately a matter of *feeling*. In a similar fashion, the jazz example above is also a matter of feeling, which cannot be precisely communicated via notation, but relies on the performer to understand the effect which is required.

However, the interest in the Miles Davis tune lies, not in the tune, but in a drum break inserted into the silent space in the middle, by drummer Tony Williams. For those who are willing to try and work it out, it would be written as follows:

Fig. 42.   *Improvised drum break from 'Seven steps to heaven'*

We can describe what Williams does, intuitively, in terms of a mathematical transformation. The drum break, enclosed between the dotted lines in the above transcription, has a duration of eighteen semiquavers, equivalent to one bar and one quaver at the stated tempo. Williams transforms this time interval into three bars of two-four time, making each crotchet of the two-four equal to three semiquavers of the original time. We might thus write it in two ways:

Fig. 43.   *Alternative ways of perceiving snare drum solo*

In each version, the two circled notes are unambiguous, and clearly serve as an introduction to the last three notes. The intention behind the break, however, is clearly to confuse the existing rhythm by introducing a completely new one, intact in itself, but only very obliquely related to the main metre, and which occupies exactly the same amount of time as the space between the two phrases. In order to come back with the ensemble at the correct time, the other instrumentalists have to preserve in memory the main metre through the drummer's attempts to destroy it. Characteristically, in this kind of situation, a sly grin may pass across the face of the drummer if the other musicians fail to grasp instantly what he is doing, and make an incorrect or ragged entry. In a sense, the drummer may be testing the rhythmic abilities of his comrades, and may well be filled with glee if he can lead them astray. In other words, it is fun.

Meyer describes an exactly similar example from Hindu music, taken from Sargeant and Lahiri (1931); interestingly, Meyer describes the situation as a contest. He writes (quoting from Sargeant), 'It often happens that a *vina* player and a drummer will engage in a friendly contest to see which can confuse the other into losing track of the *sam* (the structural beat).' And later, 'The *vina* player uses all sorts of ruses to disguise the *sam* . . . The drummer will meanwhile seek to confuse his opponent by insisting on his cross rhythms as though they were the true basic metre, playing metres of seven, or five, against the latter's four or three and so on.' This kind of rhythmic competition which takes place in Hindu music is clearly very similar to what sometimes happens in jazz, though there may well be differences in the lengths to which this is taken. By contrast, this kind of thing is most unusual in Western classical music; in fairness it must be added that the scope for this type of melodic/rhythmic interplay is necessarily greater where the performers can improvise, rather than having to adhere strictly to a written score.

The second example comes from an anthology of music prepared by Arom and Taurelle (1965), collected from amongst the Ba-Benzele pygmies. The actual piece depicted is one used as a celebration after returning from the hunt, and involves a rhythmic structure known as Djoboko. Men, women and children all participate, indicating that, in this culture, a sophisticated sense of rhythm is a norm. The piece involves flutes, percussion of various kinds, chanting and something very like yodelling. Because of the cross-rhythms used, it is impossible to specify a definite time signature for the piece, though a regular series of accents (what Mursell refers to as a takt, or regular beat) is detectable. Similarly, whilst there is a very strong sense of key, in the sense that the notes are modally and tonally consistent, the actual key is ambiguous.

The piece starts with a single performer playing a flute which produces only one note. The flute is played in a series of short non-equidistant bursts, and the player sings in between puffs. In this way, the one player produces a basic takt or beat as well as a polyrhythm, simultaneously. (Interested readers might like to try maintaining a rhythmic pattern on a child's recorder, and improvising sung passages in the gaps without any change in the pattern played on the recorder.) This introductory pattern is written below, and given a time signature of six-four. It is arbitrarily written out in the key of F. The voice part is sung in a pleasant treble voice, and the motif is shown in the top line. Simultaneously, the singer interjects a basic metre into this motif on the flute, which plays the note C'. The flute pattern is shown in the lower line.

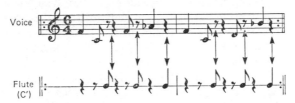

Fig. 44.   Flute/voice motifs of Ba-Benzele pygmies

The arrows indicate where the flute notes come, relative to the voice. The voice motif also changes from time to time, but the flute rhythm remains fixed. The effects of the interplay between voice and flute are interesting. At times, the flute seems to stand out from the voice (see an investigation of this phenomenon in Dowling 1973) and at such times creates a rather complicated counter-rhythm; at other times it becomes perceptually absorbed into the voice line, whereupon it becomes simply part of a tune. Perception seems to alternate between these two extremes. The first performer is very quickly joined by a second flute, whose instrument plays the note D', that is, one tone away from the first flute. As nearly as possible, the pattern played by this second flute is represented in fig. 45(a). In itself, this pattern looks very rudimentary. There is one small catch. Written in the above manner, we need to synchronize the second flute with the first by making the first beat of every bar for the second player coincide with the last quaver of every bar for the first player. In other words, viewed through Western eyes, the two rhythms do not start from the same point.

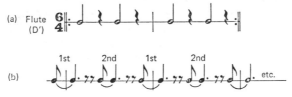

Fig. 45.   Timing of D' flute relative to C' flute

We might write it as shown in fig. 45(b). The effect of this rhythm is to imply a slow duplex metre over the existing one. However, notice where each of the D' notes falls with respect to the C' of the first player. The first D' is preceded by a C', just one quaver before. The second D' is preceded by a C', which occurs one crotchet before. Since the two flutes are only one tone apart, the effect is similar to one flute playing an ascending two-note motif, and perceptually it is almost impossible to see these tones as separate. Note that, although the cycle repeats itself, it has a peculiar lop-sided feel since the ascending two-note motif is alternately fast and slow.

As the piece continues, more patterns and voices join in; to describe the effect of each new arrival individually would take several pages. A transcription of some of the parts involved, however, is given below, up to the point where the solo singer commences; the whole thing up to this point is simply a 'backing'. The transcription should merely be taken as a sample of some of the things which are going on.

Fig. 46.   Sample of pygmy Djoboko

In the above transcription, certain parts have been written out in four-four time for clarity. These implied quadruple rhythms, however, are based on a beat which is equivalent to a dotted crotchet in the six-four rhythms. Note the tapping noise, which, in alternate bars, accentuates an on-beat, then an off-beat. Also, the clicking sound, which is displaced by a semi-quaver in alternate bars. Finally, the chant, whilst preserving its temporal form, appears to start from different points in the bar on different occasions, so that the first note is not always the first beat of a bar in terms of the way we have construed the rhythms. (The way we have construed the rhythms, in terms of Western notation, may well have nothing in common with the way a pygmy construes them.)

If one were asked to crystallize the essence of the rhythmic ability which underlies high level rhythmic performance, one might say that it consists of the capacity to mentally impose different groupings upon temporally spaced events. There can be little doubt that the ability of primitive musicians to create alternative groupings is in excess, possibly greatly in excess, of that normally displayed by Western musicians. This leads us to a very interesting point. It is extremely difficult, and for the author frequently impossible, to give a precise transcription of certain rhythmic patterns, or particular cross-rhythms, in terms of standard musical notation; and yet the whole of Western music relies on this form of notation. In other words, the system we use is inadequate for the portrayal of complex rhythms without becoming unintelligible. The bar lines operate in a tyrannical manner, insisting that the first beat always comes in the same place, and making any event which crosses a bar line into some sort of exception, to be represented by a clumsy 'tie' line, identical to that used to indicate phrasing. The basic units presuppose that any subdivision of a note is going to be made in terms of halves or quarters, so that even a simple triplet involves writing in the number 3, accompanied by the same curved line we also use for ties, and for phrasing. If, for example, one wishes to subdivide a note into five, it is again necessary to resort to numbers, as the notation alone cannot represent this event. No matter how much we divide or multiply a single beat by multiples of two, there is no way we can produce five. In other words, the notation system, which is so elegant for the representation of tunes and chords, imposes very real restrictions upon the rhythms we can employ, since it can only represent certain rhythmic events in a very clumsy and unsatisfactory manner. Although the case cannot be proved, it is not an unreasonable hypothesis that the lack of rhythmic sophistication which characterizes much of our own music stems from our adherence to written music, and the concomitant use of a system which represents notes far better than it represents rhythms. Several workers have suggested alternative notation systems, e.g. Edwards (1940). This author writes, 'Our existing system of musical notation seems like the English system of weights and measures, to have "just growed". In fact, it seems to have grown into about as needless complication as the latter.' (See also the Klavar-System, a new type of music notation.)

There are possibly other reasons why rhythmic abilities tend to be viewed rather differently from tonal abilities. As mentioned earlier, in chapter 7, studies of musical abilities tend to reveal that a separate factor exists for rhythmic, as distinct from tonal, abilities, i.e. rhythmic abilities do not appear to be closely related to abilities involving the tonal aspects of music. This finding perhaps serves to accentuate the isolation of the rhythmic aspects from those tonal attributes which receive more attention in Western music. It should be remembered, however, that the notion that tonal abilities form a single, or unitary, entity, is simply a theory. Other workers have concluded that, in fact, musical abilities are best viewed as unrelated, including the different tonal abilities. One consequence of the unitary theory has been to provide evidence for a view of rhythmic abilities as both separate and inferior. If rhythmic abilities are unrelated to tonal abilities (which together form a group), it is possible to have a high degree of rhythmic sense, and yet still be inept in those areas which form the main component of Western music. (By contrast, the atomistic theory renders such a view untenable, since all abilities are seen as basically independent, whether rhythmic or tonal.) Lundin (1967), for example, asks the question, 'Can we have individuals seriously defective in tonal appreciation who are still able to make good musical responses because of a refined perception of rhythmic groups?' He quotes Mursell, in answer to his question, by referring to the hypothetical case of a 'drummer with a jazz orchestra who is rhythmically effective but tonally inept'. The question, and its answer, have the tone of an employment agency urging potential employers to consider employing the handicapped, on grounds that they can still make a useful, if limited, contribution. The unfounded preconceptions implicit in the argument are clear. However, the notion that a drummer might pursue his occupation because he does not have the abilities which would enable him to aspire to the tonal aspects of music should apply just as much to 'drummers' in symphony orchestras as to 'drummers' in jazz bands; it is equally false in both cases. More importantly, however, the inverse of the argument can also be considered from the point of view of the unitary theory. We can ask, 'Are there individuals seriously defective in rhythmic appreciation who are still able to make good musical responses because of a refined perception of tonality?' In answer to this question, we might refer to the hypothetical example of 'the violinist in a symphony orchestra who is tonally effective but rhythmically inept'. When we turn the illustration around in this way, the real injustice of this condescending view becomes apparent. The violinist in a professional symphony orchestra, who is 'tonally effective but rhythmically inept' simply does not exist, since both kinds of abilities are demanded for the performance of his job. Similarly, the drummer, to do his job properly, also needs both kinds of abilities. It is inconceivable that he could perform in any kind of meaningful or artistic manner if the tonal aspects of the music were meaningless to him. At this level then our hypothetical 'rhythmically inept' violinist, and our 'tonally inept' drummer, are mythical creatures. True there are probably a great many bad amateur jazz bands with tonally inept drummers. There are also a great many bad amateur symphony orchestras with tonally inept violinists. The conclusion must be that, in all areas of musical performance, a serious deficit in any one musical capacity makes the achievement of a high overall standard of performance all but impossible.

The finding of a separate factor for rhythmic, as distinct from tonal, abilities, which has emerged from a great many studies, is also underscored by the different theories of rhythmic ability which have been put forward. On the whole, these theories have little to do with the tonal aspects of music, so that the distinction between rhythm and everything else is again, unfortunately, accentuated. Mursell (1937a, chapter 4) gives a good coverage of the best known theories of rhythm. Firstly, he gives an account of those theories which see rhythm as an 'instinct'; secondly, he describes those theories that view rhythm as a natural concomitant of various regularly recurring bodily processes. Basically, the instinct theory of rhythm postulates the existence of an innate rhythmic response. In other words, people respond to rhythms because such a response is inherent in their nature. The instinct notion, used as an explanation, is unsatisfactory, because instinct is a non-explanatory concept. It does, however, serve as an adequate label for particular kinds of innate (i.e. unlearned) behaviour. Unfortunately, the evidence from studies of rhythm seems to indicate that the existence of an innate 'rhythm instinct' is unlikely. Studies of the rhythmic abilities of children appear to show that they are rather poor at simple tasks such as 'keeping time'. Mursell points out that many adult observers would probably disagree with this assertion, arguing instead that children make many and varied rhythmic responses to music. Mursell insists, however, that such observers are deceived by what they see, and are too easily seduced into interpreting the actions they see as 'keeping time', when in fact nothing of the kind is happening. The movements which children appear to make spontaneously as a response to particular types of music are, according to Mursell, much more likely to be a result of the generally stimulating effect of tone; this in no way implies a true rhythmic response of any kind. The most often quoted study in this area is one carried out by Heinlein (1929) in which children 'marched in time' to music, whilst their responses were monitored by electrical contacts embedded in the walkway on which they marched. The results showed that, out of eight subjects, only one displayed any proper synchronization between his marching and the music. This finding, however, does not totally dispose of the instinct theory, since it rests on the assumption that, if a piece of behaviour is instinctive, children will automatically manifest it. This assumption is simplistic, since it overlooks the fact that many behaviours which have been regarded as instinctive (in animal studies) do not emerge until the organism has reached a particular developmental stage. Perhaps the kindergarten-aged children in this study had not yet reached the necessary stage? In an unpublished, but detailed, study of a sample of children ranging in age from five years to eight years, Pomfret (1969) found increases in the accuracy with which a 'marching' task was performed (in this example, children were asked to 'march on the table with both hands' in time to the music) as a function of increasing age; not surprisingly, a developmental effect of some kind appears to be present. She also noted that the testing situation appeared to be rather overwhelming for some of the younger subjects, and suggested that this may have prevented them from performing as well as they might have done. In evaluating Heinlein's finding, therefore, we should note both that there is a developmental aspect to rhythmic abilities, and that young children do not always do themselves justice in experimental situations.

Perhaps the main deficiency of the instinct theory, however, concerns the oversimplified view which often inheres in the very notion of instinct itself. The postulation of an instinct for rhythm, of which Seashore is a major proponent, is perhaps a carry-over from the golden era of instinct which came at the start of the century. At this time, the term 'instinct' became an all-purpose panacea for the 'explanation' of types of behaviour which were widespread but for which no obvious learning process was apparent. A survey of 500 books was performed by Bernard (1924) from which he abstracted a list of no fewer than 5,648 instincts which had been postulated by different writers. Among these were the instinct to sit in a chair (an amazing piece of luck, since we presumably inherited this trait from our distant ancestors who didn't have any chairs to sit on), and the instinct not to pick apples from your own orchard (from an evolutionary point of view, this would seem to be a strangely maladaptive behaviour pattern). The problem in using the word 'instinct' in this kind of way is that we tend to think we have explained something when we have done no such thing. Instead, we have coined a particular word to *describe* an observed pattern of behaviour; at a later point in time we use this arbitrary label as though it *explained* the behaviour. In other words, we say that a particular behaviour is caused by the presence within the organism of 'an instinct', and we infer the presence of the instinct from the behaviour. The course of the argument is thus circular, and lacks an external referent, and therefore is unhelpful. Further, it is probably incorrect to conceive of the actions of genes as taking place in a vacuum. The precise way in which they are expressed depends both on interactions between genes, and between genes and the environment. To say that a particular individual's rhythmic behaviour is the result of an instinct is therefore oversimplified, as is the attribution of differences in rhythmic abilities between individuals to different degrees of instinct. Similar caution must be observed when speaking of racial differences. A currently widespread belief, stemming no doubt from the observation that African music is rhythmically very complex, is that Negroes have a 'natural' (i.e. instinctive) sense of rhythm supposedly lacking in whites. The findings on this issue are not satisfactory, since, in the main, the only Negro groups who can, with any semblance of fairness, be tested with standardized test batteries, are those domiciled in the USA, so that most findings come from this group rather than from an African group and we have no way of knowing how far the US Negro is like his African counterpart. Mursell gives a summary of findings on this issue, and the results are contradictory. Sometimes whites do better than Negroes, and sometimes the Negroes are better than the whites; on other occasions there are no reliable differences between the groups. Mursell also outlines the problems inherent in using culturally biased tests to examine supposed differences between ethnic groups, and the objections here are well known. There may be differences between racial groups in their capacities for rhythmic response, or there may not. It should be clear, however, that, even if there are, we cannot naïvely ascribe differences in rhythmic performance to instinct. As Lundin concludes, '. . . the explanation may just as easily lie in culturalization as in inherent tendencies'.

A second theory of rhythm is based on the periodicity of bodily processes, such as heart-rate, or respiration. Thus music which proceeds at a speed below the limits of the normal pulse sounds sluggish, whilst music above this limit sounds hurried. Music which approximately coincides with heart rate is supposed to sound 'just right', and one latter-day folk myth has it that the popularity of pop music is due to such coincidence between heart-beat and tempo, which is supposed to give the music some irresistible, compulsive quality. Whilst the evidence on these more general claims is largely to be taken with a pinch of salt, the 'bodily processes' theory cannot be entirely discounted, since interesting results have been obtained in studies with children. By and large, these do *not* show rhythmical responses in children, but they do appear to show that children respond to particular kinds of rhythmic stimuli (the distinction is important). In particular, certain kinds of periodic events, such as rocking or swinging, appear to have a calming effect on babies. Mothers have probably known this for a long time, but it is nice to have it on a scientific footing. An interesting study by Korner and Thoman (1972) compared the efficacy of various soothing techniques in causing crying four-day-old children to be quiet. Of the different methods they used, the one which led to the shortest continuation of crying afterwards was one in which the baby was moved to and fro as if in a pram. None of the other methods described involved such repetitive type of stimulation, though lifting the baby and cradling it in the arms was similar in some respects, although it was not repetitive (or, as the authors describe it, '. . . . during intervention 5 the infant was given continuous linear acceleration over the thirty-second period and during intervention 2 only momentary linear acceleration was provided'). Thus, if your baby cries too much, you might try giving it some continuous linear acceleration or pushing it to and fro for a while. (Although the notion of a linearly accelerated baby might appear rather hilarious, it should be stated, in fairness to the authors, that it is often difficult to find ways of expressing such things succinctly yet with precision. Even so, the appropriation of this terminology from physics is not entirely apt since the baby was not continuously accelerated, as the authors suggest, but repeatedly accelerated. On second thoughts, therefore, mothers are strongly advised *not* to apply continuous linear acceleration as baby will thereby attain a theoretically infinite terminal velocity.) These authors refer to other studies of an equally interesting nature; for example, there is evidence to suggest that rocking at a rate of sixty to seventy oscillations per minute might be the most effective rate in stopping crying in very young babies. According to Ayres (1973) this is the speed at which women are likely to walk during the later stages of pregnancy. Also, up-and-down motion may be more effective than side-to-side. One more general conclusion, however, is of special interest here. The authors write (p. 450), 'It seems likely that the most effective soothers involve rhythms and types of motions experienced in utero.' It is possible, for example, that the regular sound of the mother's heart-beat might have a soothing effect (or alternatively, that its removal produces a change in stimulation which is disturbing). Owners of dogs may be familiar with the practice of putting a clock in the basket of a new puppy to reduce its crying at night.

Recently a fascinating hypothesis has been advanced by Barbara Ayres (1973), namely, that cross-cultural variations in the use of rhythm in music might be related to variations in the manner in which parents carry their children. The notion is that rhythm serves a major psychological function in promoting feelings of security and satisfaction, and in reducing anxiety and tension, through association with early experiences when similar rhythmic events occurred. Consequently, it is argued that children coming from cultures where they are customarily carried by the mother will associate feelings of security with the regular rhythms of the mother walking, grinding or performing other regular tasks. Such cultures should thus demonstrate regular rhythms in their music. On the other hand, it is argued, cultures in which the infants are not carried but are kept in cradles, hammocks or on cradleboards, will not be characterized by regular rhythms in their music. This hypothesis is supported when data on carrying practices from a number of different cultures are related to a preference for regular or irregular rhythm in the music of those cultures. Unfortunately, whilst the hypothesis is a most attractive one, the paper is rather speculative in several of its aspects. In the first instance, the classification of rhythms into 'regular' and 'irregular' involves some rather naïve assumptions about rhythm (as we have seen previously, whether a rhythm sounds regular or not depends very much on who is listening to it). Secondly, there are some important exceptions to the results, and the explanations of these amount to little more than guesswork. For example, it is suggested that African polyrhythms come about in tribes where the infant is carried about by different women at different times. In fact, this would, at most, subject the infant to rhythms of different speeds. To meet the psychological requirements for polyrhythmic perception, it seems more likely that the infant would have to be carried about by several women at the same time. Other exceptions to the rule are explained in similar speculative terms. Lastly, there is reason for supposing that rhythms which sound irregular, or even 'free', to Western ears, represent a more highly developed rhythm sense than the simple repetitive or regular rhythms of the West. In the Ayres paper, it is implied that a good rhythmic sense is a product of a 'carrying' environment, where the infant has more rhythmic stimulation; but it is also, at two points, implied that a good sense of rhythm means good sense of regular rhythm, i.e. 'individuals who have been carried extensively in infancy and early childhood have a *better sense of rhythm* [author's italics] and stronger preference for regular rhythm . . .', and also, 'Since the Yaghan wear little clothing their *low rhythm score* [author's italics] cannot be explained by the absence of body contact. . . .' In other words, there are two hypotheses operating, which are slightly confused. If the hypothesis is that regular rhythms are preferred in cultures where infants are carried, Ayres's data support such a conclusion. However, if, as implied later, it is the belief that carrying leads not merely to a preference for regular rhythm, but to the development of a 'better sense of rhythm', one might expect the results to be precisely opposite to those found. Although Ayres suggests that carrying infants while walking, kneading, grinding and so on leads to preferences for regular rhythms in elementary times like 2/4, 3/4, or 6/8, it is difficult to see why one should assume *a priori* that such events should be psychologically grouped in twos and threes, rather than fives or sevens or thirteens.

Despite these differences of opinion, the paper remains very interesting. In summary, one might say that the hypothesis that specific aspects of child-rearing practices affect rhythmic development remains entirely plausible, but that the specific relationship suggested by Ayres remains speculative. It is unlikely, however, that anyone would disagree with the observation that testing such hypotheses remains very difficult in the presence of the influence of other more general cultural factors upon rhythmic development.

Recent research into the influence of 'musical acculturation' upon rhythmic development has been performed by Zenatti (1976). In experiments with French children, Zenatti concludes that one manifestation of their musical acculturation is a marked preference for regular (*bien marqué*) rhythms, presumably of the type normally heard in Western music. Zenatti stresses the developmental aspects, especially the development of perceptual abilities, and also specifically musical learning (from songs and dances which the children hear) as both being important in rhythmic development. Her results also show that when rhythms are 'carried' by a tonal sequence, children's judgements are affected by the tonal nature of the material; a fact probably related to the predominantly tonal nature of 'musical acculturation' in the West. In particular, only 30 per cent of six-year-old children differentiated between two tonally identical sequences, one of which was presented with a simple rhythm (*cellules isorythmique*) and one with a syncopated (*syncopé*) rhythm (*cellules rythmiquement hétérogènes*). (Unfortunately, in the written example of this stimulus material, the second version is not merely syncopated; the elements used add up to five beats, whereas the first version is in 4:4 time. Since the metre is thus different in the two renditions, it is not certain that the difference can be simply described as one of rhythmic syncopation.) However, this task was successfully performed by seven-year-olds (71 per cent successful), suggesting a developmental difference. By contrast, melody differentiation was performed much better by both these age groups (72 per cent and 83 per cent respectively), so that results cannot be simply attributed to failure to understand the task on the part of the younger children. It is possible, however, that rhythm was simply less salient for the younger children than melody. It thus appears that Ayres and Zenatti stress different processes in the acquisition of rhythmic abilities. Ayres stresses the importance of bodily stimulation through movement, whilst Zenatti's results suggest the importance of later perceptual development, and also of a more cognitive type of learning through exposure to music occurring within the culture. The two sets of results are not comparable, however, since Zenatti's data come from a society where children are not habitually carried by the mother, and where a preference for regular rhythm would consequently have to be learned in a way different from that suggested by Ayres. Thus, unless Zenatti's findings can be shown to hold true in a 'carrying' society, there is no reason to view the two positions as contradictory.

Related to the bodily processes theory are certain studies involving the phenomenon of 'photic drive'. In photic drive, bursts of neural discharge (manifesting themselves as brain waves which can be measured) can be made to 'lock on' to a regularly flashing light. When this occurs, the electrical discharges of the brain are synchronized with the flashes of the light (Livanov and Poliakov 1945). The earliest work in this area involved rabbits, but more recent work has demonstrated similar results with human beings. In particular, some persons, particularly epileptics, have been found to be more susceptible to photic driving than others. In one form of epilepsy, attacks are accompanied by a characteristic brain-wave pattern known as the 'spike-and-wave', which commences at the start of the attack, and finishes when the attack terminates. The attacks are characterized by varying degrees of inattentiveness, and in some cases by jerks of the limbs. There is by no means always loss of consciousness during these attacks (this form of epilepsy is sometimes known as *petit-mal*, as opposed to the more striking *grand-mal*), and, in some cases, subjects are not even aware that such an attack has taken place. Furthermore, subjects are still able to discriminate sounds whilst the attack is in progress, and even able to continue making automatic rhythmic movements which they were instructed to make before the 'spike-and-wave' attack was induced (Cornil, Gastaud and Corriol 1951). There are many other studies demonstrating, amongst other things, the phenomenon of synchrony between brain waves and external regularly occuring events, and a full review of these is not necessary here.

Given findings like those above, it is very tempting to draw speculative analogies with certain aspects of pop music. For example, at a superficial level, the things which take place in photic drive experiments seem very similar to the things which go on in a discotheque, where very loud repetitive sounds occur in conjunction with stroboscopic (i.e. flashing) lighting. Furthermore, it appears that many of the dancers are apparently oblivious of anything going on around them (inattentiveness), their movements might loosely be construed as of an epileptic type (jerky), they do not totally lose consciousness, they are apparently still able to discriminate sounds, and they are able to continue making automatic rhythmic responses throughout the duration of the 'attack'. In truth, the flashing lights and incredible volume levels sometimes present in the disco can become very headachy and oppressive. However, the inference that all present are undergoing the paroxysms of some type of epilepsy, as a result of photic drive, or its auditory equivalent (or a combination of both) does not bear close examination as an explanation for the behaviour of groups of teenagers. The precise control and monitoring necessary to produce photic drive are not available in the disco, nor are all the teenagers of the highly susceptible type. The findings concerning photic drive are important, not for these simply speculative reasons, but because they demonstrate that synchrony between internal and external events takes place. This is a long way from the notion that respiration, or heart-rate, are crucial internal variables with respect to the rhythmic response, but not all that different from MacDougall's claim that feeling for rhythm is due to a basic rate of nervous discharge (MacDougall 1902). We are not here attributing the whole of the rhythmic response to a rate of nervous discharge, but simply saying that the structure of the nervous system, and the speed at which it operates are likely to have some bearing upon the perception of periodic events, and whether such events seem fast or slow. Furthermore, the fact that particular repetitive stimuli can induce a synchronous pattern of brain waves means that the possibility of a relationship between regular musical events (metre) and similar patterns of nervous discharge cannot be entirely dismissed. Finally, it is of interest to note that, in certain recent studies, particular rates of brain waves have been found to be associated with particular experiential and mood states, suggesting that particular brain-wave patterns have particular types of experiential correlates (e.g. Brown 1970, Fermi 1969, Wortz 1969, Green 1969).

However, the rhythmic response goes far beyond simple repetitive events. Such events have been defined earlier as 'metre', and rhythm is something imposed on top of the basic metre, not necessarily of a simple repetitive nature. The basic rhythmic response would seem to involve not the perception of simple regularity, but the formation of perceptual units. Any theory of rhythm which is based on voluntary bodily movements, or which assigns paramount importance to movement, would therefore seem to place the cart before the horse, or, at least, by its side. For example, Ruckmick (1913) carried out experiments in the perception of rhythm, and found that 'awareness of rhythm' was accompanied by muscular movement. The conclusion was that rhythmical forms must initiate the factor of movement in order that the impression of rhythm shall arise. This does not mean, however, that muscular movement is a cause of rhythmic perception. It could be either a concomitant, or a consequence. Indeed, it is difficult to imagine how one could, for example, tap one's foot to a rhythm that one had not perceived. On the other hand, no one can doubt that movement and rhythm are closely related. People tap their feet, shake their heads, and move in a variety of ways in response to rhythm, and sometimes these movements are probably of real value in helping to 'keep the beat'. At the heart of the matter, however, lies a purely mental process involving the subjective grouping of temporally spaced events into groups. Our own movements might be intimately related to this process, and for many people they may enhance the pleasure of the rhythmic experience, but they are not themselves the process.

What is the nature of this grouping process? Interesting experiments performed by Vos (1973) cast some light on this subject. (Vos was impressed initially by the fact that most of the empirical work on rhythmic abilities was either descriptive or historical in nature, or else highly speculative. Much of the evidence in the area comes from studies performed many years ago.) Vos presented subjects with sequences of tones which were constant in both pitch and intensity. The temporal arrangement of tones was manipulated, however, in accordance with particular statistical rules. In general terms, Vos found that metrical (or periodically structured) sequences gave rise to the subjective perception of 'measure' and of 'accent'. In other words, groups of tones were perceptually formed into units or measures, probably as a consequence of the Gestalt laws of proximity and similarity; there also arose a perceived difference in the stimulus strength of the different elements (accents) where none existed in physical terms. To put this another way, people heard accents where there were none in actuality. According to Vos, the phenomenon of rhythmic perception which he describes is not confined to music alone, but is allied to the perception of speech rhythms also.

So far as music is concerned, we need to take care about how we define 'rhythmic groups' and 'accents', since they are not to be thought of solely as properties of music. Vos clearly demonstrates that they are properties of people, as well as of musical sounds. If this is true, then logically we go even further with this analysis. Accent, or that quality of a tone which makes it sound louder than other tones, can arise due to either the perceptual phenomenon which Vos describes, or due to the manipulation of 'objective loudness' so that the difference in the intensity of tones impresses itself upon perception, i.e. accents can be purely perceptual, or can be physical. There is experimental evidence on the influence of changes in physical parameters (i.e. intensity) upon pattern perception. Using pulses of white noise (a broad band noise containing all audible frequencies), Ptacek and Pinheiro (1971) showed that an attenuation of at least 10 dB was necessary to make a 50 dB pattern 'stand out', even though the threshold for actual discrimination is only about 0·5 dB at this level. These authors, again, make a comparison with the visual figure-ground phenomenon, and also note the occurrence of spontaneous pattern reversals, mentioned in an earlier chapter. On the other hand, grouping is always a purely psychological phenomenon, and no matter how we manipulate the tones themselves, they are never grouped until they are perceived as such. There are thus two ways we can perceive accents (namely, we can perceive accents which are subjectively created, and accents which are objectively created), but only one way in which we can perceive groupings (namely, when we can impose a grouping on the stimulus elements). What appears to happen in much music is that accents are presented as parts of the music, and serve as cues which the listener uses to form perceptual groupings. We should remember, however, that accents are not essential to this process, since the rhythmic listener will generate his own accents if none are objectively present in the music, as demonstrated by Vos with tones, and, in analogous terms, by many other workers in the field of pattern perception in general. Moreover, because we have two kinds of accents (those contained in the music and subsequently perceived, and those generated solely by the listener), there is no reason to suppose that the subjective accents and the objective accents will of necessity coincide, and no basis for thinking that they ought to. One can envisage a situation in which accents are objectively placed so as to accentuate grouping cues like proximity or similarity, and also situations where the objective accents are so placed as to be at variance with the grouping cues, or even in conflict with them.

If we now consider once again the nature of largely improvised primitive music, and formally written-down music in the Western tradition, we might speculate as to how the rhythmic superiority of the former has come about. In brief, the former involves a dialectic process which is largely absent in the latter. Consider what happens when a man starts to play some sort of elementary rhythm, or rudimentary pattern of regularly recurring tones or drum beats. Regardless of his playing, subjective accents (possible alternatives to those he is playing) will arise. These accents, at first entirely internal to himself, can be made external by the simple expedient of starting to play them objectively. He is not constrained to play a part exactly as written, and thus can suggest an alternative rhythmic organization. Once this new state has been arrived at, an alternative set of internal accents may arise, and once again the possibility of making public this new rhythmic insight is possible, so that once again the level of complexity of the rhythms is changed. This process, in which an objective state of affairs spontaneously generates new internal possibilities to an individual performer, who then makes these new subjective types of organization public, is a characteristic of most rhythmically complex music systems, but is largely absent from classical music where the composer's original conception is adhered to rather more closely. Indeed, whilst minor deviations are characteristics of musical performance (Small 1937) the major evolution of totally new rhythmic patterns would be regarded as sacrilege, and would certainly alter the whole character of a piece.

The principle underlying the spontaneous organization of sounds into definite patterns appears to be similar to pattern perception in other areas, and seems to resemble what is known as the 'figure-ground' relationship. Basically, this refers to the relationship between an object and the background on which it appears. People learn from their past experience that particular visual stimuli are normally used as objects or 'figures', which occur against some sort of background. For example, in fig. 47 below, there is a tendency to see the shapes as figures, occurring against the background of the page, since this is the normal state of affairs. In fact, if a ruler is laid along the top and bottom edges of the figure, we can observe that our interpretation of what is figure, and what ground, is erroneously juxtaposed, since it is really the background which forms the figure. We are in a sense perceptually accentuating the wrong thing.

Fig. 47.   Figure-ground illusion. What is it?*

* horseshoes.

The classic illustration of the figure-ground phenomenon is contained in fig. 48 and shows the ways in which a figure and ground can be ambiguous. At one point in time we tend to see a white vase in front of a black background, whilst at another the figures seem to reverse, and we see two faces in front of a

Fig. 48. Figure-ground illusion. Two faces or a vase?

white background (Rubin 1921). If we in some way perceptually accentuate the white section, then the two 'faces' merge into, and become, the background. The reverse also happens. Now, according to Vos, the processes involved in the above figure are similar to those involved in the perception of auditory rhythm. Thus, he suggests that the Gestalt terms we have been using here, namely 'figure' and 'ground', can be identified with the accented and unaccented tones in a sequence, respectively. In other words, accents are the figures which stand out, whilst the ground comprises those tones in the sequence which do not stand out.

As we can see from the previous figure, however, the parts that stand out, and the parts that form the background, are produced as much by the listener as by the performer. It is this ability to differentiate between figure and ground which is at the heart of rhythmic ability; the person with a high degree of this faculty may be able to form a number of different possible groupings of figure and ground in a situation where others may see none at all. Given a particular metrical sequence to perform, the skilled performer has an almost limitless number of devices he can use. A basic number of beats may be subdivided into groups containing any number (of elements) which is a common factor of the first number. Thus, a sequence of thirty-six beats may be subdivided into nine units of four, four units of nine, twelve units of three, six units of six, and so forth. This is still fairly simple. It might also be divided into units of unequal length, such as five units of seven, plus one unit of one, or any other combination. In addition, the performer may choose to deliberately accentuate elements which he knows will not be accentuated perceptually by the listener, thereby presenting him with a dilemma as to who is 'right'. In other words, the performer presents rhythms which conflict with the obvious ones that the listener is probably using, and thereby shows him new ways of grouping. If the listener is not careful, he may even be seduced into a blind alley if he interprets the objective (played) accents as 'the beat' when they in fact are not. This kind of rhythmic approach is baffling to those who cannot perceive the relationship of the new groupings to the ongoing, or underlying, metrical form. The rhythm never seems to be constant, but is perpetually changing course, apparently in a purely whimsical fashion. ('The trouble with modern jazz is it's got no rhythm,' remarked one frustrated listener at a jazz concert, after his strenuous efforts to tap his foot had been foiled by his failure to locate the first beat of the bar.)

From the above, it should be apparent that rhythm and rhythmic perception can be developed to extreme levels of complexity which go far beyond simply 'keeping time'. Furthermore, whilst rhythm is highly effective when it occurs in a reciprocal complementary relationship with tonal sequences, it is in no way subservient to the tonal aspects of music unless we choose to make it so. There are musical cultures in which the rhythmic aspects have much the greatest priority, with a minor role being assigned to the tonal aspects. If we have a view of rhythm as being of secondary importance to tonality, this is only because our own musical culture often implies such a distinction by failing to exploit the possibilities of rhythm to any great extent.

13 Musicians and instruments

In the main, this book has been concerned with treating the musical person in terms of processes. In the course of this treatment, occasional anecdotes of a non-scientific nature have been included, chiefly to enliven the scene. This last chapter is different, however, and concerns itself rather more with anecdote and speculation, and rather less with scientifically respectable findings. Most of the anecdotes and speculations, however, come from musicians themselves. This makes a fitting conclusion, since much has been said about the musical person 'as machine', but very little has been said about musicians as people.

One topic which seems to interest many musicians is personality, both their own, and those of other musicians. There is little doubt in the mind of the author that there exists among musicians a number of stable beliefs or stereo-types about the personality characteristics of other musicians. They often seem willing, even eager, to describe various aspects of other musicians' personalities at great length, and the subject is clearly one that fascinates many of them. To try to put these impressions on a slightly more secure footing, a series of group discussions was held in the psychology laboratory, to which musicians from a Glasgow-based symphony orchestra were invited, on a voluntary basis. Alcoholic refreshment was provided for those who wished. The comments made were confidential, in the sense that the people making them would not be named; since not all participants were happy, or at ease, when the conversations were tape-recorded (there were some fairly indelicate speculations from time to time), the substance of the meetings was written down by a research assistant. The meetings were unstructured, other than encouraging individuals to talk about the various sections of the orchestra.

Before proceeding to the contents of the interviews, it is interesting that psychologists have so far paid relatively little attention to the topic of the personality of musicians. Books on the psychology of music deal with aspects of the 'musical mind' largely in terms of musical ability, its assessment, and its relation to other abilities; or the nature of, and propensity for, affective and aesthetic responses; or various aspects of the development of musical abilities. Information about personality types of musicians must normally be gleaned from biographical accounts of famous composers long since dead, often with extracts from their letters. Other information comes from light-hearted accounts of the musician's life, such as Malcolm Tillis's *Chords and Discords* (1960), or the accounts of events in the jazz world revealed in books by authors like

Leonard Feather (1972) and Ian Carr (1973). Books dealing with the growth and development of musical prodigies, by such authors as Revesz (1925) or Bell (1928) also give incidental information of a subjective nature about particular traits. By and large, however, there has been little systematic study of the personality of the everyday working musician. Most musicians are not Mozarts, Tchaikovskys, or Nyiregyhazys, so that studies of genius are not appropriate as descriptions of the normal, competent musician, each of whom is exceptional in his own way, but few of whom are members of that small elite with national or international reputations. Furthermore, much of this information is of an historical nature, so the degree to which it generalizes to the present is also likely to be limited.

Returning to the interviews, one of the most striking things to emerge was the particular way in which the various sections of the orchestra perceived and described other sections, often in terms which were slightly bantering and derogatory.

The main polarization, which emerged time after time in conversations, was between the brass (trombones, trumpets, tuba, etc.) and the strings (violins, violas, 'cellos). For some reason, the horns are seen as being rather different, in terms of personality, from the other brass sections. In a similar way, basses are different from the other strings. To some extent, the woodwind appear to occupy a sort of no-man's-land between, though one or two interesting comments about these instruments, particularly oboe players, were made. Below, under the headings 'Brass' and 'Strings', are given some of the characteristics which these groups attribute to each other. For example, under the heading 'Brass' appear those things which string players attribute to brass players; and under 'Strings', some characteristics which brass players attribute to string players. The information comes from twenty interviews with professional classical musicians. The results are not definitive; they are reported because they are thought-provoking, suggestive of questions which might be asked more scientifically, and also, perhaps, amusing. Whilst the author believes they have some general application, it has not been demonstrated that they do.

Brass (as seen by strings)

Slightly oafish and uncouth
Heavy boozers*
Empty vessels ('That's why they make the most noise, you see.')
Like to be in the limelight
Can't play quietly
Loud-mouthed and coarse
The 'jokers' of the orchestra
'They're extraverts, big noises, that's why they play the trumpet.'

*In fact, in the discussion sessions, the brass drank no more than other sections of the orchestra. Such a situation, however, probably says very little about normal drinking patterns.

'The brass is where all the funnies come from (he's always shouting "Hey, maestro", to the conductor).'
Don't practise
Don't take things seriously

Strings (as seen by brass)

'They're like a flock of bloody sheep.'
Precious
Oversensitive and touchy
Humourless
'They think they are God's gift to music.'
Take themselves, and the music, very seriously
A bunch of weaklings, or 'wets'
'They never go ski-ing, or climbing, or anything active in case they hurt their fingers.'

Most of the descriptions are applied in a pleasant and bantering manner and there are clearly a great many exceptions to the general stereotype; but it is interesting to speculate whether there is a deeper, more fundamental, difference between these two sections of the orchestra. It goes without saying that the brass section's perception of brass, and the strings' perception of strings, are rather different from the descriptions applied by their opposite numbers. Interestingly, however, there is still a big difference between these groups even in terms of their perceptions of themselves. By and large, the brass players seem to see themselves as a group of honest, straightforward, no-messing-about, salt-of-the-earth, good blokes. Apart from the less pejorative words used, this is not so far removed from the string-players' stereotype of the brass player. By contrast, the string players see themselves as hard-working, conscientious, aesthetic and sensitive individuals; again, a picture that can be readily translated into terms of the brass-players' stereotype. The author recently received a letter from a clarinet player who largely concurred with the string and brass categorizations. He wrote the following: 'The brass are drinkers, the strings are stinkers, and the woodwind are thinkers.' Perhaps the best psychological account of the discrepancy that usually occurs between the way we perceive ourselves and the way others perceive us comes from Robert Burns's 'To a louse':

'O wad some Power the giftie gie us
To see oursels as ithers see us.'

It would appear that horn players, bass players, and woodwind players, are on the whole categorized less consistently. Purely for interest's sake, however, one or two of the descriptions offered are given below. A few individuals, for example, described oboe players as being extremely 'neurotic' and other woodwinds as 'neurotic' to various degrees. There seemed little reason for this, until one person expanded on this with the comment (about oboes and oboe players), 'but then the instrument is neurotic anyway'. When we tackled her on the question of how an instrument itself can be neurotic, she replied by saying that the mechanical action of the oboe is extremely complicated, a veritable mass of bits of wire and metal, little springs and complicated mechanisms. As a result, our subject added, oboe players are perpetually engaged, more so than any other member of the orchestra, in a battle to keep their instruments working. It would appear that minor defects, leaks, sticking pads, and other faults are forever developing. Our interviewee argued that this, coupled with an obsession about 'reed' problems, serves to keep the hapless oboe player in a perpetual state of fear that the instrument is about to go wrong. Yet again, another instrumentalist, speaking of the double bass, argued that, intrinsically, the sight of a person wrestling with a huge outsize violin on top of a spike is funny, and that in some way a bass player has to come to terms with this funniness as an essential fact of life in order to play the instrument. The artistic-looking swayings to and fro, extravagant vibrato action, tossings of the head, and generally expressive body movements which are the first-violin player's stock in trade are not for the double-bass player, as he wrestles his monstrous and unwieldy dinosaur through a symphony, producing a level of sound which is completely absurd compared to the size of the instrument. Comments like these point obliquely to a hypothesis that the very physical structure of an instrument, and its consequent demand characteristics, require a particular type of individual to play it. Or it may be that, if a person perseveres with a particular instrument for long enough, he must necessarily develop certain traits which will emerge when he plays it, and possibly at other times too. Otherwise, he will simply not persevere. It is also probable that the demand characteristics of particular instruments are more stringent in some cases than in others, so that certain traits appear more consistently than do others.

Horn players half seem to belong to the brass, and half to a unique group. They are perceived as combining a combination of certain 'normal' brass characteristics with a little more arrogance and an air of the *prima donna* on particular occasions. One musician gave them as an example of high risk takers, and gave the untimely death of Denis Braine in a car accident as an example. Speculatively, he ventured the opinion that the widespread belief that the horn is an especially tricky and capricious instrument rubs off on most musicians, including horn players. Whether it is true or not is less important than the possibility that the belief affects the horn player's comportment. One characteristic attributed to brass players generally, and to horn sections in particular, was some degree of *esprit de corps* not found so much amongst string players. If the anecdotes are to be believed, the horn section of one particular nationally famous orchestra indulges in extreme forms of mutual copying, even to the extent of wearing identical leather jackets and sun-glasses (or 'shades') when they are off duty, and driving about in identical cars with consecutive number plates.

By contrast, string players were often described as having various petty jealousies within the sections as a whole. One musician described the difference between violin and viola players principally in these terms. Apparently, viola players in many cases come to choose that particular instrument only after they have acquired some skill on the violin, which is seemingly the more usual introduction. Consequently, viola players often tend to see themselves as having in some sense 'moved on' from the violin, and by implication therefore violin players are those who have failed to 'move on' in this way. By contrast, however, violin players see viola players as violin players who have failed to 'last the course', and who have swapped the violin for something more manageable. The phrase used to describe this was that violin players see viola players, very often, as 'failed violinists'.

The kind of anecdotes given above are very easy to come by, and most of them appear with a high degree of reliability. In the interviews, however, the musicians were asked to speculate as to the kinds of things which might cause, or help to bring about, the kind of personality/character differences which they described. Some very interesting, and highly plausible, influences were pointed out. The most obvious difference between brass and string sections, for example, concerns the numbers of people playing the different parts. Thus, in the main, the strings are characterized by groups of people engaged in playing the same notes, whilst the brass and woodwind consist of small groups of individuals playing different notes. For example, the usual division of a violin section is into two fairly large groups labelled 'firsts' and 'seconds' respectively. For most of the time the 'firsts' play a part simultaneously, and the 'seconds' play a different part simultaneously. It was pointed out that playing in a string section of this type provides a degree of security, with the occasional individual error normally swallowed up by the sound of the whole. On the other hand, the duplication of parts which we see in the violins, and to a lesser extent in other string sections, is very different from the situation existing in woodwind or brass sections where duplication does not exist to anything like the same degree. For much of the time, a player in these sections is playing his own unique part, and any error which occurs within a particular part is the handiwork of a certain individual to whom the error is normally readily attributable. This is a situation of a possibly more anxiety provoking and insecure nature. Possibly, the situation is even more extreme for leaders of sections, since these players are required to perform, on many occasions, the most difficult and most exposed parts.

Given the above situation, we might speculate about the kinds of personality attributes which could be required by these different tasks. In the first place, any player in a brass section, and particularly the section leader, is bound by the laws of probability to make an obvious and blatant mistake from time to time; clearly, this will be rarer for highly skilled performers. One requirement is, therefore, that the player in question must have the ability not to be put off or disturbed when he makes a *faux pas*. Having missed one entry, he needs the capacity to go for the next one with equal confidence and assurance, just as though the first one had been perfect. Any carry over of fear or worry from the first entry to the second is an almost certain guarantee that the second one will be missed also. In other words, the player must simply not care when he plays a wrong note, or, at least, he has got to try not to care. He might do this by adopting an air of studied indifference, or by finding the incident funny, or using other devices serving the same function. After such an incident the face of the offender often seems to wear an expression of utter and complete apathy; not the trace of a grimace, or a flicker of guilt, crosses the face of the skilled performer who has just erred. (The author recalls one lead trumpet player who had an amazing capacity to make 'screaming' entries with a high degree of accuracy. Inevitably, in the course of an evening, one or two of these do-or-die entries would come out shatteringly wrong. When this happened, there was absolutely no difference observable in the leader's behaviour. He simply went at every one with the courage of the Light Brigade, without a hint of self-recrimination or doubt. Without one or two wrong ones, there would have been no right ones, and the occasional wrong note was just as much a part of the job as the right ones, and not even worthy of comment.)

With the brass and woodwind instruments, then, there is often no place to hide when an error occurs. It is obvious who perpetrated the error, and that person must simply shrug it off as of no consequence and carry on with the job. As soon as he starts to doubt his ability, or worry about his lip, he is in danger of losing the confidence which is essential to the performance of his task. By contrast, however, the violin player in the rearward desks of a section is much less exposed and much less likely to be pinpointed by all and sundry as 'the one who just played the wrong note'. In a sense, the rank-and-file violinist is subject to less strain and pressure, and does not have to develop a mask of the type which, we hypothesize, is often developed by brass players, or section leaders. It is also interesting to speculate as to whether the image of the brass players as being heavier drinkers has some basis in fact, and whether such behaviour could be one way in which they seek to reduce the stress inherent in their jobs. In interviews, several musicians described the classical music scene in London as being especially competitive and stressful, and claimed that there was a relationship between this fact and the heavy drinking of many principal musicians in the metropolis. Drinking as a means of coping with stress cannot therefore be ruled out. According to one musician, a proportion of the London musicians are, from time to time, so nervous and tense that they are unable to take their places on the stage without a few drinks to steady them down.

It would be dangerous, however, to over-emphasize the possible importance of the factors outlined above, since there are differences between strings and brass that have nothing to do with the instrumental tasks themselves. There can be very little doubt that there is a type of class difference between brass and strings in the public imagination. Historically, the strongholds of brass in this country are the industrial towns of the North, where the brass band is still a strong institution. Names like Fairey Aviation, Black Dyke, and CWS Manchester are poles apart from the Amadeus Quartet. The essentially working-class image (myth?) of a man coming out of the pit, going home for a bite of tea and then repairing to the bandroom with his cornet wrapped up in a brown-paper bag simply has no string counterpart. Why brass, rather than strings, should have become the Lancastrian's stock-in-trade is a question to which there is no answer. However, we might note that the stereotyped image of the Lancashire man is not all that different from the stereotyped image of brass players held by string players. It may well be that many people associate the playing of brass instruments with a kind of personality supposedly found in areas where brass instruments hold sway. (Some years ago, in the course of an interview for a job, the author mentioned that he played the trumpet a little. Immediately, the interviewer put on an arch expression, and, in a voice suppos-edly imitating a Lancashire accent, said, 'Oh, ah, lad. Tha' plays t'trumpet doest'a?' and broke out in fits of hilarity. The unstated premise behind the remark, presumably, is that anyone who plays the trumpet must come from somewhere like Ramsbottom, and that this is funny.)

A final point of interest concerns the operations, or 'demand characteristics' of different instruments, and the way these affect the playing of notes at the beginning of a piece or phrase. For a number of instruments there are visual as well as tactile (touch) cues for the first note of a passage. The piano is the obvious example. If I want to play a particular note, I can see where the note is, and hold my finger over it. When the note is required, I know that the right one is going to come out because I can see my finger touching it, and simply press down. To some extent, the same may be said for a string player waiting to make his entry; though in this case the task is harder because the fingerboard of the instrument is not nicely marked out into divisions, like the piano keyboard. The woodwind player, also, is to a large extent able to know what note is going to come out in so far as he covers the appropriate combination of holes, which is the correct combination for playing that note. There is a degree of uncertainty here, though, because of the chance of unintended squeaks, or octave errors. Finally, we have the brass player, for whom the initial entry (the first note of a passage) is probably the most anxiety provoking, and also the point where mistakes frequently occur. His problem is that he has no unique, visually veri-fiable combination of finger positions, valves, or what have you; any combina-tion of valves merely locates a harmonic series and not a note. Moreover, the note which emerges depends on the degree of tension in his lips, a muscular response which is not externally verifiable until after the note is played. The very slight lip movements required to produce the different notes cannot be assessed for *a priori* correctness in the way that a finger on a string or a piano can. In a sense, therefore, this is a situation of even greater uncertainty, since every entry is a little like a step into the dark; the player has no independent way of checking his note before he plays it. The possibility of particular traits arising in response to this uncertainty is worth consideration.

It has been argued that there are differences between the sections of the orchestra in terms of the various instruments played. These differences come from various sources. Different instruments are believed to have different degrees of difficulty. The formal social layout of the orchestra places certain individuals in groups involved in the same task; others are isolated as the unique performers of a particular part, thus making some individuals more identifiable (less anonymous) than others. Furthermore, there are different social and sociological histories surrounding the different instruments; strings have a different set of sociological associations than do brass. The nature of the instruments themselves makes different kinds of demands upon the performer, in which differing degrees of risk, or more probably, risks of different kinds, are involved. Lastly, there are differences in the power of the various instruments; a lone trumpet can, if he wishes, cut through the rest of the orchestra and dominate it. Not so the violinist. From a limited number of interviews with orchestral musicians, we have observed that these kinds of differences are related to differences in the ways the various sections of the orchestra are perceived by other musicians.

If there is any substance in these observations, there are two forms it might take. Firstly, there might be a relationship between the musical instrument played, and the real, enduring personality characteristics of the player. Secondly, it might be that playing a particular instrument has a less deep-rooted relationship to personality, but instead is related to the comportment of the player in the musical situation. In other words, the effect might be a transient one which affects the person's behaviour when he is *in situ* in the orchestra, but which disappears when he moves into a different setting. This question could only satisfactorily be answered by a large-scale survey of instrumentalists, in which various aspects of personality, and the instrument played, would be the crucial variables. Unfortunately, such data does not exist, and the present information from a few unstructured interviews must be viewed with suspicion. Just for the record, it is worth noting that the musicians who took part in the interviews all agreed to fill in two short personality inventories (the EPI 1963, and the IPAT Self Analysis form 1963). Dividing up the musicians into strings, brass and woodwind revealed that the brass had the lowest average 'neuroticism' score, and the strings the highest; brass had the highest 'extraversion' score, and woodwind the lowest; and strings had the highest 'anxiety' score, and woodwind the lowest. Because of the small size of the sample, its unrepresentative nature, and the large individual differences, it is most unwise to attach any undue significance to these results. The differences are not statistically reliable. Nor do the results constitute a survey. The results are interesting curiosities, however, and a thorough study in this area could be intriguing. It would be interesting to see if the picture of the strings as 'anxious and neurotic', and the brass as 'extraverted and not-neurotic' had any truth in it, or whether it was merely an idiosyncrasy of the particular sample used. Whatever the truth of the matter, there are certainly large individual variations.

Whilst the relationship between a person's personality and the instrument he or she elects to play must remain at the level of hypothesis, there is evidence for slight relationships between certain traits and musical preferences of various kinds. Payne (1967), for example, investigated a suggestion from Cattell and Saunders (1954) that personality and temperament might be important factors relating to appreciation. She tested the hypothesis that persons with stable (not-neurotic) personalities would prefer music in the Classical idiom (e.g. Vivaldi, Haydn, Bach), whereas Romantic music (e.g. Tchaikovsky, Delius, Rachmaninoff) would be preferred by those with neurotic dispositions. In this study, forty-two composers were ranked first of all in terms of Classicism/ Romanticism, to serve as criteria for the experiment. (This classification was performed by a group described simply as 'expert musicians', and perhaps not everyone would agree with all their decisions; this is only a minor quibble.) Although Payne concluded that other factors were important in conditioning musical taste (the word 'conditioning' is the one used in the study), she also concluded that personality was one of the most powerful factors in explaining the preferences of subjects for composers rated as Classical or Romantic. More specifically, she found that, indeed, the less neurotic subjects tended to prefer music of a Classical type, whereas more Romantic music was favoured by those with higher neuroticism scores. The subjects used in the experiment were 'discriminative but non-professional listeners', and were fairly rigorously selected. They were not professional musicians however, so it is not possible to say whether the same relationship would hold good for such a group. Thus, although neuroticism scores might be a useful guide to the musical tastes of 'discriminative' listeners (again, in this case one suspects that, in the Payne study, the sample comprised discriminative listeners to *classical* music, rather than to pop or some other musical form) it is unlikely that one could predict the musical preferences of people from a normal, less selected population, nor those of the professional musician, where a great many other factors might be at work. Finally, it often seems to be the case that musicians like some Classical pieces but not others, and some Romantic pieces but not others; one set of reasons underlying these preferences, largely overlooked, is how satisfying the piece is to play, rather than simply to listen to. Like cricket, some pieces might be terrible to watch but marvellous to play, or, conversely, good to listen to but soul-destroying to play. Even in the orchestra itself, probably not all sections would agree on these issues. When Wagner comes out, the trombones rub their hands with glee, while the strings recognize the inevitable and shrug with resignation.

A recent study by Csikszentmihalyi and Getzels (1973) investigated the personalities of a sample of young artists, and produced certain tentative findings, in terms of the expectations of their careers. From the point of view of this chapter, some of their comments are of interest. For example, they write, 'There are certain intrinsic requirements for most occupations that pre-select the type of person intending to perform within their given limits. For instance, a career in classical music not only excludes people who are tone-deaf [the inadequacy of the term 'tone deaf' has been dealt with in earlier chapters: author] but also those whose personality characteristics make them unwilling to concentrate, who lack self-discipline, or dislike sedentary activities.' This statement should be considered in two separate parts. The notion that certain activities demand certain characteristics (or the alternative suggestion, that certain occupations might produce certain particular characteristics) is the one being considered in this chapter. However, the authors of this article seem to assume that musicians can be described as having the traits of concentration, self-discipline, and a liking for sedentary occupations, and that such traits have some sort of global application. This is wrong. Musicians might, in some situations, display concentration and self-discipline, but there is definitely something to be said for the notion that, in other situations, they display little or no concentration or self-discipline. There is also something to be said for the idea that, in some situations, they display less concentration and self-discipline than normal. The last suggestion, that musicians by implication prefer a sedentary way of life, is contradicted by musicians who drive rally cars, who go deep sea fishing, mountaineering and so on. Despite these criticisms, the conclusion that particular occupations have certain task requirements which have implications for personality, is a fair one. More important, however, the above study demonstrates significant differences between people engaged in different fields of art, i.e. engaged in different aspects of the same field of endeavour. (The fields compared were art education, advertising arts, and industrial arts). Though the authors describe their conclusions as tentative it is possible at least to make a subjective analogy between certain of their findings, and the hypothesis that musicians as a group might have certain personality characteristics, and also that there might be systematic differences between the personalities of musicians working in different areas of music.

In popular mythology, literature, and in films, particular stereotypes are frequently portrayed, and one wonders whether these have any basis in fact. Regularly recurring characters include the jazz genius, who fights a constant losing battle against terrible home circumstances, alcohol or drugs or both, is driven by desperation into crime, and either finds the girl of his dreams or dies a nasty death, or both. On the classical side nothing but 'cellists, violin players and pianists occur. The typical character here plays the violin, talks with an outrageous East European accent, is slightly overweight and as shortsighted as a bat. So dedicated and bound up is he with his violin, that simple tasks like making phone calls, or putting his shoes on the right feet, are things which frequently elude him. Such characters are clearly cartoons, but what lies behind them? Studies of highly talented individuals in many fields show them to be more creative, imaginative and sometimes more intelligent (though this quality may have been over-estimated), than other less talented persons, but findings with regard to more specific traits are equally interesting.

One study of individuals possessing creative talent was performed by Mackinnon (1962). He saw creativity as a 'process extended in time, and characterized by originality, adaptiveness and realization. It may be brief, as in a musical improvisation, or it may involve a considerable span of years, as was required for Darwin's creation of the theory of evolution.' The individuals studied by Mackinnon included writers, architects, mathematicians, physicists and engineers. The sample included no musicians, but creative artists, as distinct from scientists, were represented by poets, novelists, and essayists. Apart from the empirical results of the study, Mackinnon offers the subjective view that the products of these creative artists were 'clearly expressions of the creator's inner states, his needs, perceptions, motivations and the like'. His view was that the creative artist strives to externalize something inner and private. Such a view accords well with what one would expect the creative artist to be, but the view is still too vague and too broad. More specifically, it was found that creative persons were more sensitive, more self-aware and more open to their own feelings and emotions. They also appeared to give more expression to the 'feminine' side of their personalities, and were less concerned with the hypermasculinity which often characterizes less creative persons. This does not have to have specifically sexual connotations, but might simply mean they were less concerned about appearing to be totally masculine, which in some sections of society would be regarded as a sign of inadequacy or weakness. Unfortunately, the research caters less well with the creative woman, so it is not clear whether creative persons are more open to the expression of traits associated with the opposite sex, or whether the difference lies in the femininity of some of these traits. Finally, on this topic, it was found that the personality profiles of many creative persons showed a rather clear tendency towards psychopathology, though there was usually also evidence of adequate control mechanisms. There was often also a higher than usual tendency towards psychiatric disturbances like depression, hysteria, paranoia, and schizophrenia (as measured on the MMPI), though these results may be explained in terms of the candour and lack of defensiveness that creative persons often show, rather than in terms of clinical conditions. In other words, the results should not be construed to mean that creative persons are all suffering from mental illness.

Probably, the findings from creative people have general relevance for the musician also, though these results cast little light on specifically musical attributes. It is known that a number of musicians of genius have shown abnormal personality traits, and a recent book by Storr (1972) refers to some of these. The obsessional personalities of Stravinsky, Rossini and Beethoven, and the depressive and delusional states of Schumann, are amongst those mentioned. Storr, as might be expected, takes a psychoanalytic view of these cases, and discusses generally the speculative role of schizoid, manic/depressive, and compulsive/obsessional character in relation to creativity. He also deals with the issue of genius and insanity. Although Storr endeavours to show how such personality disturbance could serve a positive function in some cases, he points out that the opposite can also be true. Severe manic/depression, or schizophrenia, for example, far from helping the creative process, may well interfere directly and make work impossible. Although the cases are fascinating, it remains impossible to say how far their theoretical interpretations can be generalized into a more global statement about genius and insanity. It has been suggested many times that creative artists show more mental instability than others involved in non-artistic pursuits, but the issue remains open to doubt. Least of all has it been demonstrated that artistic genius and madness are necessarily linked, or that genius *per se* is a form of insanity.

Although the musical personality has been subjectively described many times, more precise, empirical investigations are scarce, so to a considerable degree the problems remain. Are musicians different from other people? Are trombone players different from violinists?

14 Postscript

Music, whether it be classical, or jazz, or rock-'n'-roll, is capable of creating in people experiences and states of consciousness ranging from exaltation to despair. The power of music lies in its ability to evoke such feelings. Subjectively, one might make a guess that some music is more powerful in evoking strong emotional reactions, and that some music operates at a level which looks more superficial. This subjective thesis, however, is difficult to demonstrate empirically.

For many people, classical music evokes by far the strongest reactions, and, by comparison, popular music will appear uninteresting to them. On the other hand, there are a great many people for whom the opposite is true. It is not possible to demonstrate that the difference between these two sorts of people lies in any absolute values; yet it is sometimes supposed that classical music is absolutely superior to pop, and that people who appreciate the former are preferring a better type of music, and demonstrating some type of superior aesthetic taste. The preceding chapters in this book outline some theories about musical perception, and musical ability, which suggest that the processes involved in listening to, and appreciating, music are the same qualitatively regardless of the nature of the music itself.

The aim is not to devalue certain forms of music relative to others, nor to suggest that certain forms are 'just as good as' others, but merely to show that comparative statements are nothing more than opinions. On the other hand, we have seen how music can vary in its complexity, and consequently some tunes have more potential or information if the listener can extract it. But, in the last analysis, the listener is the central variable, and whether the music is any good or not depends solely on him.

Unfortunately, in all spheres of music, there is a tendency for those who like it to try and create a mystique around their preferred music, as if by so doing they demonstrated its superiority. Thus underground pop music surrounds itself with a particular image, one consequence of which is to make it less likely that suit-and-tie-wearing 'squares' will come to their concerts, and thus the exclusivity of the music is preserved. In the field of modern jazz, a combination of terrible presentation, a take-it-or-leave-it attitude to the audience, and the half-coherent mumbling of in-jokes, serves the similar function of preserving exclusivity. With classical music, the pretentiousness tends to go in the opposite direction. The attempt to surround some music with an air of sophistication and intellectualism serves to deter those who might otherwise have come along to a symphony concert just because it was good to listen to. One consequence of these 'halo' effects is to narrow the range of types of music which people are prepared to listen to, and to cause them to espouse one type as opposed to other types, as though there were some kind of contest going on. In fact, a person is quite capable of finding his preferred level of complexity within any musical form, for the range available is vast; so one could theoretically listen to concerts by Vivaldi, Chick Corea and Frank Zappa all in the same week, and enjoy each of them on its musical merits.

It is obviously true, though in some ways unfortunate, that people do not listen to music in a social vacuum. The intrusion of social factors is often extensive, and in the main these serve to obscure many of the relationships discussed so far. It has been seen, for example, how the work on consonance and dissonance is made more difficult due to changes of fashion which cause a particular sound to be judged pleasant at one moment in history, and unpleasant at another. We have observed how musicians seem to play more carefully when they are told that a composition is 'serious', but make more mistakes if they believe it to be non-serious. Even in the field of aptitude and ability testing, which one might have expected to be rigorous and objective, there are fashions; in the present climate of opinion, normative mental testing is viewed by many as an unhelpful and unnecessary exercise, for reasons which are often ideological as much as scientific. In addition to examples like the above, there can be little doubt that the musical tastes and preferences of many people are influenced, or even dictated, by social influences rather than musical ones. It seems possible that for some people there is an important social difference between types of music, analogous almost to a social class difference. For people on one side of the 'division' to listen to the music of the 'others' amounts almost to a betrayal. One individual known by the author refused to go to symphony concerts entirely for such class reasons, since he believed symphony concerts were only attended by effete snobs who themselves only attended the concert for class reasons. Such a place, he reasoned, was not one in which a good socialist would wish to place himself. On the other hand, there are no doubt persons for whom a particular style of music has just such a symbolic meaning, i.e. a particular kind of music serves as a 'badge'. Amongst some groups of teenagers, for example, it seems likely that a liking for classical music is regarded as a sign of weakness, or as rather cissy, due to its imagined associations with disliked highbrow kinds of behaviour. The images adopted by many pop groups also reflect a class bias in terms of dress and behaviour, as sometimes does their music (e.g. Cockney Rebel; Leader of the Pack). The opposite side of the coin can also be considered. There are probably people for whom a night at a symphony concert is as much a sign of taste and refinement as an opportunity to listen to some music and to whom a liking for the music of the Rolling Stones would amount to a dangerous sign of moral and spiritual degeneration.

The present vogue for the casual concert can be seen as an attempt to lessen the class gap between types of music. André Previn has recently given much prominence to the casual classical concert, especially on television, in an attempt to make classical music appealing to a wider audience. The polo-necked or shirt-sleeved image adopted can be seen as an attempt to undermine the traditional upper-class stereotype of orchestral music by adopting a casual style of dress which implies a lower social class. Finally, lest anyone should still doubt that social influence affects musical behaviour, let them consider the closing stages of the Last Night of the Proms. This is a strange and wonderful phenomenon, involving famous singers in the singing of well-worn patriotic songs with interminable verses aided by a raucous and unruly crowd of well-natured revellers who wave flags and let off fireworks, the whole being conducted by one of the nation's leading conductors festooned in toilet rolls. The occasion is primarily a social one, a celebration, and should not be confused with a concert, to which there is a superficial resemblance. It is in fact only comprehensible in social terms.

The 'climate of the times' also influences music itself, though an examination of this process is a task for the musicologist. In the same way that different styles of painting reflect different preoccupations of the time, or different ways of viewing the world, so music can reflect particular social, economic, or even political situations. In painting, for example, Gombrich (1959) points out how different styles reflect differing beliefs about pictorial representation, rather than simple inadequacies of perception or of technique. The impressionists' intention was to represent sensation, or the way things actually look to the eye. Thus Monet's painting of Rouen Cathedral in bright sunlight is intended to look blurred, bright and indistinct, as though the eye were dazzled. In fact, however, when we look at a scene in bright sunlight, what the eye sees is not what we perceive, because the sense impression is much modified by what we know. Constable's paintings are not therefore more accurate, but represent instead an attempt to represent the truth rather than the actual sense impression. On the other hand, the so-called primitive paintings of the ancients look strange to our eyes because the artist was primarily concerned to represent what was known rather than what was seen. Thus, if an animal was known to have four legs, it had to be seen to have four legs. The fact that this might violate the laws of perspective and look odd to us is merely a consequence of our different preconceptions as to what a picture should do. Whilst the relationship between specific pieces of music and history is seen very obviously in some instances (e.g. Tchaikovsky's '1812' overture and the Napoleonic wars; or more recently the Beatles' tunes 'Eleanor Rigby', or 'She's leaving home', reflecting current social problems), the relationship between history and general musical style remains problematic. The perennial problem of whether the eighteenth-century lover of Mozart would make much sense out of Bartók, Stravinsky or Schoenberg remains unanswered.

There appear to be two hypotheses with regard to the question of how music relates to society at a given point in time. These two views are set out in a recent book by Bray and Middleton (1974). The first view is that today's 'accepted' music has always been yesterday's *avant-garde*, so that the situation existing at present, in which modern music fails to communicate, is one which recurs time after time. They distinguish between composers who accept traditional views, and those who strive to create a new style by modifying and rethinking existing aspects of music. This latter group represents the *avant-garde*. With regard to the present, they write, 'This situation has existed before and parallels can be drawn between what happened then and what is happening now. There is a recurrent pattern.' For example, at the first performance of Schoenberg's 'Second string quartet' in 1908, there was a near riot. An account of the performance reads, 'The scenes last night . . . were unprecedented in Viennese musical history; there was a downright scandal, during the performance of a composition whose author had already caused a public nuisance with other products of his.' Bray and Middleton also cite a verse from the *Boston Herald* of 1924, concerning Stravinsky:

'Who wrote this fiendish "Rite of Spring",
What right had he to write the thing,
Against our helpless ears to fling
Its crash, bash, cling, clang, bing, bang, bing?'

A second view, however, sees today's situation as unique and the failure of the music to communicate as a consequence of an attempt to transcend existing musical traditions. These attempts are viewed either as praiseworthy or as moribund according to taste. Thus, on the one hand, audiences can be blamed for being over-indulgent towards music which is seen as having no socially confirmed style and limited merit. Modern music 'is identifiable only as modern in the sense that it resembles, more or less, the music of other men of similar aspirations and similar prejudices', writes Pleasants (op. cit.). 'It expresses nothing but his own incapacity to grasp, or his unwillingness to face up to, the musician's communicative responsibility.' This, of course, takes for granted that it really *is* the musician's responsibility to communicate.

On the other hand, it is possible to take the view that modern music is unique because it is a valid reaction against musical styles which have become commercial and decadent. A quote from Weisengrund-Adorno has a distinct Marxist ring to it: 'Advanced music has no recourse but to insist on its own ossification without concession to that would-be humanitarianism which it sees through, in all its attractive and alluring guises, as the mask of inhumanity. Its truth appears guaranteed more by its denial of any meaning in organized society, of which it will have no part, . . . than by any capability of positive meaning within itself.' In other words, ugly, meaningless music is a reaction against, and a reflection of, an ugly and meaningless society; traditional musical forms have been taken over by a manipulative and commercial culture, according to this view.

Considering the 'recurring' versus the 'unique' views, it appears quite possible that both may be to some extent correct in different contexts. The situation of modern music may be in some ways unique and in other ways recurring. Only time will tell. The precise interpretation one puts on these views, however, is a matter of belief or opinion. It seems advisable, however, to distinguish between music, and arguments about music, and, as far as possible, to prevent the latter from interfering with the former. It is possible to distinguish between the views themselves, and one's likes and dislikes. For example, because a piece is supposed to be decadent, one does not necessarily have to dislike it. It is quite possible to think that a piece is decadent, and find it marvellous to listen to at the same time. On the other hand, one might find a piece artistically pure, ethically beyond reproach, but awful to listen to.

With regard to social influences in music it thus appears that there are two sets of related factors. The ones outlined immediately above represent the general 'musical climate' and provide the context within which music is listened to and composed. On the other hand, it has been argued earlier that a second set of factors of a more specific kind operates, consisting of the symbolic values we sometimes attach to music within the existing culture. Without overstressing the importance of these factors, it appears that their influence will be a divisive one whenever they lead to the rejection of certain classes of music for reasons which are essentially extra-musical.

Happily, the mythology with which some of us like to surround our music is often exploded by the musicians themselves. They appear to have a more clear-sighted view of the music itself, and are rarely led astray by the trappings. A consequence of this is that one frequently finds a far more catholic taste amongst musicians than amongst some of the people who listen to their music. Almost all areas of music contain some material of a potentially satisfying and enriching nature. There is no reason why the discerning listener should not find something to his liking in all of them. The sometimes irreverent behaviour shown by musicians towards the music they play should not be misconstrued. It enriches the total musical experience, rather than belittling it; at the same time it makes things more human and more comprehensible. One cannot be creative and sensitive for twenty-four hours a day. Indeed, in the present-day world, many of us hardly achieve these states at all.

Bibliography

ABRAHAM, O. (1901), 'Das absolute Tonbewusstein' *International Musikges*, vol. 3, pp. 1–86 (cited from Ward, 1963(b))

AITKEN, P. P. (1974), 'Judgements of pleasingness and interestingness as functions of visual complexity', *Journal of Experimental Psychology*, vol. 103, no. 2, pp. 240–4

ALLEN, D. (1967), 'Octave discriminability of musical and non-musical subjects', *Psychonomic Science*, vol. 7, no. 12, pp. 421–2

ANASTASI, A. (1961), *Psychological Testing*, 2nd ed., New York: Macmillan

ARCHER, J. (1970), 'Effects of population density on behaviour in rodents', in Crook, J. H., *Social Behaviour in Birds and Mammals*, London: Academic Press

ARNHEIM, R. (1954), *Art and Visual Perception*, Berkeley: University of California Press

AROM, S. and TAURELLE, G. (1965), *The Music of the Ba-Benzele Pygmies*, Department for Folk Art and Tradition of the Musée National, Barthelemy Goganda, Bangui, Central African Republic

ATTNEAVE, F. and OLSON R. K. (1971), 'Pitch as a medium: a new approach to psychophysical scaling', *American Journal of Psychology*, vol. 84, pp. 147–66

AYRES, B. (1973), 'Effects of infant carrying practices on rhythm in music', *Ethos* (Winter), vol. 1(4), pp. 387–404

BACHEM, A. (1948), 'Note on Neu's review of the literature on absolute pitch', *Psychological Bulletin*, vol. 45, pp. 161–2

BADDELEY, A. D. (1966), 'Short-term memory for word sequences as a function of acoustic, semantic and formal similarity', *Quarterly Journal of Experimental Psychology*, vol. 18, pp. 302–9

BADDELEY, A. D. (1968), 'How does acoustic similarity influence short-term memory?', *Quarterly Journal of Experimental Psychology*, vol. 20, pp. 249–64

BANNISTER, D. and FRANSELLA, F. (1971), *Inquiring Man: The Theory of Personal Constructs*, Harmondsworth: Penguin Books

BARRON, F., JARVIK, M. E. and BUNNELL, S. (1971), 'The Hallucinogenic Drugs', in *Readings from the Scientific American; Contemporary Psychology*, San Francisco: W. H. Freeman and Co., pp. 303–11

BARTHOLOMEW, W. T. (1942), *Acoustics of Music*, New York: Prentice-Hall

VON BEKESY, G. (1934), 'Uber die nichlinearen Verzerrungen des Ohres Ann', *Physik*, vol. 20, pp. 809–27, in von Bekesy, G., *Experiments in Hearing*, McGraw-Hill (1960), pp. 332–68

VON BEKESY, G. (1960), *Experiments in Hearing*, New York: McGraw-Hill

BELL, F. (1928), *Hugh Lowthian Bell. A Record and Some Impressions 1878–1926*, Middlesbrough: Wm. Appleyard and Sons (private circulation only)

BENTLEY, A. (1966a), *Musical Ability in Children, and its Measurement*, London: Harrap

BENTLEY, A. (1966b), *Measures of Musical Abilities*, London: Harrap Audio-Visual

BERLYNE, D. E. (1970), 'Novelty, complexity and hedonic value', *Perception and Psychophysics*, vol. 8 (5A), pp. 279–86

BERLYNE, D. E. (1971), *Aesthetics and Psychobiology*, New York: Appleton-Century-Crofts

BERLYNE, D. E., MCDONNELL, P., NICKI, R. M. and PARHAM, L. C. C. (1967), 'Effects of auditory pitch and complexity on EEG desynchronisation and on verbally expressed judgements', *Canadian Journal of Psychology*, vol. 21, pp. 346–67

BERLYNE, D. E., OGILVIE, J. C. and PARHAM, L. C. C. (1968), 'The dimensionality of visual complexity, interestingness and pleasingness', *Canadian Journal of Psychology*, vol. 22, pp. 376–87

BERNARD, L. L. (1924), *Instinct: A Study in Social Psychology*, New York: Holt

BEVER, T. G. and CHIARELLO, R. J. (1974), 'Cerebral dominance in musicians and non-musicians', *Science*, vol. 185, no. 4150, pp. 537–9

BINGHAM, H. VAN DYKE (1910), 'Studies in Melody', *Psychological Monographs*, vol. 12, p. 3

BLACKWELL, H. R. and SCHLOSBERG, H. (1943), 'Octave generalisation, pitch discrimination and loudness thresholds in the white rat', *Journal of Experimental Psychology*, vol. 33, pp. 407–19

BOOMSLITER, P. C. and CREEL, W. (1962), 'Ratio relationships in melody', *Journal of the Acoustical Society of America*, vol. 34, p. 1,276

BORING, E. G. (1923), 'Intelligence as the tests test it', *New Republic*, vol. 34, pp. 35–7

BORING, E. G. (1942), *Sensation and Perception in the History of Experimental Psychology*, New York: Appleton-Century-Crofts, p. 361

BRAY, T. and MIDDLETON, R. (1974), *Music and Society Today*, Milton Keynes: Open University

BREGMAN, A. S. and CAMPBELL, J. (1971), 'Primary auditory stream segregation and perception of order in rapid sequences of tones', *Journal of Experimental Psychology*, vol. 89, no. 2, pp. 244–9

BRINDLE, R. S. (1966), *Serial Composition*, London: Oxford University Press

BROADBENT, D. E. and ROBINSON, D. W. (1964), 'Subjective measurements of the relative annoyance of simulated sonic bangs and aircraft noise', *Journal of Sound and Vibration*, vol. 1, no. 2, pp. 162–74

BROWN, B. B. (1970), 'Recognition of aspects of consciousness through association with EEG alpha activity represented by a light signal', *Psychophysiology*, vol. 6, pp. 422–52

BRUES, A. M. (1927), 'The fusion of non-musical intervals', *American Journal of Psychology*, vol. 38, pp. 624–8

BRUSILOVSKY, L. S. (1972–3), 'A two year experience with the use of music in the rehabilitative therapy of mental patients', *Soviet Neurology and Psychiatry*, vol. 5, nos. 3–4, p. 100

CALHOUN, J. B. (1962), 'Population density and social pathology', *Scientific American*, vol. 206 (2), pp. 139–48

CAMPBELL, D. T. (1960), 'Recommendations for APA test standards, regarding construct, trait or discriminant validity', in Messick, S., and Jackson, D. N., *Problems in Human Assessment*, New York: McGraw-Hill, pp. 147–56

CANNON, W. B. (1927), 'The James–Lange theory of emotion: a critical examination and an alternative theory', *American Journal of Psychology*, vol. 39, pp. 106–24

CANNON, W. B., LEWIS, J. T. and BRITTON, S. W. (1927), 'The dispensability of the sympathetic division of the autonomic system', *Boston Medical and Surgical Journal*, vol. 197, p. 514

CARDINELL, R. L. and BURRIS-MEYER, H. (1947), 'Music in industry today', *Journal of the Acoustical Society of America*, vol. 19, pp. 547–8

CARDOZO, B. L. and VAN NOORDEN, L. P. A. S. (1968), 'Imperfect periodicity in the bowed string', Instituut voor Perceptie Onderzoek, *Annual Progress Report no. 3*, pp. 23–8

CARR, I. (1973), *Music Outside*, London: Latimer

CATTELL, R. B. (1963), 'The structure of intelligence in relation to the nature-nurture controversy', in Cancro, R. (ed.), *Intelligence: Genetic and Environmental Influence*, New York: Greene and Stratton (1971)

CATTELL, R. B. and SAUNDERS, D. (1954), 'Musical preferences and personality diagnosis', *Journal of Social Psychology*, vol. 39, pp. 3–24

CERASO, J. (1967), 'The interference theory of forgetting', *Scientific American*, vol. 217, no. 4, pp. 117–24

CHEATHAM, P. G. and WHITE, C. T. (1954), 'Temporal numerosity: III Auditory perception of number', *Journal of Experimental Psychology*, vol. 47, no. 6, pp. 425–8

CLEALL, C. (1968), 'The natural pitch of the human voice', paper presented at BPS Annual Conference (Education Section), Didsbury, September 1968

COLWELL, R. (1970), 'The development of the Music Achievement Test series', Council for Research in Music Education, *Bulletin no. 22*, pp. 57–73

CORCORAN, D. W. J. and WEENING, D. L. (1967), 'Redundancy effects in short-term memory', *Quarterly Journal of Experimental Psychology*, vol. 19, no. 4, pp. 309–18

CORNIL, L., GASTAUD, H. and CORRIOL, J. (1951), 'Appréciation du degré de conscience au cours des paroxysmes épileptique "petit mal" ', *Revue Neurologique*, vol. 84, pp. 149–51

CORSO, J. F. (1970), *The Experimental Psychology of Sensory Behaviour*, New York: Holt, Rinehart and Winston

COTTON, J. C. (1935), 'Beats and combination tones at intervals between the unison and the octave', *Journal of the Acoustical Society of America*, vol. 7, pp. 44–50

CREEL, W., BOOMSLITER, P. C. and POWERS, S. R. (1970), 'Sensations of tone as perceptual forms', *Psychological Review*, vol. 77, no. 6, pp. 534–45

CROWDER, R. G. (1973), 'Representation of speech sounds in precategorical acoustic storage', *Journal of Experimental Psychology*, vol. 98, no. 1, pp. 14–24

CROWDER, R. G. and MORTON, J. (1969), 'Precategorical acoustic storage (PAS)', *Perception and Psychophysics*, vol. 5, pp. 365–73

CSIKSZENTMIHALYI, M. and GETZELS, J. W. (1973), 'The personality of young artists: an empirical and theoretical exploration', *British Journal of Psychology*, vol. 64, no. 1, pp. 91–104

CULPEPPER, L. R. (1961), 'A study of the hearing impairments in defective singers', unpublished Ed. D. thesis, George Peabody College for Teachers, in Shuter, R. (1968), p. 160

DAVIES, J. B. (1965), 'An examination of musical IQ and musical preference', unpublished dissertation, University of Durham, Psychology Department

DAVIES, J. B. (1969), 'An analysis of factors involved in musical ability, and the derivation of tests of musical aptitude', Ph.D. thesis, University of Durham Library

DAVIES, J. B. (1971), 'New tests of musical aptitude', *British Journal of Psychology*, vol. 62, no. 4, pp. 557–65

DAVIES, J. B. (1976), 'Orchestral discord', *New Society*, vol. 35, no. 692, pp. 46–7

DAVIES, J. B. AND BARCLAY, G. (1977), 'Consonance/dissonance and the fusion of non-simultaneous tones', *Psychology of Music*, vol. 5, no. 1 (in press)

DAVIES, J. B. AND JENNINGS, J. (1977), 'The reproduction of familiar melodies and the perception of tonal sequences', *Journal of the Acoustical Society of America*, vol. 61, no. 2, pp. 534–41

DAVIES, J. B. AND YELLAND, A. (1977), 'Effects of training on the production of melodic contour, in memory for tonal sequences', *Psychology of Music*, vol. 5, no. 2 (in press)

DAVIS, R. (1961), 'The fitness of names to drawings: a cross-cultural study in Tanganyika', *British Journal of Psychology*, vol. 52, pp. 259–68

DEMBER, W. N., EARL, R. W. and PARADISE, N. (1952), 'Response by rats to differential stimulus complexity', *Journal of Comparative Physiology and Psychology*, vol. 50, pp. 514–18

DEUTSCH, D. (1969), 'Music recognition', *Psychological Review*, vol. 76, pp. 300–7

DEUTSCH, D. (1974), 'An auditory illusion', *Nature*, vol. 251, no. 5,473, pp. 307–9

DIVENYI, P. L. and HIRSH, I. J. (1974), 'Identification of temporal order in three-tone sequences', *Journal of the Acoustical Society of America*, vol. 56, no. 1, pp. 144–51

DOEHRING, D. G. (1968), 'Discrimination of simultaneous and successive tones', *Perception and Psychophysics*, vol. 3 (4B), pp. 293–6

DOEHRING, D. G. (1971), 'Discrimination of simultaneous and successive pure tones by musical and non-musical subjects', *Psychonomic Science*, vol. 22, no. 4, pp. 209–10

DORFMAN, D. D. and MCKENNA, H. (1966), 'Pattern preference as a function of pattern uncertainty', *Canadian Journal of Psychology*, vol. 20, pp. 143–53

DOWLING, W. J. (1971), 'Recognition of inversions of melodies and melodic contours', *Perception and Psychophysics*, vol. 9(3B), pp. 348–9

DOWLING, W. J. (1973), 'The perception of interleaved melodies', *Cognitive Psychology*, vol. 5, pp. 322–37

DOWLING, W. J. and FUJITANI, D. S. (1971), 'Contour, interval and pitch recognition in memory for melodies', *Journal of the Acoustical Society of America*, vol. 49, no. 2 (Part 2), pp. 524–31

DRAKE, R. M. (1933), 'Four new tests of musical talent', *Journal of Applied Psychology*, vol. 17, pp. 136–47

EAGLESON, H. V. and EAGLESON, O. W. (1947), 'Identification of musical instruments when heard directly and over a PA system', *Journal of the Acoustical Society of America*, vol. 19, pp. 338–42

EDMONDS, E. M. and SMITH, M. E. (1923), 'The phenomenological description of musical intervals', *American Journal of Psychology*, vol. 34, pp. 287–91

EDWARDS, P. (1940), 'A suggestion for simplified musical notation', *Journal of the Acoustical Society of America*, vol. 11, p. 323.

EGAN, J. P., SCHULMAN, A. I. and GREENBERG, G. Z. (1959), 'Operating characteristics determined by binary decisions and by ratings', *Journal of the Acoustical Society of America*, vol. 31, pp. 768–73

ELFNER, L. (1964), 'Systematic shifts in the judgement of octaves of high frequencies', *Journal of the Acoustical Society of America*, vol. 36, pp. 270–6

ELLIOTT, C. (1974), 'Intelligence and the British Intelligence Scale', *Bulletin of the British Psychological Society*, vol. 27, pp. 313–17

FEATHER, L. (1972), *From Satchmo to Miles*, New York: Stein and Day

FERMI, L. (1969), 'Feedback and states of consciousness: meditation', proceedings of Bio-Feedback Research Society, Panel 5

FLETCHER, H. (1934), 'Loudness, pitch and the timbre of musical tones and their relation to the intensity, the frequency and the overtone structure', *Journal of the Acoustical Society of America*, vol. 6, pp. 59–69

FLETCHER, H. and MUNSON, W. A. (1933), 'Loudness, its definition, measurement and calculation', *Journal of the Acoustical Society of America*, vol. 5, pp. 82–108

FORGUS, R. H. (1966), *Perception*, New York: McGraw-Hill

FRANCES, R. (1958), *La Perception de la Musique*, Paris: Vrin

FRANZEN, O., NORDMARK, J. and SJOBERG, L. (1972), 'A study of pitch', *Goteborg Psychological Reports*, vol. 2, no. 12, pp. 1–31

GALANTER, E. (1962), 'Contemporary psychophysics', in *New Directions in*

Psychology, vol. 1, Holt, Rinehart and Winston

GASTON, E. T. (1958), *A Test of Musicality* (manual), Kansas: Odell's Instrumental Service

GELLHORN, E. (1968), *Biological Foundations of Emotion*, Illinois and London: Scott Foresman and Co.

GESELL, A. and ILG, F. (1943), *The Infant and Child in the Culture of Today*, London: Hamilton

GESELL, A. and ILG, F. (1946), *The Child from Five to Ten*, London: Hamilton

GILLHAM, W. E. C. (1974), 'The British Intelligence Scale: à la recherche du temps perdu', *Bulletin of the British Psychological Society*, vol. 27, pp. 307–12

GOLD, D. (1969), 'Statistical tests and substantive significance', *American Sociologist*, February, pp. 42–6

GOMBRICH, E. H. (1959), *Art and Illusion*, London: Phaidon Press

GORDON, E. (1965), *Musical Aptitude Profile*, Boston: Houghton Mifflin

GORDON, E. (1971), *The Psychology of Music Teaching*, New Jersey: Prentice-Hall

GREEN, A. (1969), 'Feedback and states of consciousness: meditation', proceedings of Bio-Feedback Research Society, Panel 5

GREEN, D. M. (1971), 'Temporal auditory acuity', *Psychological Review*, vol. 78, no. 6, pp. 540–51

GUERNSEY, M. (1928), 'The role of consonance and dissonance in music', *American Journal of Psychology*, vol. 40, pp. 173–204

GUILFORD, J. P. (1967), *The Nature of Human Intelligence*, New York: McGraw-Hill

GULICK, W. L. (1971), *Hearing: Physiology and Psychophysics*, London: Oxford University Press, p. 164

GUTTMAN, N., and JULESZ, B. (1963), 'Lower limits of auditory periodicity analysis', *Journal of the Acoustical Society of America*, vol. 35, no. 4, p. 610

GUTTMAN, N. and PRUZANSKY, S. (1962), 'Lower limits of pitch and musical pitch', *Journal of Speech and Hearing Research*, vol. 5, no. 3, pp. 207–14

HALPIN, D. D. (1943–4), 'Industrial music and morale', *Journal of the Acoustical Society of America*, vol. 15, pp. 116–23

HEINLEIN, C. P. (1928), 'The affective characters of the major and minor modes in music', *Journal of Comparative Psychology*, vol. 8, p. 101

HEINLEIN, C. P. (1929), 'A new method of studying the rhythmic responses of children', *Journal of Genetic Psychology*, vol. 36, pp. 205–28

HELMHOLTZ, H. (1885), *The Sensations of Tone*, New York: Dover Publications (republished 1954)

HEVNER, K. and LANDSBURY, J. (1935), *Oregon Musical Discrimination Tests*, Chicago: C. H. Stoelting

HEYDUK, R. (1972), 'Static and dynamic aspects of rated and exploratory preference for musical compositions', Ph.D. dissertation, University of Michigan, in Walker, E. L. (1973)

HICKMAN, A. (1969), 'Musical imaging and concept formation', paper read at

Conference on Music in Education, Reading (see also Ph.D. thesis, University of Manchester, 1968)

HILLMAN, J. (1962), *Emotion* (2nd ed.), London: Routledge and Kegan Paul

HIRSH, I. J. and SHERRICK, C. E., Jr. (1961), 'Perceived order in different sense modalities', *Journal of Experimental Psychology*, vol. 62, no. 5, pp. 423–32

HOAGLAND, H. (1961), 'Some endocrine stress responses in man', in Simon, H., Herbert, C. C. and Keene, C. H., *The Physiology of Emotions*, Springfield, Illinois: Charles C. Thomas

HOUGH, E. (1943–4), 'Music as a safety factor', *Journal of the Acoustical Society of America*, vol. 15, p. 124

HOUSTON, J. P., GARSKOF, B. E. and SILBER, D. E. (1965), 'The informational basis of judged complexity', *Journal of General Psychology*, vol. 72, pp. 277–84

HOUTSMA, A. J. M. and GOLDSTEIN, J. L. (1971), 'The central origin of the pitch of complex tones: evidence from musical interval recognition', *Journal of the Acoustical Society of America*, vol. 51, no. 2, pp. 520–9

JAMES, W. (1884), 'What is an emotion?', *Mind*, vol. 9, pp. 188–205

JAMES, W. (1890), *The Principles of Psychology*, New York: Dover Publications (republished 1950)

JENSEN, A. R. (1969), 'How much can we boost IQ and scholastic achievement?', *Harvard Educational Review*, vol. 39, pp. 1–123

JENSEN, A. R. (1970), 'A theory of primary and secondary familial mental retardation', *International Review of Research in Mental Retardation*, vol. 4, pp. 33–105

JOHN, I. D. (1972), 'Some variables affecting judgements of auditory temporal numerosity', *Australian Journal of Psychology*, vol. 24, no. 3, pp. 347–52

JORGENSEN, C. (1950), 'A theory of the elements in the emotions,' in Hillman, J., *Emotion* (2nd ed.), London: Routledge and Kegan-Paul (1962), p. 40

KALMUS, H. (1949), 'Tone deafness and its inheritance', *Proceedings of the International Congress on Genetics*, Stockholm, p. 605

KERR, W. A. (1943), 'Attitudes towards types of industrial music', *Journal of the Acoustical Society of America*, vol. 15, pp. 125–30

KERR, W. A. (1945), 'Effects of music on factory production', *Applied Psychology Monographs*, (No. 5), California: Stanford University

KIMURA, D. (1964), 'Left-right differences in perception of melodies', *Quarterly Journal of Experimental Psychology*, vol. 16, pp. 355–8

KINNEY, J. S. (1961), 'Discrimination of auditory and visual patterns', *American Journal of Psychology*, vol. 74, pp. 529–41

KLAVAR-SYSTEM, *The Klavar System of Music Notation* (*Klavarskribo*), Klavarskribo Institute, Holland (67 Highbury New Park, London, N5)

KLING, J. W. and RIGGS, L. A. (1972), *Woodworth and Schlosberg's Experimental Psychology*, London: Methuen

KOESTLER, A. (1964), *The Act of Creation*, London: Pan Books

KOFFKA, K. (1935), *The Principles of Gestalt Psychology*, New York: Harcourt Brace

KOPA, J., SZABO, I. and GRASTYAN G. (1962), 'A dual behavioural effect from stimulating the same thalamic point with identical stimulus parameters in different conditional reflex situations', *Acta Physiologica Academiae Scientiarum Hungarieae*, vol. 21, pp. 207–14

KORNER, A. F. and THOMAN, E. B. (1972), 'The relative efficacy of contact and vestibular–proprioceptive stimulation in soothing neonates', *Child Development*, vol. 43, no. 2, pp. 443–53

KRAUS, M. S. (1972), 'Insignificant differences and null explanations', *Journal of General Psychology*, vol. 86, pp. 217–20

KWALWASSER, J. (1927), *Kwalwasser Test of Musical Information and Appreciation*, Iowa: Bureau of Educational Research

KWALWASSER, J. (1953), *Kwalwasser Music Talent Test*, New York: Mills Music Co.

KWALWASSER, J. and DYKEMA, P. W. (1930), *Kwalwasser-Dykema Music Tests*, New York: Carl Fischer

LAMP, C. J. and KEYS, N. (1935), 'Can aptitude for specific musical instruments be predicted?', *American Journal of Educational Psychology*, vol. 26, pp. 587–96

LANGE, C. G. (1887), *Uber Gemutsbewegungen*, Leipzig

LAWRENCE, M. (1968), 'Audition', *Annual Review of Psychology*, vol. 19, pp. 1–26

LEHMANN, A. (1914), 'Die Hauptgestze des menschlichen Gefuhlslegens', in Arnold, M. B., *The Nature of Emotion*, Harmondsworth: Penguin (1968)

LEHRMAN, D. S. (1958a), 'Effect of female sex hormones on incubation behaviour in the ring dove', *Journal of Comparative and Physiological Psychology*, vol. 51, pp. 142–5

LEHRMAN, D. S. (1958b), 'Induction of broodiness by participation in courtship and nest-building in the ring dove', *Journal of Comparative and Physiological Psychology*, vol. 51, pp. 32–6

LEWIS, D. and COWAN, M. (1936), 'The influence of intensity on the pitch of violin and 'cello tones', *Journal of the Acoustical Society of America*, vol. 8, pp. 20–2

LICKLIDER, J. C. R. (1959), 'Three auditory theories', in Koch, S. (ed.), *Psychology: A study of a Science*, vol. 1, (1959), pp. 41–144, New York: McGraw-Hill

LIPPS, T. (1885), *Psychologische Studien*, Heidelberg: Weiss, in Berlyne, D. E. (1971), p. 243 in Berlyne, D. E. (1971), Aesthetic and Psychobiology. New York: Appleton-Century-Crofts

LITTLER, T. S. (1965), *The Physics of the Ear*, London: Pergamon Press, p. 200

LIVANOV, M. N. and POLIAKOV, K. L. (1945), 'The electrical reactions of the cerebral cortex of a rabbit during the formation of a conditional defense reflex by means of rhythmic stimulation', *Bulletin of the Academy of Science*, USSR, vol. 3, p. 286

LORENZ, K. (1935), 'Der Kumpan in der Umwelt des Vogels', *Journal of Ornithology*, vol. 83, pp. 137–214, 289–413, in Thorpe, W. H., *Learning and Instinct in Animals*, London: Methuen (1956).

LOWERY, H. (1932), 'Estimation of musical capacity', *Proceeds of the Manchester Literary and Philosophical Society*, vol. 6, no. 76, p. 53

LUNDIN, R. W. (1949), 'The development and validation of a set of musical ability tests', *Psychological Monographs*, vol. 63, no. 305, pp. 1–20

LUNDIN, R. W. (1967), *An Objective Psychology of Music* (2nd ed.), New York: Ronald Press

MACDOUGALL, R. (1902), 'The relation of auditory rhythm to nervous discharge', *Psychological Review*, vol. 9, pp. 460–80

MCDOUGALL, W. (1928), *An Outline of Psychology* (4th ed., revised), London: Methuen

MCGEHEE, W. and GARDNER, J. E. (1949), 'Music in a complex industrial job', *Personnel Psychology*, vol. 2, pp. 405–17

MCGINNIS, C. S. and PEPPER, R. (1945), 'Intonation of the Boehm clarinet', *Journal of the Acoustical Society of America*, vol. 16, pp. 188–93

MACKINNON, D. W. (1962), 'The nature and nurture of creative talent', in Jackson, D. N., and Messick, S., *Problems in Human Assessment*, New York: McGraw-Hill, chapter 41.

MCLEISH, J. (1968), 'Musical cognition', *Musical Education Research Papers no. 2*, London: Novello

MADISON, T. H. (1942), 'Interval discrimination as a measure of musical aptitude', *Archives of Psychology*, no. 268

MADSEN, C. K. and MADSEN, C. H. (1970), *Experimental Research in Music*, New Jersey: Prentice-Hall

MAINWARING, J. (1931), 'Tests of musical ability', *British Journal of Educational Psychology*, vol. 1, pp. 313–21

MALMBERG, C. F. (1918), 'The perception of consonance and dissonance', *Psychological Monographs*, vol. 25, no. 2, pp. 93–133

MALTZEW, C. V. (1928), 'Absolutes Tonevewusstsein und Musikalitat', *Psychotech*, vol. Z, no. 3, p. 111, in Wing, H., 'Tests of Musical ability and appreciation', *British Journal of Psychology*, Monograph Supplement, vol. 27, (1948), p. 22

MARTIN, D. W. and WARD, W. D. (1954), 'Subjective evaluation of musical scale temperament in pianos', *Journal of the Acoustical Society of America*, vol. 26, p. 932

MASSARO, D. W. (1972), 'Perceptual images, processing time and perceptual units in auditory perception', *Psychological Review*, vol. 79, no. 2, pp. 124–45

MEIER, N. C. (1940–2), *The Meier Art Tests: 1. Art Judgement*, Iowa: University of Iowa

MERSENNE, M. (1957), *Harmonie Universelle*, (trans. Chapman), The Hague, in Pikler, A. G., 'History of experiments on the musical interval sense', *Journal of Music Theory* (1966), vol. 10, part 1, pp. 55–95

MEYER, L. B. (1956), *Emotion and Meaning in Music*, Chicago: University of Chicago Press

MEYER, M. F. (1962a), 'Helmholtz's aversion to tempered tuning experimentally shown to be a neurological problem', Journal of the Acoustical Society of America, vol. 34, p. 127

MEYER, M. F. (1962b), 'Listeners can be seduced to perceive the paradoxical ratio 51:87 as either one or another truly melodic interval', Journal of the Acoustical Society of America, vol. 34, p. 1277

MILLER, G. A. (1948), 'The perception of short bursts of noise', Journal of the Acoustical Society of America, vol. 20, no. 2, pp. 160–72

MILLER, G. A. (1962), Psychology: the Science of Mental Life, Harmondsworth: Penguin, pp. 62–5

MILLER, G. A. and HEISE, G. A. (1950), 'Trill Threshold', Journal of the Acoustical Society of America, vol. 22, pp. 637–8

MILLER, G. A. and SELFRIDGE, J. A. (1953), 'Verbal context and the recall of meaningful material', American Journal of Psychology, vol. 63, pp. 176–85

MILLER, G. A. and TAYLOR, W. G. (1948), 'The perception of repeated bursts of noise', Journal of the Acoustical Society of America, vol. 20, no. 2, pp. 171–82

MINDUS, L. (1968), 'The role of redundancy and complexity in the perception of tone patterns', unpublished M.A. thesis, Clark University, in Berlyne, D. E., Aesthetics and Psychobiology, New York: Appleton-Century-Crofts (1971), p. 211

MOLES, A. (1968), Information Theory and Esthetic Perception, Urbana: University of Illinois Press

MORAN, H. and PRATT, C. C. (1926), 'Variability of judgements on musical intervals', Journal of Experimental Psychology, vol. 9, pp. 492–500

MORTON, J., CROWDER, R. G. and PRUSSIN, H. A. (1971), 'Experiments with the stimulus suffix effect', Journal of Experimental Psychology, Monograph, vol. 91, no. 1, pp. 169–90

MUNSINGER, H. L. and KESSEN, W. (1964), 'Uncertainty, structure and preference', Psychological Monographs, vol. 78, no. 9

MURCH, G. M. (1973), Visual and Auditory Perception, Indianapolis: Bobbs-Merrill

MURSELL, J. L. (1937a), The Psychology of Music, New York: Norton

MURSELL, J. L. (1937b), Music Educators Journal (October), in Seashore, C. E., Psychology of Music (Appendix), New York: McGraw-Hill (1938)

MUZAK CORPORATION (1958), 'How Muzak affects profits', (C-1(4)28a), New York

MYERS, C. S. (1904), 'A study of rhythm in primitive peoples', British Journal of Psychology, vol. 1, p. 397

MYERS, C. S. (1928), A Text-book of Experimental Psychology (3rd ed., Part 1), Cambridge: Cambridge University Press

NEISSER, V. (1967), Cognitive Psychology, New York: Appleton-Century-Crofts

NEU, D. M. (1947), 'A critical review of the literature on absolute pitch', Psychological Bulletin, vol. 44, pp. 249–66

NEU, D. M. (1948), 'Absolute pitch – a reply to Bachem', Psychological Bulletin, vol. 45, pp. 534–5

NEWMARCH, R. (1906), *Life and Letters of Peter Ilich Tchaikovsky*, London: John Lane

NICKSON, N. (1967), *Education Through Music*, St Lucia: University of Queensland Press

NOBLE, C. E. (1964), *The Psychology of Cornet and Trumpet Playing*, Montana: Mountain Press

NORDOFF, P. and ROBBINS, C. (1973), *Therapy in Music for Handicapped Children*, London: Gollancz

NYLOF, G. (1973), 'Prestigeeffekter vid bedomning av jazzmusik', research reports from the department of sociology, Uppsala University, no. 16

OLSON, H. F. (1967), *Music, Physics and Engineering*, New York: Dover Publications

OSTER, G. (1973), 'Auditory beats in the brain', *Scientific American*, vol. 229, no. 4, pp. 94–102

PAVLOV, I. P. (1927), *Conditioned Reflexes*, New York: Dover Publications (republished 1960)

PAYNE, E. (1967), 'Musical taste and personality', *British Journal of Psychology*, vol. 58, nos. 1 and 2, pp. 133–8

PEDERSON, P. (1975), 'The perception of octave equivalence in twelve-tone rows', *Psychology of Music*, vol. 3, no. 2, pp. 3–8

PICKFORD, R. W. (1972), *Psychology and Visual Aesthetics*, London: Hutchinson

PIKLER, A. G. (1966), 'History of experiments on the musical interval sense', *Journal of Music Theory*, vol. 10, no. 1, pp. 54–95

PITTMAN, D. J. and SNYDER, C. R. (1962), *Society, Culture and Drinking Patterns*, New York: Wiley

PLEASANTS, H. (1969), *Serious Music – And All That Jazz*, London: Gollancz, in Bray, T. and Middleton, R., *Music and Society Today*, 1974, Milton Keynes: Open University Press

PLOMP, R. (1964), 'Rate of decay of auditory sensation', *Journal of the Acoustical Society of America*, vol. 36, no. 2, pp. 277–82

PLOMP, R. and LEVELT, W. J. M. (1965), 'Tonal consonance and critical bandwidth', *Journal of the Acoustical Society of America*, vol. 38, pp. 548–60

PLOMP, R., WAGENAAR, W. A. and MIMPEN, A. M. (1973), 'Musical interval recognition with simultaneous tones', *Acustica*, vol. 29, pp. 101–9

POMFRET, V. (1969), 'An investigation of rhythmic ability in young children, and its relation to short-term memory', unpublished dissertation, University of Durham Psychology Department

PRATT, C. C. (1921), 'Some qualitative aspects of bitonal complexes', *American Journal of Psychology*, vol. 32, pp. 490–515

PTACEK, P. H. and PINHEIRO, M. L. (1971), 'Pattern reversal in auditory perception', *Journal of the Acoustical Society of America*, vol. 49, no. 2 (part 2), pp. 493–8

QUASTLER, H. (1956), 'Studies of human channel capacity', in Cherry, *3rd London Symposium on Information Theory*, London: Butterworth (1955), pp. 363–9

REED, G. (1972),   *The Psychology of Anomalous Experience*, London: Hutchinson

REVESZ, G. (1925),   *The Psychology of a Musical Prodigy*, New York: Harcourt Brace

REVESZ, G. (1953),   *Introduction to the Psychology of Music*, London: Longmans Green

REYNOLDS, R. R. (1968–9),   'Replication and substantive import: a critique on the use of statistical inference in social research', *Sociology and Social Research*, vol. 53, pp. 299–310

RITSMA, R. J. (1966a),   'The "octave deafness" of the human ear', Instituut voor Perceptie Onderzoek, *Annual Progress Report*, no. 1, pp. 15–17

RITSMA, R. J. (1966b),   'The pitch of sinusoids and complex signals as affected by masking noise', Instituut voor Perceptie Onderzoek, *Annual Progress Report*, no. 1, p. 27

RITSMA, R. J. (1967),   'Frequencies dominant in the perception of pitch of complex sounds', Instituut voor Perceptie Onderzoek, *Annual Progress Report*, no. 2, pp. 5–10

RODDA, M. (1967),   *Noise and Society*, Edinburgh and London: Oliver and Boyd Paperback; Contemporary Science Series

ROSENZWEIG, M. R. (1961),   'Auditory localisation', *Scientific American* (October), pp. 132–42

RUBIN, E. (1921),   *Visuelle wahrgenommene Figuren*, Copenhagen: Gyldendalska

RUCKMICK, C. A. (1913),   'The role of kinaesthesis in the perception of rhythm', *American Journal of Psychology*, vol. 24, pp. 303–59

RYLE, G. (1949),   *The Concept of Mind*, in Hillman, J. (1962) *Emotion*, Routledge and Kegan Paul (p. 114)

SARGEANT, W. and LAHIRI M. (1931),   'A study of East Indian rhythm', *Musical Quarterly*, vol. 17, pp. 435–6

SCHACTER, S. and SINGER, J. E. (1962),   'Cognitive, social and physiological determinants of emotional state', *Psychological Review*, vol. 69, pp. 379–99

SCHOUTEN, J. F., RITSMA, R. J. and LOPES-CARDOZO, B. (1962),   'Pitch of the residue', *Journal of the Acoustical Society of America*, vol. 34, pp. 1418–24

SEASHORE, C. E. (1906),   'The tonoscope and its use in the training of the voice', *The Musician*, vol. 11, pp. 331–2

SEASHORE, C. E. (1919, 1939),   'Measures of musical talents', (original version 1919, revised 1939; latest edition 1960), New York: The Psychological Corporation

SEASHORE, C. E. (1938),   *Psychology of Music*, New York: McGraw-Hill

SERGEANT, D. (1967),   'The incidence and characteristics of absolute pitch amongst musicians', paper delivered at 3rd Conference in Research on Music Education, University of Reading

SERGEANT, D. (1970),   'The measurement of discrimination of pitch', 10th Conference on Research in Music Education, University of Reading

SHACKFORD, C. (1961), 'Some aspects of perception I', *Journal of Music Theory*, vol. 5, p. 1

SHACKFORD, C. (1962a), 'Some aspects of perception II', *Journal of Music Theory*, vol. 6, no. 2, pp. 66–90

SHACKFORD, C. (1962b), 'Some aspects of perception III: Addenda', *Journal of Music Theory*, vol. 6, no. 2, pp. 294–303

SHANNON, C. E. and WEAVER, W. (1949), *The Mathematical Theory of Communication*, Urbana: University of Illinois Press

SHUTER, R. (1968), *The Psychology of Musical Ability*, London: Methuen

SIVIAN, L. J. and WHITE, S. D. (1933), 'On minimum audible sound fields', *Journal of the Acoustical Society of America*, vol. 4, pp. 288–321

SKINNER, B. F. (1972), *Beyond Freedom and Dignity*, London: Jonathan Cape

SLOBODA, J. (1974a), 'The eye–hand span – an approach to the study of sight reading', *Psychology of Music*, vol. 2, p. 2

SLOBODA, J. (1974b), 'The musician's eye: evidence for reorganisation of visual memory', paper delivered at BPS Annual Conference, 1974

SMALL, A. M. (1937), 'An objective analysis of artistic violin performance', University of Iowa studies in the *Psychology of Music*, vol 4, pp. 172–231

SPEARMAN, C. (1927), *The Abilities of Man, their Nature and Measurement*, London: Macmillan

SPEARMAN, C. and JONES, L. W. (1950), *Human ability*, London: Macmillan

SPELT, D. K. (1948), 'The conditioning of the human fetus in utero', *Journal of Experimental Psychology*, vol. 38, pp. 375–6

STEVENS, S. S. (1934), The attributes of tones', *Proceedings of the National Academy of Science, USA*, vol. 20, pp. 457–9

STEVENS, S. S. (1935), 'The relation of pitch to intensity', *Journal of the Acoustical Society of America*, vol. 6, pp. 150–4

STEVENS, S. S. and DAVIS, H. (1938), *Hearing: Its Psychology and Physiology*, New York: Wiley and Sons

STEVENS, S. S., VOLKMANN, J. and NEWMAN, E. B. (1937), 'A scale for the measurement of the psychological magnitude of pitch', *Journal of the Acoustical Society of America*, vol. 8, pp. 185–90

STORR, A. (1972), *The Dynamics of Creation*, Harmondsworth: Penguin

STROUD, J. (1955), 'The fine structure of psychological time,' in Quastler, H. (ed.), *Information Theory in Psychology*, New York: Free Press

STUMPF, C. (1898), 'Konsonanz und Dissonanz', *Beitrage zur Akustic und Musikwissenschaft*, vol. 7, pp. 1–108, in Boring E. G. (1942), *Sensation and Perception in the History of Experimental Psychology*. New York: Appleton-Century-Crofts, pp. 359–63

SWANWICK, K. (1973), 'Musical cognition and aesthetic response', *Bulletin of the British Psychological Society*, vol. 26, pp. 285–9

SYMMES, D., CHAPMAN, L. F. and HALSTEAD, W. C. (1955), 'The fusion of intermittent white noise', *Journal of the Acoustical Society of America*, vol. 27, no. 3, pp. 470–3

TAYLOR, C. A. (1965), *The Physics of Musical Sounds*, London: English Universities Press

TAYLOR, R. (1970), *Noise*, Harmondsworth: Penguin

TEPLOV, B. M. (1966), *Psychologie des Aptitudes Musicales*, Paris: Presses Universitaires de France

THACKRAY, R. (1969), *An Investigation into Rhythmic Abilities*, Music Education Research Papers, no. 4, London: Novello

TILLIS, M. (1960), *Chords and Discords: The Life of an Orchestral Musician*, London: Phoenix House

TOBIAS, J. V. (1970), *Foundations of Modern Auditory Theory*, vol. 1, pp. 407–47, New York: Academic Press

DE TROCH, D. (1974), 'Validité intrinsèque de contenu d'une batterie de tests d'aptitude musicale (étude critique)', Centre de Psychologie Experimentale et Comparée, Université de Louvain, pp. 119–42

TROTTER, J. R. (1967), 'The psychophysics of melodic interval: definitions, techniques, theory and problems', *Australian Journal of Psychology*, vol. 19, pp. 13–25

UHRBROCK, R. S. (1961), 'Music on the job; its influence on worker morale and production', *Personnel Psychology*, vol. 14, pp. 9–38

VALENTINE, C. W. (1914), 'The method of comparison in experiments with musical intervals and the effect of practice on the appreciation of discords', *British Journal of Psychology*, vol. 7, pp. 118–35

VALENTINE, C. W. (1962), *The Experimental Psychology of Beauty*, London: Methuen

VAN DE GEER, J. P., LEVELT, W. J. M. and PLOMP, R. (1962), 'The connotation of musical consonance', *Acta Psychologica*, vol. 20, pp. 308–19

VERNON, P. E. (1934–5), 'Auditory Perception: (I) the Gestalt approach', *British Journal of Psychology*, vol. 25, no. 3, pp. 265–81

VERNON, P. E. (1968), 'What is potential ability?', *Bulletin of the British Psychological Society*, vol. 21, pp. 211–19

VITZ, P. C. (1964), 'Preferences for rates of information presented by sequences of tones', *Journal of Experimental Psychology*, vol. 68, no. 2, pp. 176–83

VITZ, P. C. (1966), 'Affect as a function of stimulus variation', *Journal of Experimental Psychology*, vol. 71, no. 1, pp. 74–9

VITZ, P. C. (1972), 'Preference for tones as a function of frequency (Hertz) and intensity (decibels)', *Perception and Psychophysics*, vol. 2 (1B), pp. 84–8

VOS, P. G. (1973), 'Pattern perception in metrical tone sequences', Psychological Laboratory, *Report 73*, University of Nijmegen, ON 06, pp. 1–15

WALKER, E. L. (1973), 'Psychological complexity and preference: a hedgehog theory of behaviour', in Berlyne, D. E., and Madsen, K. B. (eds.), *Pleasure, Reward, Preference*, New York: Academic Press (1973)

WARD, W. D. (1954), 'Subjective musical pitch', *Journal of the Acoustical Society of America*, vol. 26, no. 3, pp. 369–80

WARD, W. D. (1962), 'On the perception of the frequency ratio 55:32', *Journal of the Acoustical Society of America*, vol. 34, p. 679

WARD, W. D. (1963, a and b), *Absolute Pitch* (a) Part one, *Sound*, vol. 2, no. 3, pp. 14–21; (b) Part two, *Sound*, vol. 2, no. 4, pp. 33–41

WARD, W. D. (1970), 'Musical Perception', in Tobias (ed.), *Foundations of Modern Auditory Theory*, vol. 1, pp. 407–47, New York and London: Academic Press

WARREN, R. M. and OBUSEK, C. J. (1972), 'Identification of temporal order within auditory sequences', *Perception and Psychophysics*, vol. 12 (1B), pp. 86–90

WARREN, R. M. and WARREN, R. P. (1970), 'Auditory illusions and confusions', *Scientific American*, vol. 223, pp. 30–6

WEBSTER, J. (1954), 'Intonation errors due to discontinuities in the valve mechanisms of trumpets', *Journal of the Acoustical Society of America*, vol. 26, pp. 932–3

WEDIN, L. (1972), 'Evaluation of a three-dimensional model of emotional expression in music', no. 349, Reports from Psychological Laboratories, University of Stockholm

WEGEL, R. L. and LANE, C. E. (1924), 'The auditory masking of one pure tone by another, and its probable relation to the dynamics of the inner ear', *Physiological Review*, vol. 23, pp. 266–85

WEICK, K. E., GILFILLAN, D. P. and KEITH, T. A. (1973), 'The effects of composer credibility on orchestra performance', *Sociometry*, vol. 36, no. 4

WEVER, E. G. and BRAY, C. W. (1937), 'The perception of low tones and the resonance-volley theory', *Journal of Psychology*, vol. 3, pp. 101–14

WHISTLER, H. S. and THORPE, L. P. (1950), *Musical Aptitude Test*, Los Angeles: California Test Bureau

WHITE, B. W. (1954), 'Visual and Auditory Closure', *Journal of Experimental Psychology*, vol. 4, pp. 234–40

WHITE, C. T. (1963), 'Temporal numerosity and the psychological unit of duration', *Psychological Monographs: General and Applied*, vol. 77, no. 12, (whole no. 575)

WHITE, W. B. (1937), 'Practical tests for determining the accuracy of pianoforte tuning', *Journal of the Acoustical Society of America*, vol. 9, pp. 47–50

WHITE, W. B. (1939), 'New system of tuning pianos', *Journal of the Acoustical Society of America*, vol. 10, pp. 246–7

WHITTLE, L. S. and ROBINSON, D. W. (1974), 'Discotheques and pop-music as a source of noise-induced hearing loss', *Report Ac66* (March), National Physical Laboratory

WICKELGREN, W. A. (1965), 'Acoustic similarity and retroactive interference in short-term memory', *Journal of Verbal Learning and Verbal Behaviour*, vol. 4, pp. 53–61

WICKELGREN, W. A. (1966), 'Consolidation and retroactive interference in short-term recognition memory for pitch', *Journal of Experimental Psychology*, vol. 72, no. 2, pp. 250–9

WILSON, SIR ALAN (1963), *Noise: Final Report*, Committee on the Problem of Noise, London: HMSO, Cmnd 2056

WINCKEL, F. (1967),   *Music, Sound and Sensation: a Modern Exposition*, New York: Dover Publications

WING, H. D. (1948a), 'Tests of musical ability and appreciation', *British Journal of Psychology*, Monograph supplement, vol. 27

WING, H. D. (1948b), 'Standardised tests of musical intelligence', available through the National Foundation for Educational Research (NFER)

WING, H. D. (1962), 'A revision of the Wing Musical Aptitude Test', *Journal of Research in Music Education*, vol. 10, no. 1, pp. 39–46

WITKIN, H. A., OLTMAN, P. K., CHASE, J. B. and FRIEDMAN, F. (1971), 'Cognitive patterning in the blind', in *Cognitive Studies*, vol. 2, *Deficits in Cognition*, Hellmuth, J. (ed.), New York: Brunner-Mazel (1971)

WORTZ, E. (1969), 'Feedback and states of consciousness: Meditation', proceedings of Bio-Feedback Research Society, Panel 5

YOSHIDA, T. (1965), 'An investigation on how industrial music in Japan goes on', 5th International Congress on Acoustics, Liège, M56

ZENATTI, A. (1969), 'Le développement génétique de la perception musicale', *Monographies Françaises de Psychologie*, no. 17, Centre National de la Recherche Scientifique

ZENATTI, A. (1973), 'Etude de l'acculturation musicale chez l'enfant dans une épreuve d'identification mélodique', *Journal de Psychologie*, vol. 70, pp. 453–64

ZENATTI, A. (1976), 'Jugement esthétique et perception de l'enfant entre 4 et 10 ans, dans des épreuves rhythmiques', *L'Année Psychologique*, vol. 1, pp. 93–115, Presses Universitaires de France

ZIPF, G. K. (1949),   *Human Behaviour and the Principle of Least Effort*, Mass: Addison-Wesley

ZWICKER, E. (1961), 'Subdivision of the audible frequency range into critical bands', *Journal of the Acoustical Society of America*, vol. 33, no. 2, p. 248

ZWICKER, E., FLOTTORP, G. and STEVENS, S. S. (1957), 'Critical bandwidth in loudness summation', *Journal of the Acoustical Society of America*, vol. 29, pp. 548–57

Index of Subjects

Index of Names